SLAVERY

SLAVERY

History and Historians

PETER J. PARISH

Westview Press
A Member of the Perseus Books Group

Published by Westview Press, A Member of the Perseus Books Group

Designed by Cassandra J. Pappas

Library of Congress Cataloging-in-Publication Data

Parish, Peter J.
    Slavery: history and historians/Peter J. Parish.—1st ed.
        p.   cm.
    Bibliography: p.
    Includes index.
    ISBN 0-06-437001-1
    ISBN 0-06-430182-6 (pbk.)
    1. Slavery—United States—History.   2. Afro-Americans—History—To
1863.   3. Slavery—United States—Historiography.   4. Southern States—History—
1775–1865.   5. Southern States—History—1775–1865—Historiography.   6. Afro-
Americans—History—To 1863—Historiography.   I. Title.
E441.P367   1989   88-45051
973'.0496073—dc19

---

95 96 97 98 99 AC/HC 10 9 8 7 6 5 4 3 2 1
          99 AC/HC 15 14   (pbk.)

PERSEUS
POD
ON DEMAND

For Helen

Contents

Preface

There are times when it is hard to avoid the feeling that historians may unintentionally obstruct the view of history. Our students are sometimes better equipped to reel off the views of the leading authorities in a particular field than to develop a genuine understanding of what happened in the past. Ever-increasing specialization, particularly in such popular and densely populated fields as American history, has encouraged historians to concentrate on conversation—and controversy—with their professional colleagues at the expense of their obligation to present a clear view of the past to a broader audience.

Controversy frequently sets the pace of historical inquiry. Adversarial history has been a powerful stimulus to new discovery and fresh interpretation, but its constructive achievements have not been without cost. Aspirants to membership in the guild of professional historians commonly seek to make a name for themselves by challenging the views of one of the established authorities. Professional historians, absorbed in their long-running controversies, have sometimes left their students and the wider history-reading public bewildered and confused in the face of yet more disagreement among the experts.

There is no better example of this general point than the historiography of slavery in the South. During the last three decades, there has been an unprecedentedly rich outpouring of new work on the subject. It has included some of the great books of modern American historiography. The dimensions of the subject have expanded dramatically as new or neglected aspects of it have been opened up—above all those relating to the lives of the slaves themselves. We have all benefited from fresh insights and perspectives, new evidence, and new techniques for exploiting this evidence.

Controversy has operated as both cause and effect of this forward surge in the study of slavery. This is as it should be and as it must necessarily be. Our understanding of slavery has gained enormously from the cut and thrust of the historians' debates, but there is also a danger that real historical situations and the real participants in them may be obscured in the dust of the gladiatorial combat between one historian and another. There is no good reason why a wider readership should not have access to the riches amassed by the distinguished historians of slavery during recent decades. History has the enormous advantage that, unlike some of the social sciences, it has not yet completely wrapped itself in a professional jargon which serves to exclude those outside the inner circle. But how is a wider audience to tune in to the multiplicity of voices which have spoken so eloquently on the history of slavery? How is it to come to grips with the intricacies of the debate and share its real excitement?

The purpose of this book is a modest one. It examines some of the more important and illuminating recent work on slavery in the hope of identifying crucial questions and basic themes, and defining some of the main areas of controversy. Its aim—or at least its aspiration—is to offer a few signposts, perhaps even a simple map, to guide those coming afresh to this fascinating subject as they make their way through the thickets of rival interpretations and the fog of historical battle. At an early stage of the enterprise, I abandoned any pretense of comprehensiveness and chose to concentrate on some of the most conspicuous landmarks. The modern golden age of the historiography of slavery, ushered in by Kenneth Stampp and Stanley Elkins, came to a climax with the publication of the major studies of John Blassingame, Robert Fogel and Stanley Engerman, Eugene Genovese, Herbert Gutman, and Lawrence Levine during the 1970s. One of my aims in this book has been to measure the conclusions of these outstanding landmarks in the study of slavery against the findings of recent and more specialized studies dealing with particular aspects of the history of slavery or with particular localities within the slaveholding South. If the seventies were the decade of the grand synoptic overview of the South's "peculiar institution," the eighties have been the decade of the in-depth study. With one or two exceptions, the telescope has given way to the microscope.

I come to this discussion of the controversial institution of slavery with views of my own, but, I trust, with no axe to grind. It may be some small advantage to the author of a study of this kind that he has not himself been a combatant in any of the major controversies—and that he is able to view the subject from a safe distance and a transatlantic perspective. I have tried to avoid succumbing too often to the temptation of a bland "much might be said on both sides" approach to areas of controversy, but it is important to establish common ground where it does exist. In the excitement of historiographical attack and counterattack, it is not altogether unknown for scholarly controversialists to exaggerate their differences, or even to erect targets simply for the purpose of knocking them down again.

I take this opportunity to express my deep gratitude to those who have helped me in the preparation of this book. My first and most conspicuous debt is to that large and distinguished band of historians of slavery, on whose work I have fed parasitically for many years. One of the justifications for a book of this kind, and one of the great pleasures in working on it, derives from the sheer quality of so much of the modern historiography of slavery. As my acquaintance with the work of the historians of slavery has broadened and deepened, so too has my admiration and appreciation increased.

Second, I should like to thank my students at the universities of Glasgow and Dundee, and now at the Institute of United States Studies, University of London. They have always been ready to challenge my facile generalizations and to rescue me from at least some of my prejudices and misconceptions; they may even recognize in what follows ideas which I have begged, borrowed, or stolen from them. Year after year, they have also demonstrated how widely shared is the fascination with the subject of slavery. I treasure the comment of one student who, after a lively discussion on the slave family, said to her friend as she left (but within my earshot), "I didn't know history could be about interesting subjects like that!"

My third debt is to the British Association for American Studies. It was for BAAS that I wrote a pamphlet titled *Slavery*, which was published in 1981, and that pamphlet served as the springboard for this project. BAAS has placed no obstacle in the way of this attempt to write a short book which takes the pamphlet as its starting point. I am particularly grateful to my good friend Donald Ratcliffe, of the University of Durham, who, as the first editor of the BAAS pamphlets series, provided a superb critique—both rigorous and constructive—of the first draft of the pamphlet. It was Cass Canfield, Jr., of Harper & Row, who first saw the makings of a book in the original pamphlet, and who, with a judicious mixture of patience and firmness, has coaxed me toward completion of the project.

Finally, I thank my family for many things, from patience and moral support to practical assistance—and above all for their determination that I should retain something of that sense of proportion which is one of the historian's most essential qualities. My wife, Norma, has as always maintained a domestic environment which has robbed me of excuses to avoid or delay my work—and she has shown tact and restraint in limiting her references to domestic slavery in the Parish household. My daughter, Helen, remains healthily unimpressed by what I am attempting to do, but at least she has not been deflected by my poor example from her intention to read history when she goes to university. I dedicate this book to her as one of the coming generation of historians.

In a book which consists largely of discussion of the work of other historians, there is the obvious danger that any and every paragraph may give offense to someone. I offer my apologies to any of my fellow historians who may feel that I have been less than just or less than fair, and I accept responsibility for any errors of fact, judgment, or interpretation. If this book serves in some small way to broaden appreciation of one of the great debates among modern historians, I shall be more than content.

PETER J. PARISH

1

The Paradoxical Institution:
Complexity and Controversy

In the American South, as elsewhere, slavery rested upon a basic contradiction: Its guiding principle was that slaves were property, but its everyday practice demonstrated the impossibility of living up to, or down to, that denial of the slave's humanity. The master learned to treat his slaves both as property and as men and women; the slaves learned how to express and affirm their humanity even while they were constrained in much of their lives to accept their status as chattel.

For all the harsh lines of status and class, race and color, which divided owners and slaves, both were caught up in a complex web of compromise, adjustment, inconsistency, ambiguity, and deception. Slave society was the society of the double standard, adopted for its own convenience by the slave-owning class and forced upon the slaves by the simple need to survive. For the master, there were the competing needs of profit and paternalism, economic interest and social standing. The master claimed the absolute right of an owner over his property, but he was also restrained by the conventional morality of his time, his own standards of decency, the precepts of his religious faith, and the pressure of the white community. Owners weighed both their interests and their principles when they debated the balance between kindness and severity, the carrot and the stick, persuasion and coercion, in their management of the slaves.

For their part, slaves were obliged to strike their own balance between resignation and rebellion, accommodation to the facts of

1

slave life and resistance to the dominance of their masters. In their daily lives they strove to reconcile the demands of survival with the impulse to assert their autonomy. They struggled with persistence and ingenuity to create and maintain a life of their own in a situation where, in the nature of things, a large part of their lives could never be their own. They hated slavery but could not maintain total hatred of slave owners and their families. They could fight or take flight or they could lapse into complete submissiveness, but for most of the time most slaves steered a complex, devious, opportunist, occasionally inconsistent, sometimes bewildered, often subtle course between those two extremes. While bracing themselves to support the crushing weight of the master's authority, they succeeded in creating out of their African heritage and their American environment a distinctive African-American culture and life-style, with its own institutions, its own pattern of relationships, and its own communal bonds.

Lawrence Levine has highlighted some of the more acute paradoxes of slavery for both masters and slaves.

> Slaveholders who considered Afro-Americans to be little more than sub-human chattels converted them to a religion which stressed their humanity and even their divinity. Masters who desired and expected their slaves to act like dependent children also enjoined them to behave like mature, responsible adults. . . . Whites who considered their black servants to be little more than barbarians, bereft of any culture worth the name, paid a fascinated and flattering attention to their song, their dance, their tales, and their forms of religious exercise. The life of every slave could be altered by the most arbitrary and immoral acts. They could be whipped, sexually assaulted, ripped out of societies in which they had deep roots, and bartered away for pecuniary profit by men and women who were also capable of treating them with kindness and consideration and who professed belief in a moral code which they held up for emulation not only by their children but often by their slaves as well.[1]

In their sharply different ways, whites and blacks, masters and slaves, learned to live with slavery by learning to live a lie. They divided their lives into compartments, did not prize consistency too highly, evaded rather than confronted some of the inherent contradictions of slave society, and blurred the harsh lines of the system by bargain and compromise.

Slavery abounded in further paradoxes and contradictions. It owed its very existence in North America to the rise of capitalism in Europe, and yet it provided the foundation for a distinctive Southern social and economic order which lived uneasily with full-blown nineteenth-century capitalism—or, indeed, in the opinion of Eugene Genovese and others, was basically incompatible with it.[2] The products of slave labor, cotton above all, were crucial to the northern Atlantic economy in the mid–nineteenth century and constituted by far the most important item in the export trade of the free-enterprise capitalist American economy.

There was an even more tangled relationship between slavery and American liberty, republicanism and democracy. If the American colonies were in most respects the freest society in the eighteenth-century world, that society already bore within it the malignant tumor of a well-established system of racial slavery. The irony of a Declaration of Independence affirming that all men were created equal, but drafted and signed by large-scale slave owners, was not entirely lost upon the Revolutionary generation, but may have seemed less blatant than it does today. Be that as it may, slavery marched on into the nineteenth century, advancing in area, numbers, and economic performance. But increasingly it became an anachronism in a rapidly changing world, and an anachronism above all in a country which saw itself—and was perceived by others—as the standard-bearer of liberty and democracy. For Southern whites, however, slavery and liberty were inextricably intertwined; indeed, their conception of the latter depended upon the preservation of the former.[3] When the states of the Deep South seceded in 1860–61, they did so in defense of their freedom as they understood it. That freedom included the right to hold their slave property, and to take it with them into the western territories. It is the final paradox of the history of Southern slavery that this dramatic bid to defend it in fact sealed its fate during the next four years. Without secession and Civil War, it is virtually inconceivable that slavery would have been abolished during the 1860s.

Some of the contradictions and paradoxes of slave society were inherent in the system. Others may have been more apparent than real, in view of the remarkable diversity of slavery in the American South. There can be no greater mistake than to regard slavery as monolithic. It evolved more than two centuries before it reached its prime in the pre–Civil War decades, and some major interpretations have given too little weight to this most important historical dimension of change over time. Indeed, it has even been suggested that intense concentration on the study of slavery in the immediate antebellum decades has placed undue emphasis on certain features which may have been atypical of the history of Southern slavery as a whole.[4] What is beyond all question is that slavery was, throughout its history in North America, a growing, changing, mobile, flexible, and variable institution.

It varied greatly not only from time to time but from place to place—from the border states to the deep South, from Virginia and the Carolinas through Alabama and Mississippi to Texas. In fact, the slave population was spread very unevenly across the South, and even within individual states. There were large areas of "slave" states which contained few slaves, if any at all, in their population. This was most conspicuously true of the Appalachian region, including western Virginia and North Carolina, eastern Kentucky, and Tennessee; but it occurred elsewhere, too—for example, in those large areas of the state of Missouri which were not close to the Missouri or Mississippi rivers. Even in the heartland of the Deep South, there were marked contrasts within Georgia and Alabama, for example, between those areas with a heavy concentration of slaves and those with only a scattered few. The spectrum ran all the way from Appalachian counties, where there were no slaves at all, to Adams County in Mississippi, where there were fifty slaves for every white person. One consequence of these variations was a considerable degree of geographical separation between white yeoman farmers and Negro slaves in some, but by no means all, regions of the South.

These local variations within the South were a reflection, in part, of the demands imposed by the cultivation of various staple crops. Here, another complication—and even another contradiction—in the overall pattern of Southern slavery presents itself. In the picture of the South during its antebellum maturity, cotton occupies the dominant position, and rightly so. Yet, on the other hand, some of the areas with the largest concentrations of slave population and of slave ownership, and areas which conjure up the most vivid and enduring images of Southern plantation society, were not provinces of the realm of King Cotton. The tobacco plantations of the Chesapeake Bay area (especially of Virginia), the rice plantations of the coastal areas of South Carolina and Georgia, and the sugar plantations of Louisiana were the backgrounds from which emerged many of the grandees of the Southern slaveholding aristocracy. All may well be regarded as quintessentially Southern, and yet all were exceptions to the rule. Indeed, one historian, James Oakes, has depicted these very areas as outmoded outposts of an older paternalist tradition of slave ownership, increasingly isolated from the dynamic, expanding, business-oriented slave society, based mainly on cotton, which prevailed elsewhere.[5] It is questionable whether such significant parts of the total picture, which happen to have been geographically on the margin of the old South, can be pushed quite so far to the margin in other respects.

Of all the sources of the diversity of Southern slavery, none is more important than the size of the individual slaveholding unit. This was influenced by both regional and historical factors, and also the requirements of particular crops. Understandably, but in some ways misleadingly, historians have given most of their attention to the larger plantations, many of which have left extensive records behind them, whereas the small farmer, owning perhaps one family of slaves, seldom had the time or need or perhaps the ability to record farm activities in detail. The stock image of the slave environment is the great plantation, with its scores or even hundreds of slaves. In fact, in the mid–nineteenth century, half of the total number of slaveholders owned no more than five slaves each; on the other hand, a majority of bondmen and bondwomen belonged to holders of twenty or more slaves. As in so many other matters, the distribution of the slave population looks very different according to whether it is viewed from the slave's or the owner's point of view. If "typical" is taken at its simplest to mean membership of the majority, then the typical slave did not belong to the typical owner. Clearly, for the slave who was one of a handful working for, and often alongside, a master cultivating a family farm of modest size, every aspect of daily life, including any sense of belonging to a slave community, was very different from the experience of a slave who was one of thirty or fifty or one hundred on a large plantation.

Slavery was a system of many systems, with numerous exceptions to every rule. In addition to the typical field hands, there were domestic servants, craftspersons and artisans, and overseers and drivers. Beyond the farms and plantations, there were urban slaves, industrial slaves, and hired slaves, and there were a quarter of a million free blacks in the South who lived constantly in the shadow of slavery. The individual slave might well have experienced a variety of owners, environments, and occupations during a lifetime.

Finally, the variety of slavery arose from the variety of human nature. Slave owners and slaves, like other people, could be honest or dishonest, weak or strong, responsible or irresponsible, humane or sadistic, puritanical or lecherous, sober or drunk, stable or neurotic, intelligent or stupid. If the impact of slavery on the slave depended on the character or the mood of the master, the response of the slave to his or her situation depended on individual resources of character, will, endurance, and adaptability, and the sustaining power of the slave's family, community, faith, and way of life. Behind all the generalizations, the models, and the stereotypes about the planter class, the slaveholding mentality, the slave personality, and the slave community, there lies the history of millions of individuals living out their daily lives. One of the peculiarities of the peculiar institution of slavery is to be found in the distinctive pattern of human relationships it required or encouraged.

Both the multifaceted character and the inner tensions and contradictions of Southern slavery have colored the historical debate on the subject. They have helped to stimulate controversies of great intensity and to produce something of a roller-coaster effect, as successive schools of interpretation have soared into prominence and then plunged into the critical depths. Some of the major American historians of the second half of the twentieth century—Kenneth Stampp, John Hope Franklin, Eugene Genovese, Herbert Gutman, Lawrence Levine, and John Blassingame,[6] for example—have contributed powerfully to the modern debate about Southern slavery. Curiously, however, much of the modern historiographical argument has been shaped by three major but deeply flawed works which aroused such a powerful critical reaction that they rewrote the agenda of slavery studies.

The first of these was the work of the pioneer Southern historian of slavery, Ulrich B. Phillips, which was based on extensive research in plantation records but also on a deep attachment to the old South and a belief in black racial inferiority. In *American Negro Slavery,* published in 1918,[7] he treated the slave as the beneficiary of a patriarchal but unprofitable institution designed to maintain the South's cardinal principle of white supremacy. The framework established by Phillips and his followers cast the slaves themselves primarily in the role of objects, whether as victims or beneficiaries. The focus was on slave "treatment," as well as on the performance of the slave economy and the efficiency or inefficiency of slave labor. One of the remarkable features of the Phillips interpretation was its longevity. It survived for thirty years, at least, as the conventional wisdom on the subject, but the critical reaction against it eventually gathered momentum and found its definitive expression in 1956 in *The Peculiar Institution,* a work by distinguished Northern historian Kenneth Stampp.[8] Basically, Stampp accepted the framework Phillips had constructed, but, more than matching his predecessor's research in the plantation records, he completely overturned Phillips's conclusions. Stampp saw the slave as the maltreated victim of a profitable economic system; in a nutshell, where Phillips had viewed slavery as mild but inefficient, Stampp saw it as harsh but profitable.

Just a few years after Stampp had set his seal on the debate over a slavery conducted according to one set of terms, Stanley Elkins shifted the argument to very different ground. His *Slavery: A Problem in American Institutional and Intellectual Life,* first published in 1959,[9] was a work of great intellectual audacity, based on a methodology which had little connection with conventional historical research and arriving at conclusions which were challenging or outrageous, according to one's point of view. Elkins depicted the slave as the psychic casualty of an all-embracing repressive system and sought to emphasize his point by comparing the psychological damage suffered by slaves on the Southern plantation to that inflicted upon inmates of the Nazi concentration camps. Elkins's *Slavery* is the supreme example of a book which has exercised a profound influence, not by the persuasiveness of its arguments, but above all through the questions it raised, the massive critical response it elicited, and the new work it stimulated. Whatever the gaps in his arguments and the flaws in his methodology, Elkins did more than anyone else to set the agenda for the next generation of historians of slavery. His influence is to be measured not in the band of disciples and converts he inspired, for their numbers were few, but in the army of critics he goaded into fresh thinking about a whole range of different questions.

Ironically, for one who had stressed the depersonalizing impact of slavery upon the slaves, one consequence of Elkins's work was to encourage long-overdue recognition of the slave as a person. In the thirty years since Elkins's book first appeared, historians have discussed not only the extent to which the slave personality resisted, or succumbed to, the extraordinary stresses of bondage, but the means by which slaves succeeded in constructing and maintaining a life-style, a set of values, and a culture which was distinctively their own. Phrases such as "the slave personality," "the slave community," and "slave culture" have become part of the common parlance of the historians' debate. Instead of appearing as the victim or object to whom things happened or were done, the slave has emerged, in the work of historians such as Genovese, Gutman, Levine, Blassingame, and many others, as an active participant not only in the development of his or her own life-style, but in the overall history of the peculiar institution. The presentation of a slave's-eye view of slavery has raised many questions, and so far has perhaps produced rather fewer answers, but it has irreversibly altered our understanding of the whole subject.

If any one book has matched or even surpassed Elkins's *Slavery* in the furor its publication provoked, it was surely Robert Fogel and Stanley Engerman's *Time on the Cross*, which appeared in 1974.[10] In what was intended to be a model of the application of quantitative methods to a major historical problem, *Time on the Cross* returned the focus to the economics of slavery, but their work ranged widely over many aspects of slave life, from diet and housing to opportunities for individual advancement, and from sexual morality to religious observance. Fogel and Engerman claimed that slave-based Southern agriculture was both efficient and profitable, and that the slave benefited in many ways, not least because considerate treatment of a valuable capital asset was to the financial advantage of profit-seeking slave owners. Breaking both the Phillips and Stampp mold, they described an institution which was at once mild, efficient, and profitable.

Like Elkins a decade and a half earlier, Fogel and Engerman found that the sensation which publication of their work had initially produced was followed by a barrage of criticism and counterattack questioning both their methodology and their conclusions. What had at first sight seemed provocative and innovative struck many historians, on further reflection, as misconceived or simply mistaken. On the other hand, however much some of Fogel and Engerman's conclusions have been rebutted or even discredited, it is surely true to say that, in the wake of *Time on the Cross,* discussion of the efficiency and profitability of slavery—and discussion of many other aspects of slave society—will never be the same again. New questions have been raised and old ones reopened, and both the agenda of problems for discussion and the range of techniques available for their investigation have been extended still further.

The decade of the 1970s witnessed something like an earthquake in the historiography of slavery. In addition to *Time on the Cross,* it saw the publication of other major reinterpretations of the institution of slavery, and particularly of slave life, from the pens of Genovese, Gutman, Blassingame, and Levine, which have had and will certainly continue to have a pervasive and constructive influence on our understanding of the subject. The decade of the 1980s has not produced towering historiographical landmarks of this kind, but rather a large number of more specialized studies of particular aspects of slavery, or of slavery in particular circumstances or localities—studies which absorb, but at the same time test and even challenge the findings of the previous decade. This is an important and healthy phase in the study of the subject. On one hand, the clash and the clamor of historical controversy generates great excitement and stimulates fresh thinking. On the other, the swing of the historiographical pendulum and the tendency toward polarization in historical debate can occasionally result in distortion or exaggeration and may obscure the everyday realities of slave life a century and a half ago.

There is an almost irresistible tendency to define the issues in a series of excessively rigid dichotomies. It does not help to insist on the complete dominance of profit seeking over paternalism (or vice versa) in the thinking of slave owners; the two were not mutually exclusive in slave owners' minds, whatever the demands of logic or ideology may dictate to modern historians of slavery. Similarly, it is not helpful to place the emphasis exclusively on either punishment or incentive in discussing the master's control of his work force; the two were combined and balanced in one system of management and discipline. Among the slaves, unyielding rebelliousness or utter docility were both exceptions to the general rule; the great majority of slaves maneuvered in the broad ground between these extremes. The debate over the relative influence of the African heritage and the American environment in shaping slave culture has to accept sooner or later that a distinct Afro-American culture evolved from the intermingling of the two.

Again, there is a dichotomy. On one hand, insistence on the high degree of autonomy in the slave community can be carried to the absurd extreme of writing the master's authority almost completely out of the picture; on the other hand, it would be grossly misleading to ignore or belittle the interior life of the slave community.

In reality, the very essence of Southern slavery lay in the tension between these various conflicting forces, and many others besides. Beset on all sides by the multifarious pressures of the institution which shaped their lives, slaveholders sought to achieve the best they could from it, and slaves to avoid the worst. At the heart of all the contrasts and contradictions which surrounded slavery lay the greatest paradox of all—the existence of an expanding and deeply entrenched system of human bondage in the midst of a society which treasured freedom as its fundamental principle and its greatest glory.

NOTES

1. Lawrence W. Levine, *Black Culture and Black Consciousness: Afro-American Folk Thought from Slavery to Freedom* (New York, 1977), 114.

2. Eugene D. Genovese, "Slavery: The World's Burden," in Harry P. Owens, ed., *Perspectives and Irony in American Slavery* (Jackson, Miss., 1976), 27–50. See also Elizabeth Fox-Genovese and Eugene D. Genovese, *Fruits of Merchant Capital: Slavery and Bourgeois Property in the Rise and Expansion of Capitalism* (New York, 1983).

3. For a fuller discussion of this point, see below 134–136.

4. Peter Kolchin, "American Historians and Antebellum Southern Slavery," in William J. Cooper, Michael F. Holt, and John McCardell, eds., *A Master's Due: Essays in Honor of David Herbert Donald* (Baton Rouge, La., 1985), 109–110. For a recent general history of Southern slavery which stresses change over time, see John B. Boles, *Black Southerners, 1619–1869* (Lexington, Ky., 1983).

5. James Oakes, *The Ruling Race: A History of American Slaveholders* (New York, 1982), 196–201.

6. For full references to the works of these and other leading historians of slavery, see the bibliographical essay, 167–188.

7. Ulrich B. Phillips, *American Negro Slavery: A Survey of the Supply, Employment and Control of Negro Labor as Determined by the Plantation Regime* (New York, 1918; reprint, Baton Rouge, La., 1966). Among Phillips's other writings, see especially his *Life and Labor in the Old South* (Boston, 1929; reprint, 1963).

8. Kenneth M. Stampp, *The Peculiar Institution: Slavery in the Ante-Bellum South* (New York, 1956).

9. Stanley M. Elkins, *Slavery: A Problem in American Institutional and Intellectual Life*, third ed. (Chicago, 1959; revised, 1976).

10. Robert W. Fogel and Stanley L. Engerman, *Time on the Cross:* volume I, *The Economics of American Negro Slavery* and volume II, *Evidence and Methods* (Boston, 1974).

2

The Making of an Institution

The most familiar images of Southern slavery relate to the fully fledged mature institution of the last generation before the Civil War. A certain timeless, changeless, static quality has attached itself to those images. But slavery had not always been like that; the peculiar institution had its own peculiar history. The slave South was not a fixed point but a changing historical process. The two centuries from 1619 to the 1820s shaped the character of both Southern slavery and the black American experience.

Differences of time and place etched a variegated pattern into the history of slavery during the colonial period, as Ira Berlin in particular has emphasized.[1] The decades on either side of 1700 mark a crucial turning point between the first long phase of slow and uncertain evolution during the seventeenth century and the firm consolidation and rapid expansion of slavery in the eighteenth century. Geographically, there were three distinct areas where slavery took shape (and, in two of them, took root) in the British North American colonies. First in time, numbers, and importance was the Chesapeake Bay region of Virginia and Maryland, where tobacco was the main staple crop. Second, from the 1670s onward, were the coastal settlements of the Carolinas (especially South Carolina), and later of Georgia, where heavy concentrations of slave labor were used in the cultivation of subtropical crops such as rice and indigo. Third, it must not be forgotten that slaves were far from unknown in some of the Northern colonies. There the slave population was much more scattered, but at their eighteenth-century peak in New York, slaves and free blacks numbered up to 15 percent of the total population.

There is nothing clear-cut about the beginnings of slavery on the

11

North American mainland. It is impossible to name one specific date at which slavery began its long history there. The first blacks were brought to Virginia on a Dutch ship in 1619—the same year, ironically, in which the first representative assembly in North America, the Virginia House of Burgesses, also met. But blacks were only one (and for decades only a comparatively minor one) among the various possible answers to the chronic labor shortage of a new colonial society. Their status as slaves was not established at the outset, but rather was very slowly clarified over time.

Indeed, in the sixteenth and early seventeenth centuries, slavery was very much an institution of the tropical and subtropical latitudes, and in the New World was a product of the Spanish and Portuguese empires rather than the British. The slave trade linked three continents, but South America and the Caribbean were its focal points in the New World, with North America little more than an offshoot. It was the Portuguese and the Dutch who dominated the trade for a long period. It is impossible to be precise, but in the four centuries between 1450 and 1850, over ten million—perhaps nearer twelve million—slaves were transported from Africa, but only just over half a million (less than 5 percent of the total) were imported into areas which are now part of the United States. Jamaica, Cuba, and Haiti each imported many more slaves than the whole of the North American mainland. Yet, in stark contrast, by 1825 the Southern states of the United States had the largest slave population of any country in the New World, amounting to well over one-third of the total.[2] Here is one striking piece of evidence of the very unusual character of Southern slavery. Such a history of growth and development was quite unforeseen and unforeseeable in the seventeenth century. It is one more of the paradoxes of Southern slavery that the smallest importer of slaves into the Americas should by the nineteenth century have the largest slave population.

Blacks were part of the beginnings of American history, but their numbers remained very small throughout the seventeenth century. For fifty years at least, they were counted in hundreds rather than thousands, and even after a spurt in the closing years of the century they totaled only twenty-six thousand in 1700, 70 percent of them in Virginia and Maryland. As long as numbers remained small, sharp differentiation of status between slaves and free men could be delayed. Similarly, although from the outset blacks were regarded as different and there was widespread prejudice against them, early Chesapeake society did not impose a rigid system of racial discrimination. Indeed, for much of the seventeenth century, there was probably easier and more informal social contact between whites and blacks, at least at the lower end of the social scale, than in most later periods of American history. Free blacks owned property, including land and even indentured servants, sued and testified in the courts, and served on juries.

Historians have conducted a vigorous if somewhat unproductive debate as to whether racism encouraged the development of slavery or slavery stimulated racism. The most convincing explanation, offered by Winthrop Jordan and others, is that the institution of chattel slavery and the clear belief in the racial inferiority of the African marched hand in hand, with each supporting and reinforcing the other.[3] Support for both intensified as the demand for black labor increased, and particularly as the black population grew and became more heavily concentrated in certain areas.

If there is danger in using hindsight to apply the rigid pattern of discrimination which prevailed in the nineteenth century to the early history of black Americans, it is equally misleading to ascribe more modern notions of individual freedom and legal and social status to the early seventeenth century. The assumption that the distinction between freedom and servitude must always be clear and unambiguous flows naturally from the attitudes and social structure of modern Western society. However, things looked very different in the more hierarchical European society, shaped by the presence or the legacy of feudalism, from which the settlers came. A majority of the seventeenth-century settlers arrived with some limitation on their freedom, most commonly as indentured servants bound to a master for a period of years before obtaining their full freedom. Servant and slave were terms which were virtually interchangeable, or at least greatly overlapping. When the life expectation of new arrivals was so limited, there was little incentive to buy a slave rather than hire an indentured servant for five or seven years; in either case, the obligation might well prove to be for life—and indentured servants were cheaper. The process of defining a distinct slave status involved establishment of the principle of servitude for life (and indeed hereditary servitude), and relegation of the slave to the status of a mere chattel.

There was little need in the early years to hasten this process. The Chesapeake settlements were founded in the expectation of relying upon white labor of one kind or another—and tobacco, which soon became the staple crop, did not require slave labor in the way rice or, later, cotton would. However, during the last quarter of the seventeenth century, the situation was changing both in the Chesapeake Bay area and further to the south. A decline in the English birthrate and the opening up of new colonies to the north of Maryland and Virginia reduced the supply of indentured servants. Inducements offered to settlers included relaxation of the terms of indentured servitude—which in turn sharpened the contrast between white freedom and black bondage. Increasing competition for land in Virginia between the established planters and younger men (often former indentured servants) created friction within the white community, which manifested itself in Bacon's Rebellion in 1676. Possibly for the first time in American history, but certainly not for the last, greater insistence on black inferiority was seen as a means of reducing tension among whites. As life expectancy improved, landowners began to see greater advantage in a permanent labor force of black slaves rather than continued reliance on less reliable white labor.[4]

The result was a rapid increase in the black population around the turn of the century and a series of moves to define its servile status. It is a remarkable fact that the number of African slaves imported into the Chesapeake Bay area in the first decade of the eighteenth century was more than double the entire total for the seventeenth century. The Royal African Company had already begun to bring more slaves directly from Africa (in contrast to earlier arrivals, who came mainly from the Caribbean). When the company lost its monopoly of the slave trade in 1698, other merchants eagerly entered the business. It was not only the rapid rise in black numbers but the more obviously "alien" character of the arrivals directly from Africa that accelerated the evolution of both a much more explicit and formal system of racial discrimination and a legally defined system of chattel slavery.

During the same period, developments in the Carolinas led to the creation of another base for Southern slavery. South Carolina was virtually a transplant from the Caribbean, particularly from Barbados, and its population included a substantial black element from the early days. The climate was not encouraging to white labor, and once rice cultivation developed in the 1690s, black workers were even more in demand. Their skills and knowledge made a crucial contribution to the rice culture of the Carolina low country, but they paid a heavy price in years of arduous toil in foul and unhealthy conditions. Racial distinctions were always present, but in the early years of the eighteenth century, blacks—who now constituted a majority of the population—were actively involved in every aspect of South Carolina society. As Peter Wood expresses it, "servants and masters shared the crude and egalitarian intimacies inevitable on a frontier."[5]

However, by 1720, blacks outnumbered whites by almost two to one, and many were concentrated on large plantations, the owners of which spent much of their time away in Charleston. There was increasing separation between the races and increasing fear and anxiety among whites. Legislation steadily reduced black autonomy, intensified discrimination, and introduced tighter controls. Tension between the races bubbled to the surface from time to time and exploded in the localized, short-lived, but alarming Stono Rebellion in 1739, in which up to one hundred blacks took part. In the aftermath of Stono, imports of slaves were drastically reduced and the Negro Act of 1740 severely curtailed black rights and freedoms and laid the foundations of the South Carolina slave code, which endured for over a century. Blacks remained a majority, but an unequivocally enslaved majority. In Peter Wood's words, by the time the Revolution came, "too many had been reduced too soon into too thorough a state of submission."[6]

The half century before the American Revolution was a period of consolidation and reinforcement of what was now a firmly based slave system. Slavery's geographical spread was quite wide in the South, and even in the North, but its real numerical strength and economic and social importance were still concentrated around its two main Atlantic bridgeheads, the tobacco-growing area of Virginia and Maryland and the subtropical rice and indigo region of South Carolina and Georgia. This was the period when many of the enduring and distinctive features of Southern slavery assumed their recognizable shape.

The key to many of these eighteenth-century developments lay in the growth of the slave population. This was the result in part—but only in part—of the substantial rise in slave imports from Africa. During the peak period from 1740 to 1760, there were over a hundred thousand new arrivals on American shores, and Charleston in particular became a major slave-trading port. The proportion of African-born among the black population was at its highest in this same period. However, in the longer term, the other source of population growth—by natural increase—was even more significant. Among slave imports, there had always been a preponderance of males—probably at least two males for every female. This imbalance between the sexes, combined with the severe effects of the Atlantic crossing and the initial shock of the New World upon female fertility, meant that the first generation of slaves did not even reproduce their own population, let alone produce a natural increase. In the normal course of events, the numerically smaller second generation would have a balance between the sexes, and, if its health and living and working conditions met certain basic standards, a natural increase in population was likely to follow. There were other factors, too. The overall increase in the black population, its greater density, the growth of larger-scale ownership in some areas, and improvements in communications made it easier for slaves to find mates and for some kind of family life to develop. Whatever the precise combination of factors at work, the beginnings of a sustained natural increase transformed the future prospects of slavery in the South.

The conspicuous growth of the slave population had very mixed effects. On one hand, the white population, and slave owners in particular, felt the need to tighten their control and formalize the system in various ways. This need was intensified by economic concerns, as slave labor was now the basis of a flourishing Atlantic trade based on tobacco in Virginia and Maryland and rice and other subtropical products in the Carolinas. The Southern colonies enacted—and frequently strengthened—legal codes which reinforced the authority of the master, placed further restrictions on the slaves, and underlined distinctions based on race and color. Masters themselves resorted to tougher punishments and stricter discipline. Slaves imported directly from Africa often struck their owners as more alien than earlier arrivals from the Caribbean, and therefore in need of much tighter control. On the other hand, as the numbers of the American-born increased, masters found themselves dealing with a slave population which had known no other life but slavery, and habits of submissiveness could be inculcated from infancy.

In many respects, therefore, and in what was often still a fairly primitive frontier society, Southern slavery was at its harshest in the pre-Revolutionary era. Yet, at the same time, and for many of the same reasons stemming from population growth, slaves were beginning to develop their own distinct community life, based on families, kinship networks, and shared experience. Adversity and tighter control cruelly limited slave horizons, but also stimulated a very powerful reaction—and closer physical proximity and larger numbers provided the environment in which that response could develop.

While the effects of conditioning imposed by white society from the cradle to the grave were clearly important and often damaging, slaves did not necessarily learn from their masters only the lessons they were intended to learn. Moreover, masters concerned themselves predominantly with the working lives of their slaves and were often content to ignore the slaves' other life, which went on in the quarters after working hours or on days of rest. It was in these limited but precious hours that the patterns of the life of the slave community were gradually taking shape. Out of those patterns grew a distinctive Afro-American culture, synthesizing elements both from the African heritage (personified in slaves recently arrived from Africa) and from the pervasive white influence which dominated so much of slave life. Here again, the eighteenth century was of vital importance in the historical evolution of slave life in the South.[7]

All in all, this was the period which, in Duncan MacLeod's apt phrase, "witnessed the transformation of the southern colonies from societies with slaves into slave societies."[8] Then the American Revolution signaled another critical phase, laden with new ironies and paradoxes, in the history of the peculiar institution. Slaves were more than passive observers or victims of the War of Independence. Both sides used them as frontline soldiers, or more often in a variety of ancillary roles; much the larger numbers were engaged on the British side. Many slaves saw opportunities for seeking individual freedom during the Revolutionary war, and as many as fifty thousand may have been evacuated with the British forces in the closing stages—although some later returned.[9]

Wider significance attached to the uneasy coexistence of the ideals of the Declaration of Independence and the substantial, inconvenient fact of Negro slavery. Although the idea of some kind of symbiotic relationship between black bondage and their own freedom had taken root in many Southern minds, it was hard to escape completely the embarrassing implications of slavery for the principles and rhetoric of the Revolution (and vice versa). However, many supporters of the revolutionary cause succeeded either in compartmentalizing their thinking, so that the republican liberties of whites could be kept distinct from the emancipation of enslaved blacks, or in reducing the problem to one of priorities and assigning to emancipation a rather low place. The conservative face of the Revolution showed in a profound respect for property rights, which included property rights in slaves, and in an abiding fear of upsetting the delicate mechanisms of slave society. Most importantly and ironically of all, that conservatism found a new emphasis in the more explicit racism which buttressed the defense of slavery after the Revolution. As Duncan MacLeod and others have shown, whatever the difficulties of reconciling the revolutionary principle of political freedom with the institution of slavery, Americans of the Revolutionary generation managed to retain both their philosophy and their peculiar institution of slavery by redefining the humanity of the Negro. The free society of the infant republic was an even more consciously and explicitly white society than its colonial predecessor.[10]

Some historians, including Kenneth Stampp,[11] have seen the Revolution as a great missed opportunity to get rid of slavery, but in fact there was never much likelihood that such an opportunity would have been widely perceived, let alone seized. In 1787, the framers of the Constitution employed various circumlocutions to avoid using the actual word "slavery," but they gave the institution tacit recognition and protection where it already existed. In 1790, the first federal census counted over 650,000 slaves in the Southern states—a sizable element in a total U.S. population of less than four million. The generation of the founding fathers, not altogether surprisingly, shrank from the formidable task of tackling the problem of slavery head-on, although it was not averse to attacking its weaker points. Such an approach stored up trouble for the future. In the meantime, there was comfort in a posture of resigned acceptance of the burdens the institution laid upon white shoulders, or in the often expressed prediction that slavery might die, sooner rather than later, from natural causes.

There were, however, members of the Revolutionary generation who could not live with the contradiction between white freedom and black slavery. A number of slaveholders, particularly in the coastal counties of Maryland and Virginia—though only a small minority of the total—arranged for the manumission of their slaves during and after the Revolution. The free black population of the South multiplied several times over between 1776 and 1800, but even in the Chesapeake Bay region it was still very heavily outnumbered by the slave population. The city of Baltimore was the only place in the region where there were more free blacks than slaves. With hindsight, it is possible to see the beginning of the process which would eventually make Maryland as much a state with free blacks as a slave state, but as Richard Dunn has observed, the experience of Virginia was very different. There, during the early period of the United States, slavery was still expanding and strengthening its grip.[12]

More generally, there was no fundamental crisis of Southern confidence in slavery in the wake of the Revolution. Nor was there a desperate crisis facing the future economic viability of slavery. The notion, once widely held, that slavery was on its last legs economically in the closing decades of the eighteenth century has little evidence to support it, although there was some uncertainty about its long-term future. In fact, the center of gravity of slavery in Virginia was moving westward, as the slave population increased in the central part of the state and slaveholding became more deeply entrenched there. In the low country of South Carolina and Georgia, also, slavery was growing rapidly and consolidating its strength during and after the Revolution.[13] What even its most ardent champions could scarcely have foreseen a generation earlier was the new era of dramatic and galloping expansion upon which slavery was about to embark, from the 1790s to the 1820s. Far from showing any inclination to fade and die, slavery was in many ways revitalized during those decades.

Paradoxically, the new expansion took place within limits which were themselves being defined with increasing sharpness. It is true that the wave of post-Revolution manumissions soon subsided, and legal and social pressures discouraged further resort to them. But, if constraints within the South weakened, restrictions imposed from outside gained strength during the following decades. In the North, where slavery had much shallower roots, the awkward questions raised by the ideology of the Revolution found a more receptive audience. During or after the Revolution, the Northern states all committed themselves to the abolition of slavery, although the process was painfully slow in some cases. The Northwest Ordinance of 1787 kept slavery out of the vast territory to the north of the Ohio River, although for more than thirty years attempts were made to break down that barrier. The stage was set for the parallel and competitive expansion of freedom and slavery into the great central valley of the United States. In 1820, the Missouri Compromise barred slavery from most of the huge Louisiana Purchase and, in fact, left slavery with little further scope for expansion in the remaining territories of the United States as they then existed. Fears about the ability of supply to keep pace with demand for slave labor were raised by the ban on the importation of slaves imposed in 1808. The Constitution had prevented any such ban before 1808, but Congress lost no time in acting once it had the constitutional authority to do so. Mass movement of slaves into the Deep South and the southwest sowed the seeds of slavery's relative decline in the upper South. By the 1830s the rising abolitionist movement in the North added moral strictures to the territorial restrictions on slavery.

Despite external moves to circumscribe slavery, the practice actually was given a new lease on life during this same period. Its westward surge shifted the whole center of gravity of the South's peculiar institution dramatically from the upper South to the Deep South and from east to west. The key to that expansion lay in cotton. In the agriculture of the colonial South, cotton was a very minor crop indeed; in the generation after 1790, it came into power in its Southern kingdom. Demand, technology, land, and labor came together to launch the cotton boom. The demand came from across the Atlantic, above all from Britain, where technological innovation put cotton mills in the forefront of the industrial revolution. Southern ability to meet that demand depended on another, and simpler, technological development—the cotton gin. This invention removed the great bottleneck which had hitherto plagued cotton growing—the removal of the lint from the seeds. Other important factors were the development of new strains of cotton which could be successfully grown over wide areas of the South, and the availability of suitable land. With the removal of the Native Americans from large areas, South Carolina and Georgia became the first major cotton states; but, particularly after the War of 1812, settlement poured on to the rich soil of the black belt in Alabama and Mississippi, which became the heartland of the cotton kingdom.

Slave labor supplied the other necessity of that expanding realm.

Cotton has a long growing season and requires a substantial amount of steady toil, but the peak demand for labor occurs when the crop has to be picked. Growers found that, by cultivating corn as well as cotton, they could make more effective year-round use of their labor force. Cotton offered the further advantage that slave labor could be employed in its cultivation almost equally effectively on large plantations or on much smaller farms. The spread of cotton cultivation was accompanied by a large-scale movement of slaves, often over long distances, to the new lands of Alabama and Mississippi. Since the Revolution, there had already been considerable movement of slaves from Virginia into Kentucky and Tennessee, much of it in groups as owners moved westward, taking their families and their slaves with them. The longer-distance migration to the southwest encouraged the development after 1815 of a more organized slave trade, which was much more disruptive in its effects upon the slaves, and particularly upon their families.

As the cotton crop increased by leaps and bounds—it almost tripled in the decade after the War of 1812—both the area of slavery and the number of slaves also grew rapidly. The latter trend continued in spite of the abolition of the external slave trade in 1808, the earliest date at which its cessation was allowed under the Constitution. In anticipation of that event, something like a hundred thousand slaves from Africa were brought into the United States between 1790 and the ending of the trade—and almost forty thousand of them arrived at Charleston alone in the last few years before 1808.[14] Many of these new arrivals from Africa were taken immediately deep into the interior to be employed in cotton cultivation; they suffered with particular acuteness from feelings of isolation, disorientation, and bewilderment.

After the closing of the external slave trade, however, it was conclusively demonstrated that the natural increase of the slave population would be able to sustain the continued expansion of the slave South. By 1830, the number of slaves had passed the two million mark. This capacity for growth and potential for further growth were the most astonishing features of the whole period. Slavery, and the economic and social system which rested upon it, showed qualities of flexibility, adaptability, mobility, and expansiveness which were largely unsuspected at the time when U.S. independence was achieved. The institution of slavery and many thousands of individual slaves were part of the history of westward expansion and the American frontier experience.

Between 1790 and 1830, the Southern scene had been transformed; a new staple crop had risen to dominance, new lands had been opened up, many new people had entered the slaveholding class, and many existing owners had exchanged old locations for new. Inevitably, it was the slaves themselves who commonly suffered the severest growing pains of a society on the move and on the make. They were coerced into a great forced migration, often over long distances, and were obliged to start all over again the process of putting together some kind of family and community life of their own. Even those who were spared long-distance moves often encountered similarly unsettling experiences. Richard Dunn has shown that large-scale slave owners in Virginia frequently shifted slaves from one to another of their scattered properties.[15]

By 1830, Southern leaders could proudly assert their confidence in their distinctive slave society. Slavery was flourishing as a labor system, a social institution, and a device for control of one race by another. It had proved beyond a doubt its capacity for growth and its potential for further expansion. However, in other ways it was also fragile and vulnerable, and behind the confidence of its protagonists and propagandists lurked anxieties which could never be entirely suppressed. Slavery was now a sectional and no longer a national institution; it was exceptional—an unmistakably peculiar institution which set the South apart not only from the North but from almost the entire Atlantic world; it was an uneasy institution, sensitive to outside attack and disturbed by uncertainties within.[16]

It was a system which lived on, by, and with fear. Slaves were compelled by force of circumstances to fear their masters; non-slave-owning whites felt threatened socially and economically by blacks, whether slave or free; and all Southern whites shared the constant, nagging fear of servile insurrection—and, in 1831, the Nat Turner uprising in Southampton County, Virginia, fed that fear anew. The whole white South feared outside interference or domination. Parts of the upper South and the Atlantic seaboard feared for the future of slavery on their exhausted or depleted soils. Slave owners generally feared for their social status, their economic well-being, and their personal security, should their peculiar institution come to an end. Indeed, the fear which subsumed many of the others was dread of the consequences—economic ruin, social chaos, and racial anarchy—which, it was generally believed, would follow the abandonment of slavery.

Two prominent features of Southern slavery conspired to add to the paradoxes of the system. First, slavery was explicitly and essentially racial. The line of race and color drawn between master and slave was so firm that the few exceptions did not threaten it. This line dictated the formal rigidity of the master-slave relationship, the difficulty and relative rarity of manumission, and the twilight existence of the free black community. There were few escape hatches of any kind, and the color of a slave's skin marked him or her indelibly. Bondage was a life sentence and a hereditary one. Stanley Elkins attributes the harsh lines and the severity of this slave system to its origins in "unrestrained capitalism."[17] Racism, at least as much as capitalism, may have been the villain of the piece, and the one no doubt reinforced the other.

The other unquestionable—indeed unique—mark of slavery in the Southern states was the natural increase of the slave population. In all other slave societies of the New World, the slave population failed to reproduce itself and was sustained or increased only by constant injections of new slaves from Africa. In the Caribbean, in particular, the system was one of rapid and ruthless exploitation of the slaves to the point of exhaustion, sickness, and death, and then their replacement by fresh stock. In the Southern colonies—and later, states—of North America, the demographic pattern was quite different, partly because the ravages of infectious diseases were less severe, and partly because there was less voracious demand for the products of the eighteenth-century South than for West Indian sugar—and therefore less temptation to seek high profits by ruthless exploitation and exhaustion of the labor force.[18] On a small Caribbean island, land was at a premium but fresh supplies of slaves were quite readily obtainable; in the South, land was plentiful but the supply of labor had to be carefully husbanded. In contrast to the continuing preponderance of males in slave populations elsewhere, the near-balance of the sexes in the South had been producing a natural increase for many years. After the abolition of the external slave trade in 1808, the South depended on its own resources for its future slave labor force. It was now more clearly than ever in the interest of slaveholders to provide at least the minimal material and social conditions which would foster (or at least not discourage) slave fertility.

The juxtaposition of two features—rigidity and harshness on one hand, a measure of concern for slave living standards on the other—helps to explain one of the inner contradictions of the whole system.[19] Southern slavery sought to combine two apparently incompatible elements. It totally denied any rights to the slave, aimed to reduce the slave to a state of total dependence, and tried to confine him or her inescapably within the system. Yet, at the same time, it made material provision for the slave superior to that provided by other systems of bondage, moderated the severity of the system in its practical day-by-day application, made room for an element of paternalism in the master-slave relationship, and used the mediating influence of tacit compromise and "double-think." The slave society of the double standard was the product of a very distinctive historical and demographic background which had been evolving over at least two centuries.

NOTES

1. Ira Berlin, "Time, Space and the Evolution of Afro-American Society on British Mainland North America," *American Historical Review* 85 (1980): 44–78.

2. The most authoritative analysis of the slave trade is Philip D. Curtin, *The Atlantic Slave Trade: A Census* (Madison, Wis., 1969). Herbert S. Klein, *The Middle Passage: Comparative Studies in the Atlantic Slave Trade* (Princeton, N.J., 1978) includes discussion of the importation of slaves into the North American mainland. A useful modern treatment of the whole subject is James A. Rawley, *The Transatlantic Slave Trade: A History* (New York, 1981).

3. Winthrop D. Jordan, *White over Black: American Attitudes Toward the Negro, 1550–1812* (Chapel Hill, N.C., 1968), 80–2.

4. The debate among historians about the evolution of slavery in the Chesapeake Bay area during the seventeenth century is skilfully summarized in Boles, *Black Southerners,* chapter 1, with references to important articles in various journals on 217–8. Edmund S. Morgan, *American Slavery, American Freedom: The Ordeal of Colonial Virginia* (New York, 1975) is a study of major importance. See especially chapter 15 for the switch of emphasis from indentured servitude to slavery in the late seventeenth century.

5. Peter H. Wood, *Black Majority: Negroes in Colonial South Carolina from 1670 through the Stono Rebellion* (New York, 1974), 96.

6. Ibid., 326. The brief account in this chapter of the development of slavery in South Carolina relies heavily on Wood's authoritative study.

7. Eighteenth-century developments are discussed in the later chapters of Morgan, *American Slavery, American Freedom,* and in Ira Berlin, "Time, Space

and the Evolution of Afro-American Society." Among Allan Kulikoff's various articles, see in particular "The Origins of Afro-American Society in Tidewater Maryland and Virginia, 1700–1790," *William and Mary Quarterly*, third series, 35 (1978): 226–59. See also Thad W. Tate, *The Negro in Eighteenth-Century Williamsburg* (Charlottesville, Va., 1966); Gerald W. Mullin, *Flight and Rebellion: Slave Resistance in Eighteenth-Century Virginia* (New York, 1972); and Betty Wood, *Slavery in Colonial Georgia, 1730–1775* (Athens, Ga., 1984).

8. Duncan J. MacLeod, "Toward Caste," in Ira Berlin and Ronald Hoffman, eds., *Slavery and Freedom in the Age of the American Revolution* (Charlottesville, Va., 1983), 229.

9. The standard work is Benjamin Quarles, *The Negro in the American Revolution* (Chapel Hill, N.C., 1961). See also Ira Berlin, "The Revolution in Black Life," in Alfred F. Young, ed., *The American Revolution: Explorations in the History of American Radicalism* (DeKalb, Ill., 1976), 349–82.

10. Duncan J. MacLeod, *Slavery, Race and the American Revolution* (Cambridge, 1974). See also Oakes, *The Ruling Race*, 28–33. An essay of seminal importance is William W. Freehling, "The Founding Fathers and Slavery," *American Historical Review* 77 (1972): 81–93.

11. Kenneth M. Stampp, "Slavery: The Historian's Burden," in Owens, *Perspectives and Irony*, 153–7.

12. Richard S. Dunn, "Black Society in the Chesapeake, 1776–1810," in Berlin and Hoffman, eds., *Slavery and Freedom in the Age of the American Revolution*, 49–82.

13. Ibid., 51–2, 59–74, 81; Philip D. Morgan, "Black Society in the Lowcountry, 1760–1810," in ibid., 83–108, 140–1.

14. Allan Kulikoff, "Uprooted Peoples: Black Migrants in the Age of the American Revolution, 1790–1820," in ibid., 149–50, and more generally, 143–71. For some observations on the ironic consequences of the ending of the external slave trade, see Carl Degler, "The Irony of American Negro Slavery," in Owens, ed., *Perspectives and Irony*, 4–7.

15. Richard S. Dunn, "A Tale of Two Plantations: Slave Life at Mesopotamia in Jamaica and Mount Airy in Virginia, 1799 to 1828," *William and Mary Quarterly*, third series, 36 (1977): 32–65.

16. Much of this discussion of the transformation of slavery in the period 1790–1830 is based on Freehling, "The Founding Fathers and Slavery." This crucial period may have received less attention from historians than it deserves, but see the extremely important essay by Willie Lee Rose, "The Domestication of Domestic Slavery," in *Slavery and Freedom*, William W. Freehling, ed. (New York, 1982), especially 20–8.

17. Elkins, *Slavery*, third ed., 52–80.

18. For a good brief discussion, see James A. Henretta, *The Evolution of American Society, 1700–1815: An Interdisciplinary Analysis* (Lexington, Ma., 1973), 57–63.

19. Eugene Genovese has explored this duality within the slave system, and placed it within the context of his particular ideological perspective. See his *Roll, Jordan, Roll*, 49–70.

3

The Labor of the Slaves

Despite the growing awareness among historians of the importance of the earlier history of slavery in North America, it remains true that our knowledge and understanding of the peculiar institution are greatest in its last few decades. Inevitably, much of the discussion of slave work patterns, the economics of slavery, and the life of the slave community must remain centered on slavery in its maturity, at what proved to be its historical peak in the antebellum South. It must be remembered, however, that during the last three or four decades of its history, slavery was still an expanding and evolving institution. For example, although the absolute numbers of slaveholders and slaves were still increasing rapidly, the proportion of Southern white families who owned slaves showed some decline in the immediate pre–Civil War period—from a little more than a third in 1830 to a little more than a quarter in 1860.[1] In the same period, there was a small but not insignificant increase in the average number of slaves per slave owner.

The census of 1860 showed that there were nearly 4 million slaves out of a total population of 12.3 million in the fifteen slave states. The proportion of slave to white population varied greatly from area to area, with the heaviest concentrations in the Deep South. In South Carolina and Mississippi more than half the population were slaves, and in Louisiana, Alabama, Florida, and Georgia the slave population was more than two-fifths. In no other state did slaves amount to one-third of the population; in Maryland, the proportion was 13 percent, in Missouri 10 percent, in Delaware a mere 1.5 percent. Overall, there were some 385,000 slave owners out of about 1.5 million white families (and a total white population of 8 million).

Fifty percent of slave owners owned no more than five slaves, and only 12 percent owned twenty or more. At the summit of the Southern social pyramid were the ten thousand owners with more than fifty slaves, including three thousand with more than one hundred. The majority of slaveholders were therefore small-scale owners, but large-scale ownership by a small minority meant that more than half the slaves lived on plantations with more than twenty slaves. John Boles has pointed out the interesting statistical coincidence that, in 1850, 73.4 percent of slaveholders owned less than ten slaves, but at the same time precisely 73.4 percent of slaves lived in units numbering more than ten.[2]

Various conclusions may be drawn from these statistics. First and foremost, they emphasize the variety of slavery in terms of location, distribution of population, and size of unit of ownership. Even within one individual state, the overall figures for slave ownership fail to show wide local variations between the coastal plain and the hill country of the interior, the black belt and the pine barrens, or in the case of a border state like Missouri, between the concentration of slaves along the Missouri River itself and their virtual absence from much of the rest of the state.

Second, behind all the census figures lies the fundamental but often forgettable fact that three-quarters of Southern white families owned no slaves at all. Numerically at least, the typical white Southerners were small farmers cultivating their own soil, not infrequently on the move from one area to another, and in many respects not unlike their Northern counterparts, except that they lived cheek-by-jowl with slavery and accepted its social and racial imperatives as well as its economic repercussions. The other side of this coin reveals that the great plantation owner with his hundreds or at least scores of slaves—a figure so central to the legend and the romance of the Old South—belonged to a tiny minority of the white population. Such men headed perhaps one-half of one percent of all Southern white households. They were, of course, powerful and influential far beyond their small numbers, but they were atypical in more than just the numerical sense. The plantations of many of the largest slave owners cultivated, not cotton, the great Southern staple, but either sugar, in Louisiana, or rice, on the coasts and sea islands of South Carolina and Georgia. In his remarkable study of the spectacularly wealthy rice plantations on the Waccamaw River in South Carolina, Charles

Joyner points out that, in 1860, twenty-nine of the eighty-eight Southern slaveholders who owned more than three hundred slaves were rice planters. No fewer than seven of them owned plantations on the Waccamaw. At the very apex of slave ownership were the fourteen men who owned more than five hundred slaves; nine of them were rice planters, and three of those planted on the Waccamaw. One of those three, Joshua Ward, was the only planter in the whole South who owned more than one thousand slaves.[3]

The third set of conclusions to be drawn from the bare statistics depend upon interpretation of the evidence. To say that one-quarter of Southern white families owned slaves in 1860 is a neutral and objective statement of fact. On the other hand, to say that *only* one-quarter of those families owned slaves is to offer a judgment, or at least an interpretation. It implies, as various historians have done, that slave ownership was the privilege of a relatively small minority of the Southern white population, and that Southern society was dominated by a slave-owning oligarchy. However, Otto Olsen has argued powerfully that the figures should be seen in a very different light. If attention is confined to the states that eventually became part of the Confederacy, 31 percent of white families owned slaves in 1860. In South Carolina and Mississippi, almost half the white families owned slaves; in four more states of the Deep South, one-third or more of the white families owned slaves. These figures, says Olsen, represent "an amazingly large, rather than a small, base of support for any economic order." The fairest kind of comparison, he argues, is with other forms of property ownership in other periods. For example, in 1949, only 2 percent of American families held stock worth $5,000 or more—roughly equivalent in today's terms to the worth of one slave. No doubt by the 1980s the percentage will have increased considerably, but not to a point where it would come anywhere close to the figures for slave ownership in the Old South. "Slavery," says Olsen, "appears a good bit less oligarchical in several significant economic respects than twentieth century free labour capitalism. The ownership of slaves was spread among a remarkably broad proportion of the white population, and the extent of this investment was central to Southern white unity before, during and after the Civil War."[4]

This picture of slavery is largely borne out by James Oakes in his study of Southern slaveholders, *The Ruling Race*. He divides the slave owners broadly into three categories. At one extreme were the small elite of great planters who have commanded so much of the limelight in both Southern mythology and Southern historiography. Oakes sometimes shows an excess of zeal in his determination to redress the balance and relegate this group to the sidelines or the backwaters of Southern society. At the other extreme was the large number of owners of no more than five slaves. Members of this group commonly worked alongside their handful of slaves in the fields and shared with them the ups and downs of their lives, their generally precarious economic situation, and their frequent moves in search of a fresh start. Between these two contrasting classes of large planters and small, struggling farmers were the substantial numbers of middle-class masters, whom Oakes sees as very much the backbone of Southern slave society. They were often ambitious, upwardly mobile men, constantly seeking to acquire more land and more slaves, and often combining their land ownership with pursuit of other business or professional interests, as shopkeepers, artisans, doctors, teachers, and, most notably perhaps, as lawyers.[5]

For members of all three classes, slave ownership was an indication of status and a vehicle of upward mobility. But they invested in slaves, and yet more slaves, chiefly for their labor, and it is appropriate that any more detailed consideration of the South's peculiar institution should begin with the work slaves were required to undertake. Before all else, a slave life was one of toil.

The great majority of slaves were employed in agriculture, or in occupations relating to it. Although slaves were widely used in general or mixed farming, most worked on the cultivation of the great staple crops of the South. The census of 1850 offered estimates (which may be little more than reasonable guesses) of the numbers employed in the production of the major crops. Out of 2.5 million slaves directly employed in agriculture, it calculated that 350,000 were engaged in the cultivation of tobacco; 150,000 in sugar; 125,000 in rice; 60,000 in hemp; and a massive 1,815,000 in cotton.

The considerable variety in the nature and organization of slave work derived not only from the range of crops under cultivation but also from the size of the farm or plantation. The working life of the slaves of smaller owners was not in many respects very different from the lot of the farm laborer elsewhere. The owner worked with the slaves and supervised them directly, and the working relationship—

indeed the whole way of life—was obviously less organized and formalized than on the plantation. There was no scope for the more elaborate managerial structure and the specialization of labor which was a feature of large plantations. "I have no overseer," wrote one farmer, "and do not manage so scientifically as those who are able to lay down rules; yet I endeavor to manage so that myself, family and negroes may take pleasure and delight in our relations."[6] Not all small owners shared a similar disposition or similar priorities, and the slaves of such owners were, more directly than most, at the mercy of the moods and whims of individual masters.

Much less has been said and written about slavery in this kind of environment than on the large plantation. It was the great planters, after all, who left the most substantial historical record. There is inadequate information, too, about slaves belonging to what Oakes calls the middle-class owners. However, some historians—Paul Escott and Orville Burton,[7] for example—incline to the view that such slaves probably experienced some of the harshest working conditions. They suffered from the worst of both worlds: They lacked on one hand the close working relationship with the owner of a small farm, and on the other hand the security, order, and sense of belonging to a sizable slave community provided by the larger plantation.

Among plantation slaves, around half were normally full-time field hands, although efficient owners were always striving to increase that proportion. The relentless routine of the seasons required more labor in the fields at some times, less at others. On cotton plantations, the hoe was the main implement in the hands of gangs of field hands as they toiled in the sun under regular supervision to clear the grass and weeds which always threatened to overwhelm the cotton plants. Some planters preferred the task system to the gang system, particularly in rice-growing areas. Under this system, each hand was assigned a task for the day and could stop work early when he or she had completed that task. Opinions were divided on the merits of this system. It offered an incentive to the slaves, but its opponents believed it encouraged hasty and careless work and left some slaves with time on their hands. James Henry Hammond tried to abolish the task system on his South Carolina plantation, but pressure from his slaves obliged him to restore it at least in a modified form.[8]

Working hours were long—traditionally from sunup to sundown—but recognized breaks during the day were generally observed, and slaves as well as freemen rested on the Sabbath. There were times, too, when bad weather or the season of the year relieved the burden of work the field hands shouldered. The peak demand for labor came at the end of the season, at cotton-picking time, when every available hand, whatever his or her normal occupation, was needed in the fields. Indeed, the productivity of the cotton plantation was limited more by this bottleneck at the point of picking than by the work rate or efficiency of the slave labor force throughout the year. The Old South had the capacity to grow more cotton than it could pick, and until that problem was solved, there was little incentive to mechanize or modernize the earlier stages of cotton cultivation.

Plantation slaves were classified as full or fractional (half, quarter, etc.) hands, with the old, the younger children, and the expectant and nursing mothers regarded as equivalent to something less than a full field hand. Slaves who were not working in the fields were full-time or part-time domestics, craftspersons, mechanics, gardeners, blacksmiths, carpenters, millers, seamstresses, or general workers. Skilled workers were often important figures in the work of the plantation and in the life of the slave community. Household staff on some of the grander plantations were sometimes encouraged to give themselves a few airs and graces, but elsewhere the distinction between domestic servants and field hands was much less clear-cut. A maid in the big house might share a cabin with a field-hand husband and their children. At peak times, domestic slaves were often required to work in the fields.

The organization and supervision of a substantial slave work force demanded considerable managerial skill. The subject was endlessly debated in Southern newspapers and journals. However, as James Oakes has emphasized, there was often a world of difference between the ideal as expounded in print and the reality as practiced amid all the vagaries of weather, pestilence, fluctuating prices, and the irrepressible humanity of the owner's slave property.[9] On plantations large enough to justify such a management structure, the master would employ an overseer, usually white but very occasionally black, who bore a considerable load of responsibility and shielded the owner from some of the more tedious and unpleasant aspects of slave ownership. The overseer was very much a man in the middle, under pressure from the master and often unpopular with the slaves. Required to maximize the crop while dealing fairly with the slaves, he lived from one insoluble dilemma to the next.

Beneath the overseer in the hierarchy were the slave drivers, men drawn from the ranks of the slaves themselves and often taking responsibility for much of the day-to-day running of the plantation. On smaller plantations, where no overseer was hired, the slave driver was often in a position of authority if, for example, the master was absent. On farms where management was less formally organized, there was often a senior figure or a natural leader among the small slave work force who acted as driver in all but name. The slave driver occupied a position which was prestigious but precarious. He was put in a position of trust by the master and enjoyed certain privileges and perquisites; but always he had to be sensitive to the feelings of his fellow slaves, among whom he may have enjoyed a measure of respect but in whom he could all too easily inspire jealousy and resentment. The position of the slave driver summed up many of the tensions, dilemmas, and conflicting pressures of day-to-day slave life.[10]

Several issues relating to the work of slaves have excited historical controversy. How hard did slaves in fact work? What were the relative roles of sanctions and rewards in forcing or persuading slaves to work hard? Was slave labor efficient? What was the attitude of slaves themselves toward their work? The view which prevailed for many years was that slaves worked long and hard simply because they were forced to under the threat of the lash, but that they achieved no high level of efficiency. In relative terms, low efficiency was made tolerable by the low cost of slave labor. Kenneth Stampp's interpretation belongs broadly to this school of thought, but he also offers a balanced appraisal of the role of incentives—a garden plot, permission to sell produce from it, extra holidays or passes to leave the plantation, and even money payments and crude profit-sharing schemes. But he sees incentives as but one weapon—and a subsidiary one—in an armory of slave control which included firm discipline, demonstration of the master's power (symbolized by the whip), and the inculcation of a sense of slave inferiority.[11]

Fresh interest in these, as in so many issues, was generated by the remarkable conclusions of Fogel and Engerman in their highly controversial book, *Time on the Cross*. Their case for the efficiency of slave labor depends heavily not only upon the advantages of organization and manipulation of a large labor force but on the superior quality of the work force itself. Far from being lazy or incompetent, slaves were, they argued, more efficient and industrious on average than their free white counterparts. Their masters had not merely organized them effectively but had imbued them with the Protestant work ethic, a drive toward self-improvement through their own efforts.

The superiority of slave workers was not, according to Fogel and Engerman, the result of abnormally long hours, constant and brutal punishment, or ruthless exploitation. In their estimation, slaves worked shorter hours and fewer days in the year than contemporary free workers, and the extent of whipping has been grossly exaggerated. Fogel and Engerman even claimed that slaves received as "income" (though not of course as cash income) something like 90 percent of the product of their labor—which compared very favorably with the income of wage-earning employees.

In the *Time on the Cross* version of slavery, the carrot largely replaces the stick, and great emphasis is placed on the array of incentives offered to slaves. Within the ranks of slave labor, it is suggested, there was a series of grades tantamount to a career structure, by means of which the cooperative or industrious slave might be promoted to one of a variety of skilled or supervisory occupations. The slaves were not brutalized but socialized.[12]

Time on the Cross provoked an immediate and highly critical reaction which undermined or overturned many of its conclusions.[13] In the longer run, for all its serious flaws, it has helped to stimulate a more considered reappraisal of many aspects of slave work—as indeed of slavery in general—often in the form of more specialized or local studies which have put the book's arguments to the test, and often, though not invariably, found them wanting. In one of the essays in *Reckoning with Slavery*, the most comprehensive of the immediate counterblasts to *Time on the Cross*, Herbert Gutman and Richard Sutch rebutted point by point much of the case of Fogel and Engerman on the work of the slaves—and did so with a degree of success many have found conclusive. At the heart of their argument is the well-supported charge that the conclusions of *Time on the Cross* relied on the rigid application of a model rather than the evaluation of a mass of detailed evidence. Such evidence as was cited—on whipping, for example—was slender, all too often atypical, and not infrequently misunderstood. The lash was used much more often than Fogel and Engerman allowed, and the number of promoted posts available to slaves was far fewer than they claimed. Equally serious is the danger of arguing backward from consequences to causes. A hierarchy of jobs is not the same as a career structure. Its existence does not prove that it was being systematically used as an incentive scheme.[14]

The sustained debate over punishments, rewards, and incentives since the publication of *Time on the Cross* has given new depth to our understanding of slave life and slave labor. Some general conclusions may be drawn from all the controversy. Clearly, the use of rewards and incentives, even if widespread, would not in itself prove that coercion was unimportant in making slaves work hard. It is surely in the nature of a slave system that force, or the threat of force, is fundamental and all other methods are secondary. The two basic conditions which set the pattern of slave control were the fact or the threat of punishment (whether by whipping or some other means) and the generally poor prospects of successful and permanent escape.

Within the limits of the coercive framework thus clearly established, slaves might well have been receptive to the idea of making the best of their lot and gaining rewards for extra effort or skilled work. At the same time, masters were able to resort to techniques of persuasion, mediation, and compromise, including inducements and payments of various kinds. They did so for sound economic reasons, but they had other motives too. It was often easier and more convenient to tread softly. It made for a quieter life and it avoided, in the daily routine, pushing the logic of slavery to its extremes of inhumanity. The relentless use of unbridled repressive force would have been a heavy drain on the slave owners as well as an appalling ordeal for the slaves. Furthermore, a policy of such total and unrelieved repression would only have served to create a force of hopelessly dependent and inefficient workers. As master of a large plantation, James Henry Hammond came to realize the value of inducements which might win the allegiance of his slaves, or at least their reluctant cooperation. But he turned to such expedients only after he had established his authority by a policy of severe and often brutal punishment, based on frequent recourse to the lash. In other words, he was following a policy much favored by schoolteachers, drill instructors, and prison guards throughout the ages—a policy of asserting authority by initial toughness and then showing flexibility and offering concessions from a position of strength.[15]

It was only the presence or the threat of coercion which permitted the resort to persuasion. Coercion could be relaxed if, and only as long as, gentler measures worked. It is possible to turn against Fogel and Engerman a quotation they use from a set of instructions to plantation managers:

> The object of all punishment should be, 1st, for correction to deter the offender from the repetition of an offence, from the fear of the like certain punishment; and, 2nd, for example to all others, shewing them that if they offend, they will likewise receive certain punishment. And these objects and ends of all just punishments can be better obtained by the certainty than by the severity of punishment.[16]

Punishment served as deterrent and as example to others. If it continued to serve its purpose without constant application, all well and good. But infrequent resort to the exercise of a power may testify to its importance and effectiveness rather than the opposite. Rewards and incentives were the superstructure built upon the foundation of coercion.

In one of the most often quoted passages in his accounts of his travels in the slave South, Frederick Law Olmstead commented on the discipline and concentration of a large hoe gang at work in the fields. In *Time on the Cross* the quoted passage ends as follows:

> I repeatedly rode through the lines at a canter, with other horsemen, often coming upon them suddenly, without producing the smallest change or interruption in the dogged action of the labourers, or causing one of them, so far as I could see, to lift an eye from the ground.

In *Reckoning with Slavery* the critics take Fogel and Engerman to task, rightly, for omitting the next sentence:

> A very tall and powerful negro walked to and fro in the rear of the line, frequently cracking his whip, and calling out, in the surliest manner, to one and another, "Shove your hoe, there! Shove your hoe."

Unfortunately, the critics spoil a good point by themselves omitting the short sentence which follows:

> But I never saw him strike any one with the whip.[17]

The full extract reveals much more about the nature of slave control than any one piece of it carefully edited to serve as ammunition for historical controversy.

Clearly, in the case of rewards as well as punishments, there was both an exemplary and a ritual significance in the actions of the slaveholder. There is, however, an important distinction between concessions or rewards granted to all the slaves on a plantation, and payments or incentives available only to a few with some particular skill or responsibility. When the master, accompanied by his wife, distributed gifts to the assembled slaves on Christmas morning, or permitted an extra day's holiday after a period of intense labor, or paid money to a skilled worker, or allowed him or her to keep some of the profits of his or her craftsmanship, he may have been making a statement about his self-image as a benevolent paternalist, but he was also demonstrating the inducements and rewards available to some or all of his slave workers.

Similarly, when all the slaves were summoned to witness a whipping meted out to some offending or recalcitrant bondman or bondwoman, the master was making a statement about his power and his authority. Charles Joyner emphasizes the ritual aspect of such occasions:

> When a master supervised—or administered—punishment, no less than when he dispensed gifts and favors, he did so in rituals that contrasted the dependent position of the slave with his own status of dominance. . . . Thus formalized public punishment dramatized in a particularly acute way, free of etiquette, euphemism, and illusion, the enforcement of rules of deference and social behavior.[18]

Like several other historians, Joyner is also skeptical about the claim of Fogel and Engerman that slaveholders successfully imbued their slaves with something akin to the Protestant work ethic. In his in-depth study of South Carolina rice plantations, he shows that, while slaves did respond to the specific incentives offered to them, they did not swallow whole the values which underlay them. He suggests that slaves had some success in superimposing the communal values derived from their African heritage upon the individualist, competitive ethos of their white masters. More generally, slaves could surely take pride in a job well done, a crop safely gathered in, a furrow plowed straight and true, or a fence neatly mended—but their pride was in their own achievement and did not imply a surrender to any values imposed by the master. In Joyner's words:

> If they were efficient workers *within* the system of paternalism, they were also effective workers *of* the system, and they knew how to work it for their own ends.[19]

This kind of observation offers a salutary reminder that slaves were not just passive participants but active contributors to the labor system under which they were forced to live. No one has presented a more compelling argument and a richer accumulation of evidence to support this perspective on slavery than Eugene Genovese, particularly in his most substantial book, *Roll, Jordan, Roll: The World the Slaves Made.* He eschews the complicated statistics of *Time on the Cross,* but threatens his readers with the danger of a leap out of the cliometrical frying pan into the ideological fire. A Marxist historian who has fought notable battles with others on the left, Genovese has been much influenced by the Italian thinker Antonio Gramsci and is anything but an evangelist for the gospel of economic determinism. Rather, he has used the concepts of paternalism and hegemony on the master's side, and the complex balance between accommodation and resistance on the slave's side, to build up a subtle picture of the web of interdependence between owner and owned. Genovese analyzes the slave system and the master-slave relationship in terms of class as well as racial conflict, and depicts the slave's relationship with his or her master and work as a variant of the class struggle under capitalism. However, Genovese excels above all in depicting the intricate network of human relationships within a slave society. The foreground of Genovese's picture of slave life and work generally carries conviction, whether or not the reader is receptive to the ideological background.

"The slaveholders," says Genovese, "presided over a plantation system that constituted a halfway house between peasant and factory cultures." Slaveholders sought to impose upon their slaves a discipline and an attitude to work which the system required but which they did not admire or practice themselves. (The belief that hard work is extremely beneficial for other people is not of course confined to the slave-owning planters of the Old South.) The slaves sought to defend themselves as best they could against an enforced system of exploitation and an imposed set of values. "The plantation system served as a halfway house for Africans between their agricultural past and their imposed industrial future," says Genovese. The slaveholders "had their way but paid a price" in concessions to the slaves.[20]

Much more convincingly than Fogel and Engerman, Genovese describes the balance between coercion and persuasion in the slave system. He recognizes that slaves often did cooperate and respond to incentives, but he shows a sensitivity to the compromises and contradictions required to cope with the problems of daily life which entirely eludes the authors of *Time on the Cross*. There is a sense of history and of the human predicament in the one work which is missing in the other. Genovese may sometimes tend to exaggerate the explicit and conscious element in the striking of the balance between the two sides; at times his description resembles the formal, ritualized processes of bargaining in modern labor relations—although other studies show the skill of the slaves, for example, in converting privileges into rights. What Genovese does convey with great insight is the subtle interplay between coercion and conciliation on the part of the master, and deference and defiance on the part of the slaves.

In Genovese's view, slaves could and did work hard, but they resented the regularity and routine the system imposed. They could be goaded or encouraged into special effort at peak periods of the year, and found some fulfillment and heightened sense of community in such common exertion. However, for most slaves it was difficult to relate the toil which occupied most of their waking hours to the satisfaction of family and personal needs. They were not paid, and their rewards seemed in no way commensurate with the quantity or quality of their labor. They usually lacked the satisfaction as well as the responsibilities of a wage earner.

There may be some overstatement here in what is basically an important observation. Genovese concedes that some skilled plantation slaves and some industrial slaves may have achieved a sense of involvement and even satisfaction in their work—and the influence of rewards and incentives may have extended a little beyond these limited groups. More generally, a great many slaves surely perceived at least an indirect connection between their labor and its products, and the conditions in which they lived. They were shrewd enough to know that a good crop and a prosperous farm or plantation would yield not only profits to their owner but also indirect benefits to them in the shape of larger rations, improved housing, or increased privileges. Conversely, hard times, poor crops, financial losses, or insolvency for the owner could lead to hardship for the slaves, and even major upheaval and disruption of family life if the master felt compelled to dispose of some of his slave property.[21]

This question may serve to illustrate one of the difficulties facing modern historians—accustomed to life in an urban, industrial society—in seeking to understand the work patterns, the attitudes to work, and the working relationships of the slave society of the Old South. Southern historian John Boles has expressed a healthy skepticism about the description of the cotton plantation as a "farm-factory." He goes on to emphasize that latter-day notions of regularity, routine, and discipline—even of fixed hours or clear division between work and play—do not really apply to nineteenth-century farming and production of staple crops for distant markets. Seasonal fluctuations, the varying hours of daylight, the changing moods of the weather, reliance on animals rather than machinery, the diseases which afflicted both humans and other animals, and the multifarious tasks involved in running any farm or plantation all mounted to a series of challenges to regularity and organization. The work of the plantation and its slave labor force must be analyzed on its own terms, and not judged by the standards of late twentieth-century technology and managerial techniques.[22]

Such considerations also apply to some of the other controversial conclusions of *Time on the Cross*—for example, those attempting to measure the degree of exploitation of the slaves. It may be doubted how precisely it is possible to estimate the slaveholder's "rate of expropriation" of the fruits of slave labor—or at least whether any average or aggregate figure has much real meaning. Certainly, most of the critics seem to agree that the 10 percent (or possible 12 percent) rate of expropriation calculated by Fogel and Engerman is a serious underestimate, and suggest that the true figure may have been nearer to 50 percent.[23]

If attention is turned to more specific issues, evidence offered in *Time on the Cross* itself can supply unintended clues to the existence of a system of harsh exploitation. For example, in seeking to explain why the demand for slave labor in agriculture was inelastic—that is, why free labor did not compete with it—Fogel and Engerman concede that even if planters had been willing and able to offer small white farmers wages 50 percent above their normal earnings, they would not have been tempted to form themselves into a labor gang. The reason lay in the "negative nonpecuniary income" of slave workers.[24] Negative nonpecuniary income is a remarkable euphemism; in plain language it means that the work was unpleasant and unattractive to a degree which could not be overcome, in the eyes of free workers, even by large financial inducements. Whatever the inducements, free men would not voluntarily undertake work which slaves were compelled to do.

In her biography of James Henry Hammond, Drew Gilpin Faust gives an account of one attempt to substitute free white workers for black slave labor. Both the motives and the outcome were not exactly in accordance with the *Time on the Cross* model. Hammond was anxious to reclaim a large area of swamp for agricultural development but feared the effect of work in such an environment on the health of his slaves. He therefore hired a crew of Irish laborers to undertake the work, but discharged them within three months because of their drunkenness and generally unsatisfactory performance. James Oakes tells of a Virginia planter who hired Irish laborers for similar unhealthy work. "A negro's life is too valuable to be risked at it," he said. "If a negro dies, it's a considerable loss, you know." At other times, Hammond occasionally employed local landless whites as extra plantation laborers, but his view was that "white hands won't stick," and that their unreliability disrupted the plantation routine. There was clearly more to the relative advantages and disadvantages of slave and free labor than the calculation of "negative nonpecuniary income."[25]

One other feature of slave work to which Fogel and Engerman refer is what they describe as "the extraordinarily high labor participation rate" of the plantation work force. This meant that "virtually every slave capable of being in the labor force was in it." In the free labor system, about one-third of the total population was in the work force. In the slave system, the proportion was two-thirds.[26] "The extraordinarily high labor participation rate" is in fact another neutral-sounding phrase which is a euphemism for something extremely unpleasant. It means, in fact, that women and children, the aged and the handicapped, even expectant and nursing mothers, were all required to work. This was the consequence of compulsion, not of incentives. Moreover, they were made to work intensively, under constant supervision. Comparisons are hazardous even when they are not odious, but many recent authorities support the conventional view that slaves worked longer hours and had fewer days off even than nineteenth-century industrial workers, and certainly longer hours and fewer days off than free blacks after the Civil War.[27] As a general rule, slave labor was both intensive and extensive.

Questions concerning the work of the slaves show how far the controversy provoked by *Time on the Cross* has helped to shape the agenda for recent debate and further study, though few of the book's conclusions remain unchallenged or unscathed. The work of Genovese and others will almost certainly prove more durable, not least because it never loses sight of the interconnections between slave labor and many other aspects of the South's peculiar institution and the life of the slave community. Slave work is central to the study of slave society. It leads directly into consideration of even broader issues—on one hand, the overall efficiency and profitability of the Southern slave economy, and on the other, the quality of slave life, the nature of the slave personality, and the development of slave culture.

NOTES

1. For discussion of the implications of this trend, see below, 60.

2. Boles, *Black Southerners*, 107. See also 75–6. Some of the implications of the statistics on slave ownership are discussed in Oakes, *The Ruling Race*, 37–41.

3. Charles Joyner, *Down by the Riverside: A South Carolina Slave Community* (Urbana, Ill., 1984), 34.

4. Otto H. Olsen, "Historians and the Extent of Slaveownership in the Southern United States," *Civil War History* 18 (1972): 101–16, especially 111–3, 115–6.

5. Oakes, *The Ruling Race*, chapter 2, "Master-Class Pluralism," especially 37–40, 51–2, 57–65.

6. Willie Lee Rose, ed., *A Documentary History of Slavery in North America* (New York, 1976), 362.

7. Paul D. Escott, *Slavery Remembered: A Record of Twentieth-Century Slave*

Narratives (Chapel Hill, N.C., 1979), 56–7; Orville V. Burton, *In My Father's House Are Many Mansions: Family and Community in Edgefield, South Carolina* (Chapel Hill, N.C., 1985), 182–4.

8. Drew Gilpin Faust, *James Henry Hammond and the Old South: A Design for Mastery* (Baton Rouge, La., 1982), 74–5, 92.

9. Oakes, *The Ruling Race*, 153–79.

10. There is a considerable literature on the organization and management of slave labor. See for example William K. Scarborough, *The Overseer: Plantation Management in the Old South* (Baton Rouge, La., 1966); William L. Van Deburg, *The Slave Drivers: Black Agricultural Labor Supervisors in the Antebellum South* (Westport, Ct., 1979); James O. Breeden, ed., *Advice among Masters: The Ideal in Slave Management in the Old South* (West-

port, Ct., 1980). For an excellent brief discussion, see Boles, *Black Southerners*, 112–6 and, for a revealing study of one locality, see Joyner, *Down by the Riverside*, 65–70.

11. Stampp, *The Peculiar Institution*, 141–91.

12. Fogel and Engerman, *Time on the Cross*, volume I, 5–6, 148–57.

13. See Paul A. David, Herbert G. Gutman, Richard Sutch, Peter Temin, and Gavin Wright, *Reckoning with Slavery: A Critical Study in the Quantitive History of American Negro Slavery* (New York, 1976), and Herbert G. Gutman, *Slavery and the Numbers Game: A Critique of "Time on the Cross"* (Urbana, Ill., 1975).

14. Gutman and Sutch, "Sambo Makes Good, or Were Slaves Imbued with the Protestant Work Ethic?" in David et al., eds. *Reckoning with Slavery*, 55–93.

15. Faust, *Hammond*, 72–5, 89–90. The brilliant account and analysis of Hammond as slave master in chapters 5 and 6 provide a valuable litmus test for some of the generalizations in *Time on the Cross*.

16. Fogel and Engerman, *Time on the Cross*, volume I, 240.

17. Ibid., 205; David et al., *Reckoning with Slavery*, 92–3; Frederick Law Olmstead, *A Journey in the Back Country* (1860; reprint, New York, 1970), 82.

18. Joyner, *Down by the Riverside*, 57, and, for a broader discussion of punishments and incentives, 50–7.

19. Ibid., 89. See also 57–9 on the persistence of African traditions in the face of the master's control. Like Faust's study of Hammond, Joyner's work puts

many of the conclusions of *Time on the Cross* to the test, implicitly or explicitly, in the context of one local situation.

20. Genovese, *Roll, Jordan, Roll*, 286, 292, and, more generally, 285–324.

21. See Boles, *Black Southerners*, 80–2, for some shrewd observations about the extent to which self-interest and self-respect influenced the attitude of slaves towards their work.

22. Ibid., 78–9.

23. Fogel and Engerman, *Time on the Cross*, volume I, 153–7; David and Temin, "Slavery: The Progressive Institution?" in David et al., eds., *Reckoning with Slavery*, 186–9, 195–202; Richard Vedder, "The Slave Exploitation (Expropriation) Rate," *Explorations in Economic History*, 12 (1975): 453–7; Roger L. Ransom and Richard Sutch, *One Kind of Freedom: The Economic Consequences of Emancipation* (Cambridge, 1977), 203–12.

24. Fogel and Engerman, *Time on the Cross*, volume I, 235–8.

25. Faust, *Hammond*, 130, 132; Oakes, *The Ruling Race*, 174.

26. Fogel and Engerman, *Time on the Cross*, volume I, 207–9.

27. See for example Paul A. David and Peter Temin, "Slavery: The Progressive Institution?" in David et al., eds., *Reckoning with Slavery*, 209–14, and Blassingame, *The Slave Community*, 250–1. See also Genovese, *Roll, Jordan, Roll*, 301–9, for some shrewd comments on the distinction between regular work and hard work and on the compulsive need of slaveowners to believe that their black slaves were naturally lazy and had to be driven to work hard.

4

The Business of Slavery

The performance of slavery as an economic institution was affected by all kinds of factors—social and racial, moral and personal, political and psychological. There is obviously deep feeling and bitter experience behind the confession of the economic historian Gavin Wright that "in the real world of uncertainty, the attempt to distinguish 'economic' from 'noneconomic' motives was hopeless."[1] Slavery was a labor system and the foundation of a distinctive economic system, but it was much else besides.

The obvious yardstick for measuring the economic performance of slavery might seem to be profitability, but initial discussion of the profitability of slavery raises more questions than it answers.[2] The first question is simply, profitable for whom? The answer must depend on whether slavery is being assessed as a business or as a system. If as a business, one must ask whether it was profitable for the individuals, groups, and interests involved in it: the slaveholders most conspicuously of all—or perhaps some slaveholders and not others—but also merchants and middlemen, and less obviously in the post–*Time on the Cross* debate but necessarily, the slaves themselves. On the second point—slavery as a system—one must ask whether the community or society as a whole benefited from slavery. Did the economy of the South gain or lose by it?

The next crucial distinction is between absolute and relative profitability. On one hand, the question may simply be whether, on average, slave owners made a profit or a loss. In Kenneth Stampp's sensible formulation, did the average antebellum slaveholder over the years earn a reasonably satisfactory return from his investment?[3] On the other hand, the question may be whether he could have made a greater profit by dispensing with slavery and using his resources differently. Similarly, for the South as a whole, there is a distinction between the question "Did the South gain or lose by slavery?" and the question "Could the South have done better without slavery?" Was the often assumed or alleged backwardness of the South a historical reality, and if so, was it the consequence of addiction to slave labor?

This last question may prompt a further inquiry into how far it is possible to isolate the impact of slavery from all the other factors which affected the performance of the Southern economy in general and Southern agriculture in particular. For example, questions of climate and soil are obviously involved. It so happened that the abundance of suitable soil in many parts of the South, the length of the growing season, and not merely the level but the seasonal pattern of rainfall combined with the availability of slave labor to make the region singularly well suited to cotton cultivation.[4] The South was ideally placed to meet the huge and rising demand for cotton from Britain and Western Europe, and from the northern United States— and in the pre–Civil War decades was supplying four-fifths or more of that market.

One other related—and important—distinction remains: Profitability and efficiency are not quite the same thing. Profit may result, and often does result, from efficiency, but it may also arise from other causes—ruthless and extravagant exploitation of forced labor or virgin land or natural resources, or a monopoly or near-monopoly position as supplier of a product in urgent demand.

The economic fortunes of slavery—subject to booms and slumps like almost any other business—fluctuated between one time or place, or indeed one person and another. Its profits, and the methods of making them, differed between the upper South and the lower South, or between the Atlantic seaboard and the lower Mississippi Valley, or between cotton and sugar plantations. Profits varied obviously, too, from one owner to another, according to the owner's business acumen, management skills, social aspirations, intelligence, and luck, not to mention the size of the owner's farm or plantation and the quality of the land. Profitability still depended on individual ability.

When all the appropriate qualifications have been made, there is now broad acceptance that many slave owners made reasonable—and sometimes handsome—profits in the pre–Civil War decades. Most authorities now agree that they received a return on their investment which was in line with, if not superior to, that available elsewhere.[5] Such a finding clearly undermines the old view of Ulrich B. Phillips and his followers that slavery often laid a burden of unprofitability upon the planters, which they shouldered because they supported and maintained the institution for other reasons. However, it does not follow that because slavery yielded a good return, profit was the only motive and ambition of slaveholders. The slave owner was not necessarily a capitalist pure and simple, just because he or she happened to make money.

The, fundamental priorities of slavery and Southern slave society are involved in this discussion. If slavery was above all a rational economic system devoted to the pursuit of profit, those who controlled it would have retained their investment in it only as long as it continued to show greater profits than alternative forms of enterprise or labor organization. However, if slavery was even more important for other reasons—as an instrument of social adjustment or racial control, or as a status symbol—owners may have been content to maintain it for those reasons alone, as long as it did not prove cripplingly unprofitable. There is abundant evidence on one hand that slaveholders were keenly aware of considerations of profit and loss, and plantation records show that many larger owners kept very detailed accounts and responded in a sophisticated way to movements in prices and market conditions. On the other hand, it seems likely that, if they could have read the refined, complicated, and somewhat esoteric arguments deployed in the modern debate over the economics of slavery, many would have found them unimpressive and even irrelevant—not to say unintelligible. At the same time, they surely saw slavery in a broader context; it was at the center of a well-established way of life to which they were both accustomed and attached, and the disruption or demise of which they feared above all else.

The presentation of the case for the slaveholder as businessperson was carried to new extremes by Fogel and Engerman, although it is worth recalling the extent to which Stampp had prefigured some of the more sober conclusions of *Time on the Cross*. Fogel and Engerman argue that the profitability of the business of slavery was derived from the efficiency of Southern slave agriculture, which they attribute to good management, a high-quality work force, and the economies of scale which slavery made possible. They were even bold or rash enough to put a precise figure on their claim for the superior efficiency of Southern agriculture; it was, they said, 35 percent more efficient than Northern agriculture based on free labor. This figure is derived from the "geometric index of total factor productivity," through which efficiency is measured by the ratio of output to the average amount of the inputs of land, labor, and capital.[6]

The heated debate which ensued between economic historians brandishing their computers and mathematical equations as they charged into the most recent publication of their opponents seems somewhat dated from the perspective of the late 1980s. It will suffice to offer two examples of the hazards of employing the geometric index to compare like with unlike. First, Northern land values were generally higher than Southern because of urban-industrial development and improvements in transportation. The Northern input of land was therefore higher in money terms than the Southern, and the ratio of output to input therefore was lower. If the index is rigidly followed, Northern agriculture is thus shown to be less efficient because the Northern economy as a whole was more advanced!

The second objection, concerning cotton, is more fundamental. Gavin Wright has argued convincingly that the insatiable demand for cotton, and the unique ability of the South at this time to meet that demand, held the key to the performance of Southern slave agriculture. Furthermore, he says, if undue reliance is placed on the evidence of the census of 1860, the efficiency of Southern agriculture will be greatly exaggerated because 1859–60 was a time of unparalleled boom for cotton producers. The profits of Southern planters owed less to the exceptional efficiency of slave labor or to the economies of scale than to being in the right place at the right time to satisfy an exceptional demand.[7] This does not, of course, mean that slave-based agriculture was inefficient and unprofitable; far from it. But it does call into question the superior efficiency claimed for it, and the explanation for that superiority. At the very least, it does not follow that, because Southern agriculture used slave labor and because it showed a profit, its profits were the result of its labor system and nothing else. Cotton and slavery were inextricably linked. The heaviest concentrations of the slave population were in the main cotton-growing areas (and also in a few smaller areas of rice and sugar cultivation). Cotton largely determined the value of slaves, and slave property was the most important form of wealth in the South. What the authors of *Time on the Cross* attributed to the labor system may more accurately be ascribed to the crop and the demand for it.

Gavin Wright challenges the claims made for the economies of scale which the employment of slave labor made possible. It is true that, although the median size of Northern and Southern farms was similar, the *average* size of farms in the cotton South was twice that in the Northwest. The Southern figure is distorted by the larger plantations, whereas there were very few farms in the North with more than five hundred acres. On the other hand, it is also true that cotton could be successfully and profitably grown on small and medium-sized farms as well as on large plantations. Wright discerns no significant evidence of economies of scale as such on the larger plantations. What is clear is that productivity rises in step with the proportion of cotton in the total output of a farm or plantation. Every 1 percent increase in the cotton share was accompanied by a 1 percent increase in the output per worker. The crucial advantage of the larger planter, with a substantial slave work force, lay, not in economies of scale but in his ability to devote a larger share of his production to cotton rather than to other crops. Wright calculates that "when output is valued at market prices, cotton comprised about one-quarter of the output of typical slaveless farms, but three-fifths or more for the largest slaveholding cotton plantations."[8]

Why should this have been so? Why didn't all farmers maximize the proportion of cotton in their total output? First, it is important to remember that, for all the dominance of cotton and other staple crops in discussion of Southern agriculture, cotton amounted in 1850 to only one-quarter of total Southern agricultural output, and tobacco, sugar, and rice together to less than another 10 percent. In the case of cotton, where the main constraint upon production came in the picking of the crop, planters and farmers alike had spare capacity to devote to the cultivation of other crops. The largest Southern crop was not in fact cotton but corn, which was cheap to grow, and, very conveniently, could be both planted and harvested at times different from cotton. Among other things, corn provided food for livestock, notably hogs—and the South had two-thirds of the hogs in the United States in 1860. The consequence of the compatibility of cotton and corn production was to make the South virtually self-sufficient as far as food was concerned (although there were local imbalances), while it was also producing its great staple crops for export to distant markets. Corn also provided a vital element of stability and security, especially for the smaller farmer.[9]

This is the key to an explanation of why the larger slaveholders devoted so much more of their production to cotton, and thus benefited from the greater efficiency provided by a larger cotton share of total output. The choice of priorities facing Southern farmers and planters was between pursuit of maximum profit, with the attendant risks, and the achievement of greater security by concentrating first on subsistence farming, and then in addition growing some cotton for cash. In Wright's words:

> This is not because the physical output of cotton was less certain than that of corn . . . but because using cotton as a means of meeting food requirements involved the combined risks of cotton yields, cotton prices and corn prices. The man who grows his own corn need only worry about yields.[10]

The choice was not, of course, an absolute one between subsistence farming and exclusive concentration on staple crops; it was a matter of striking a balance between market and nonmarket activity. Wright has traced what he calls a crop-mix continuum, with the share of cotton in the mix steadily increasing as one moves up from small to medium-sized farmers, and on to smaller and then larger plantations.[11] In his illuminating study of the area around Augusta, Georgia, J. William Harris provides supporting evidence of the way in which farmers balanced the goals of maximum profits, represented by cotton, and security, represented by corn. However, he does somewhat modify the Wright argument by showing the strong market orientation of some owners of medium-sized or even quite small farms.[12]

On the whole, the large cotton producer was more in control of his fate above all because he was in control of the allocation of slave labor time between market and nonmarket activity. The small producer was more concerned to keep the wolf from the door and to avoid a crisis which might force the sale of hard-won land, or (if they were owned in the first place) some or all of the farm's handful of slaves. The Southern small farmer also faced a disadvantage which did not beset the Northern counterpart, whose cash crops, such as wheat, were also food crops. However hard the times, the Southern farmer could not eat cotton or feed it to the hogs.

Gavin Wright has not only rebutted the argument that economies of scale explain much of the efficiency of Southern slave owners, he has also exposed the unrealistic and ultimately false comparison attempted in *Time on the Cross* between Northern and Southern agriculture. In doing so, he and others have undermined the case for the superior efficiency of Southern slave-based agriculture. Whatever the display of cliometric ingenuity, it is surely impossible to make a fair and illuminating comparison between a large-scale planter with fifty or a hundred slaves producing cotton for export, and the characteristic Northern family farm employing little if any labor outside the family and producing a variety of cereal and animal products, with the prospect of selling any surplus on the open market. The two operations are different in scale, structure, and purpose—and in their social and economic context. There was nothing in Northern agriculture comparable to the Southern cotton plantation.

Specifically, comparison between Southern slave labor and Northern wage labor is not possible—and not valid historically—because there was hardly any wage labor on Northern farms. The question is not so much why plantations became so large but why Northern farms remained so small. The answer lies in the chronic and desperate shortage of farm labor for hire in the North and Northwest. Land was abundant, and most men aspired to be farmers rather than farm workers. The size of the family farm was limited by the amount of labor the family itself could provide. In the South, the presence of slavery altered the whole position; the farmer or planter could purchase as many slaves as financial resources permitted.[13]

The safer conclusions to be drawn from this discussion of the business of slavery might be summarized as follows. First, slavery was on the whole profitable for most owners, and the prodigious expansion of both the cotton-growing area and the volume of the crop in the half century before the Civil War would surely seem to bear this out. But the precise measurement of profit is difficult because of the many factors involved, and the answers will vary according to the criterion of profitability adopted. Second, the profitability of Southern agriculture depended heavily on its ability to meet the massive world demand for cotton. Third, the efficiency claimed for slavery was essentially allocative rather than productive—that is, it depended not on higher output per worker, or economies of scale as such, but on the ability to allocate more of the work force to the cultivation of cash crops.[14] Fourth, any attempt at precise measurement of the superior efficiency of Southern slave agriculture over Northern free agriculture is riddled with hazards and pitfalls. Fifth, maximization of profit may not always, even in purely economic terms, have been the highest or wisest priority of slave owners; there was always the need to balance short-term gain against longer-term well-being, and for smaller owners questions of security and self-sufficiency loomed large and altered the ratio of nonmarket to market activity. Finally, the business of slavery was always affected by noneconomic considerations arising from the centrality of slavery in the whole Southern way of life.

Indeed, the debate among economic historians about profitability has run parallel with another debate about the character, outlook, and motivation of the Southern slaveholding classes. In a nutshell, it is a debate over paternalism or profits, and which of the two occupied a higher priority in the minds of slaveholders. Fogel and Engerman are among the more emphatic of a large number of historians who regard slaveholders as essentially capitalists deeply imbued with the acquisitive instincts and the profit-making impulses of their kind—just a Southern variation on the nineteenth-century theme of the American businessperson and entrepreneur. The outstanding modern proponent of the alternative view of the slaveholder as paternalist is Eugene Genovese. In various writings over the last three decades, he has depicted the slave South as a precapitalist society which needed to use the apparatus of capitalism—banks and credit and merchants—to conduct its business with the outside world, but which in its internal structure and social relationships remained something different. In one of his earlier statements of this theme, Genovese emphasized that the basis of the position and power of the planters was their slave ownership:

> Theirs was an aristocratic, antibourgeois spirit with values and mores that emphasized family and status, had its code of honor, aspired to luxury, leisure and accomplishment. In the planters' community paternalism was the standard of human relationships. . . . The planter typically recoiled at the notion that profit is the goal of life; that the approach to production and exchange should be internally rational and uncomplicated by social values;

that thrift and hard work are the great virtues; and that the test of the wholesomeness of a community is the vigor with which its citizens expand the economy.

The planter was certainly no less acquisitive than the bourgeois, but an acquisitive spirit is compatible with values antithetical to capitalism. The aristocratic spirit of the planters absorbed acquisitiveness and directed it into channels that were socially desirable to a slave society: the accumulation of land and slaves and the achievement of military and political honors.[15]

Genovese stressed that paternalism necessarily implied neither lack of acquisitiveness nor an attitude of total benevolence toward the slaves. If paternalist owners assumed a responsibility for their slaves, they also strove constantly to maintain and reinforce the utterly dependent status of those slaves.[16]

No recent historian has more flatly contradicted Genovese's view of slaveholder paternalism than James Oakes. In *The Ruling Race: A History of American Slaveholders,* he agrees that the accumulation of land and slaves was the prime motive, perhaps even the obsession, of nineteenth-century slaveholders, but he regards this as proof that they were a class of acquisitive entrepreneurs and capitalists, dominated by a materialist ethos and dedicated to free-market commercialism. He describes the intense pressures in Southern white society toward material success—and the ownership of more and more slaves was regarded as the yardstick of that success. The thrust of his argument is summarized in this description of the slaveholding entrepreneurs:

> They actively embraced the capitalistic economy, arguing that sheer material interest, properly understood, would prove both economically profitable and socially stabilizing. But this intense devotion to the capitalistic spirit of accumulation had done much to diminish the influence of paternalistic ideals within the slaveholding class, and that spirit was never successfully reconciled with the conflicting devotion to stability and social harmony. This was the contradiction that rendered paternalism so anachronistic to the nineteenth-century South.[17]

Genovese and Oakes are powerful and articulate recent protagonists in a debate which has continued for half a century or more about the nature of Southern slave society. When, after decades of controversy, historians find themselves at such directly opposite poles as Genovese and Oakes, it may be appropriate to ask whether the clash of rival schools of thought is promoting or obstructing a genuine understanding of a historical situation. Have the interpretations of historians become so schematic that they begin to look dogmatic? Have powerful arguments, based on deeply held convictions, strayed too far from the often untidy and many-sided historical reality of the Old South? It may be possible to reduce the controversy to more manageable proportions, without having to settle for some feeble and inadequate compromise.

First, it helps to be clear about which slaveholders are under discussion. This controversy has become not only a war of words but a war about words, and the participants have sometimes been talking past each other. Genovese's emphasis is upon the planter class, the larger slave owners who in his view—and the view of many others—exercised a dominant influence in Southern society far beyond their actual numbers. Clearly, the paternalist ethos is more likely to have characterized this group than, for example, small farmers owning two or three slaves. With some justice, Genovese's critics have accused him of treating the words "planter" and "slaveholder" as almost interchangeable; however, Genovese has said that "the rough parvenu planters of the Southwestern frontier" did their best to follow the pattern of the older, more established areas of the South. In sharp contrast, Oakes puts the emphasis on the much more numerous slaveholders who were not "planters," who owned two or three, or five or ten, slaves and who were in his view individualistic, upwardly mobile, and ardent in their pursuit of profit, to the exclusion of paternalist values or anything else. This is no doubt a useful corrective to the concentration on the larger planters which has been a feature of so much of the historiography of slavery. Unfortunately, in his enthusiasm to make his case, Oakes often seems to neglect or ignore evidence to the contrary. He attempts simply to sweep the planters and their tradition of paternalism aside and to dismiss them as an atypical and anachronistic minority on the geographical and economic margins of Southern society.[18]

Surely, as various historians have shown, there was a broad spectrum, or a continuum, of slave ownership, running from the small farmer through the medium-sized landowner to the great planter—and there is abundant evidence, too, of the preeminent position and influence of the planter class in Southern society and politics. The social composition of Southern slaveholders does not break down simply into two opposite extremes of struggling small farmers and great planters—and no one has made that point more effectively than Oakes.[19] Similarly, the individual slaveholder, great or small, did not commit unreservedly or exclusively to the goal of either paternalism or profit. Just as, in their economic calculations, individual slaveholders struck their own balance between market and nonmarket activity, so too in their broader socioeconomic priorities they struck a varying balance between paternalism and profit seeking.

Part of the difficulty derives from the sophistication of much of the modern historical argument, which tends to ascribe an unrealistic degree of self-consciousness and self-examination to the slaveholders of the Old South. One may legitimately doubt whether the normal, busy, sensible slaveholder sat down each day, or week or year, and asked himself whether he was a paternalist or a capitalist—or whether there was indeed any unbearable tension or inconsistency in being both. In the abstract, of course, it may not be difficult to demonstrate such an inconsistency, but Southern slaveholders are not the only people who have lived their daily lives without finding the burden of such illogicality insupportable. Ironically, Oakes himself concedes this very point—and thus undermines much of his own neat and tidy argument—in the course of a discussion of the influence of religion on slaveholders:

> As humans, masters were by definition complex beings, capable of holding to contradictory values, motivated by principles at odds with their behavior, torn by irreconcilable impulses intrinsic to their way of life.... Among its many rewards, slavery offered masters the luxury of ambivalence.[20]

The "luxury of ambivalence" among slaveholders may help to clear the smoke of battle among historians. After all, the ownership of slaves was a measure of both wealth and status, and there was no need to opt exclusively for one or the other.

In fact, a number of historians have now questioned the existence of the kind of dichotomy between paternalism and profit which Oakes describes. Reviewing *The Ruling Race*, Steven Hahn suggests that, even if Oakes is right about the slaveholders' acquisitiveness, "there are no necessary implications for their culture and ideology." He asks,

"After all, what landed elite in modern history, no matter how reactionary, has not been acquisitive?"[21] Genovese has made a very similar point more than once. Even Stanley Engerman, one of the authors of *Time on the Cross,* conceded the point, or rather asserted it unequivocally:

> There need be no overriding conflict between paternal attitudes and the drive to make money. Indeed, the characteristics which some have associated with paternalism—good care . . . and personal involvement—seem to have been seen by planters as a way to higher profits as well. . . . The sometimes proclaimed conflict between paternalistic attitudes and a response to economic incentives is, for some issues, an artificial and unnecessary one.[22]

In a valuable case study of one large planter, Drew Gilpin Faust has shown how James Henry Hammond was equally determined to transform his plantation into a profitable enterprise and to project himself as a beneficent master who would guide the development of those he regarded as backward people entrusted to his care by God.[23]

The balance between paternalism and profit seeking varied from master to master, according to a whole range of factors, including size of holding and economic conditions—and also time. In his analysis of broad social changes in nineteenth-century America, Thomas Bender has argued that many social historians have greatly exaggerated the speed and comprehensiveness of the transition from a way of life based on the local community to a more complex, interdependent modern society. In particular, attitudes, values, and relationships often changed much more slowly than the rate of technological and economic development.[24] Similarly, it seems likely that, at the very least, Oakes has exaggerated the rapidity and the completeness of the switch to commercialism and the entrepreneurial ethos in the minds of slaveholders.

Indeed, one subplot of the main debate over paternalism and profits has been concerned with the direction of change over time. Oakes claims that, between the Revolutionary era and the Civil War, whatever paternalist tradition existed in the South was overtaken and overwhelmed by the rising capitalist values of an expanding slave-owning society of men on the make. This challenges directly Genovese's argument that, having been in the eighteenth century essentially an economic system and a labor system, slavery became the basis of an increasingly paternalist social order—particularly after the ending of the external slave trade in 1808. Placing the argument both within his own ideological frame of reference and the broader international context, Genovese argues that the early spread of European capitalism called forth a new system of slavery in the New World which in time proved incompatible with the consolidation of the capitalist world order. Slave owners then assumed the mantle of the landed aristocracy in Europe by resisting the advance of the very capitalist system which had spawned them.[25]

With or without Genovese's ideological assumptions, it is possible to detect a change in the character of Southern slave society as it not merely took firm root but expanded and became an essential part of the established Southern order. If slaveholders enjoyed the "luxury of ambivalence," success and expansion also allowed them the luxury of escape from purely profit-related considerations—though not of course completely. In a justly famous essay, "The Domestication of Domestic Slavery," Willie Lee Rose has described the process. Eighteenth-century Virginia planters, according to Rose, were more concerned with the state of their crops than with establishing paternal relations with their slaves. But, emphasizing the evolutionary character of slavery, she suggests that in the nineteenth century the South was "domesticating" slavery, taming its earlier harshness and consolidating it as an integral part of Southern society. "The Old South was actually engaged in a process of rationalizing slavery, not only in an economic sense, but also in emotional and psychological terms," she says.[26]

Much of the discussion of slavery as a business also applies to slavery as a system. The debate over profitability applies not only to the individual or plantation but to the Southern economy as a whole. It was perfectly possible, of course, for slavery to be a good business proposition for slaveholders but a poor economic proposition for the South in general. It would not be easy to demonstrate that it promoted the economic well-being of the non-slave-owning sections of the community—and the nonslaveholders were the large majority of the population. On one hand, it is true that slave ownership did provide a kind of escalator by which people might rise in Southern society, and Oakes has stressed the extent of upward (and presumably downward) mobility in Southern society and the frequency with which individuals moved in and out of ownership of one or two slaves.[27] On the other hand, there were wide disparities in wealth among the Southern population, and this reflected the wide gap between the great planters and the poorer whites. Although the overall inequality in the distribution of wealth was little different among the white population of the North and the South, the Northern figures were distorted by the situation in the cities, where there was a substantial propertyless class—and of course such a comparison leaves out the 40 percent of the Southern population who were Negro slaves and owned no property at all.[28] In much of the South, the poorer whites lived in constant dread of the day when they might have to compete with freed slaves, but in fact they were suffering all the time from wage levels depressed by competition from slave labor. Slavery was a rich man's joy but often a poor man's plight.

If the cotton boom held the key to Southern prosperity, then parts of the South felt the strain of sharing only indirectly in it, if at all. Various historians, including William Freehling, have shown that slavery was a declining institution in parts of the border states and the upper South before the Civil War.[29] Cotton had converted slavery into the peculiar institution particularly, but not exclusively, in the Deep South and the Southwest. It has long been thought—and this view was reinforced by the pioneering cliometric work of Alfred H. Conrad and John R. Meyer—that the states of the upper South boosted their flagging fortunes by selling their surplus slaves to the Deep South and the Southwest. However, Fogel and Engerman sought to show that the scale and importance of the domestic slave trade had been greatly exaggerated. It is an incontrovertible fact that there was a forced migration of several hundred thousand slaves across the South in the half century or so before the Civil War— perhaps as many as a quarter of a million in the peak decade of the 1850s alone. The controversy is about how they were transferred from the Old South and the upper South to Alabama, Mississippi, and Louisiana, and later to Arkansas and Texas. Fogel and Engerman claim that the great majority were not sold, but either moved with their owners or were sent by them to their new lands to the west. The point is important because sale was likely to mean sudden and permanent separation from family and the local slave community, whereas movement in a group usually mitigated such horrors. Various critics, notably Richard Sutch and Herbert Gutman, have undermined the argument presented in *Time on the Cross* and laid bare its slender basis in the evidence.[30] Precise conclusions on this subject are difficult, but it seems clear enough that slave sales formed a significant part of the long-distance transfer of slaves to the Deep South and the Southwest, and that they were economically important to the upper South. When the large number of local sales is taken into consideration, there is no doubt that sale, or the prospect of sale, was indeed a looming threat in the lives of most slaves.[31]

Slave trading could be a very profitable business, particularly for larger firms such as Franklin and Armfield. They bought between one thousand and twelve hundred slaves each year for transfer to the Southwest. Most of these were shipped from Virginia to New Orleans, and some were then sent upriver to Natchez and other places. But each year the company sent some slaves overland—perhaps one hundred and fifty—under the supervision of only three or four whites. The slaves walked a distance of several hundred miles and the journey took seven or eight weeks. Although the slave trade was an important cog in the machinery of the Southern slave economy, slave traders were ill-regarded in Southern society and were often treated with disdain even by the very planters who relied on their services.[32]

There is now broad agreement among historians that, although the internal slave trade was active, the systematic breeding of slaves for market was very rare. The slave stud farm may have existed but it was exceptional.[33] However, this was an era of large families and rapidly growing population, both slave and free; owners were well aware of the marketability of their slaves, and fecundity added to the value of a young female slave. It would be fair to say that slaveholders were ready to exploit the fertility of their slaves but seldom sought to increase it by forced mating. They enjoyed the profits of coition without coercion.

The much larger question arising from the discussion of slavery as a system concerns its relationship with what some have called the economic "backwardness" of the South. So many factors are involved, and so many different criteria might be applied, that it is virtually impossible to isolate the retarding effect, if any, of slavery alone. On one hand, there is a strong presumption that slavery imposed a certain rigidity and inflexibility upon the Southern economy, that the dead weight of the slave system prevented the South from seizing new opportunities, that low levels of literacy and skill inhibited economic growth, and that the depressed living standards of many Southerners,

·white and black, reduced the consumer capacity of the home market.

On the other hand, when the Civil War came, slavery and the economic system based on it were not in imminent danger of collapse through inefficiency or unprofitability. Demand for cotton was at its peak, slave prices were rising, and Southern planters expressed confidence in their economic prospects. The notion that agriculture based on slave labor necessarily led to soil exhaustion has been shown to be more of a myth than a fact. Whatever its problems, slavery had also demonstrated a measure of flexibility and resilience as a labor system—for example, in the employment of some slaves in the towns and cities or in mills and factories.

In fact, the South was paying the penalty of success—but a success which was very narrowly based. The South clearly lagged behind the North in urban-industrial development, but that can be interpreted as testimony to the vigor, not the sickness, of the Southern slave economy. Once again, the explanation lies in the peculiar advantage of the South in meeting the booming world demand for cotton. Gavin Wright has argued persuasively that that boom had reached its peak in the 1850s and that the South would have faced an economic crisis within the next decade or two with or without the Civil War. For the first half of the nineteenth century, the cotton/slave economy had grown and prospered by responding to the early surge of a new product in a new market. But that could not go on forever, and was in fact about to level off, as later history demonstrated.

Moreover, the South had met the surge in demand by extensive rather than intensive growth. Cotton cultivation had expanded into new land and had employed more slaves; on the other hand, says Wright, there is no evidence of genuine productivity gains in Southern agriculture in this period. "The pattern of rapid but primarily extensive growth, without major productivity gains, was characteristic of American agriculture generally, at least before 1850."[34] From around the middle of the century, Northern agriculture, based on the family farm and still short of labor for hire, resorted increasingly to mechanization; in contrast, Southern agriculture continued to rely on slave labor, as it concentrated more than ever on meeting the demand for cotton. As if to bear this out, J. William Harris's study of the area around Augusta, Georgia, reveals a strong trend in the 1850s among both planters and farmers toward cotton at the expense of the other crops. Harris argues that it was not slavery alone but also other factors, such as the climate and the lack of adequate local markets, which hindered any movement toward diversification. However, he adds that slavery did limit crop choices by enabling and encouraging farmers to respond to world demand for cotton, by removing incentives to overcome the problems involved in growing other crops, and by helping to create an essentially rural economy and restricting the local market.[35]

The combined forces of cotton and slavery kept not only Southern agriculture but the whole Southern economy on a straight and narrow path which led to rejection of other choices, and consequent retardation. The very success (and the profits) of plantation slavery and cotton cultivation removed any incentive to switch from agriculture to industrial and urban development. Some historians claim that slavery had proved its capacity to adapt to factory and cities, but in the particular situation of peak cotton demand in the 1850s, slaves were actually drawn out of the towns and onto the plantations because they could be more profitably used there. In towns they could be replaced by white immigrant workers; on the plantations they were irreplaceable.[36] There are many other factors—political, social, and psychological, as well as economic—involved in the analysis of the limited development of urban and industrial slavery. These will be discussed in Chapter 6.

The divergent paths of the Southern slave economy and the Northern free labor economy in the mid–nineteenth century may be clarified by drawing a distinction between growth and development. The Southern economy grew extensively, while the Northern economy diversified, urbanized, and industrialized. Development in the North fostered the process of sustained economic growth. In contrast, the South enjoyed the ephemeral advantage of being the dominant supplier of cotton to the world market, a position which offered limited-term enjoyment of profit not necessarily linked to real efficiency, but not the long-term prospect of sustained growth. Perhaps, after all, the argument leads back to the conclusion of Lewis C. Gray, who almost half a century ago saw in slavery "the near-paradox of an economic institution competitively effective under certain conditions, but essentially regressive in its influence on the socio-economic evolution of the section where it prevailed."[37] While the South expanded along one line, the North was branching out in many new directions.

In one of their more intriguing comparative ventures, Fogel and Engerman claimed that, in terms of the level of per capita income, the Southern states would have ranked fourth in the world in 1860, behind only Australia, the northern United States, and Great Britain. (The presence of Australia, with its tiny population, in this exalted company might have given them pause for thought!) The cotton boom might offer an explanation of the high place of the South in this list relative to most European countries. But the figure for the South was still only 73 percent of that for the North in 1860. However, Fogel and Engerman went on to separate the Northeastern from the North Central states. They then showed that the level of per capita income was 14 percent lower in the North Central states than in the South. Again, perhaps, cotton gave the South an advantage.[38] But the crucial point is surely that it is the Northeast which enjoyed an enormous lead over the South, presumably because of its urban-industrial development. The effect of slavery, whether by its success or its failure, in inhibiting such development in the South surely cannot be ignored or explained away.

Even in the midst of the booming 1850s, the Southern slave economy faced a number of dangers and problems, some external and others internal. First was the looming sectional crisis over the further extension of slavery, which aroused deep anxiety in the minds of those who believed that slavery must expand or die. If the crisis were to lead to the disruption of the Union, the economic consequences would be unpredictable but could be dire. Second was the danger, no doubt less discernible at the time than with hindsight, that the cotton bubble would burst and thus deprive the slave economy of its most conspicuous advantage. Third, the relative decline of slavery in the border states and the upper South was a disturbing indication of the uneven spread of the benefits of the cotton boom.

Finally, there was evidence of a widening gap between slaveholders and nonslaveholders throughout the South. Though still impressively high, the proportion of slaveholders in the total white population was declining, and by 1860 was down to 25 percent. More alarming still was the fact that the wealth of the average slaveholder was growing much faster than that of the average nonslaveholder; by 1860, the slaveholder was ten times as wealthy as the nonslaveholder. Much of the explanation lay in the rising price of slaves.[39] If one already owned slaves, one could enjoy the benefit of the steady rise in their value; if one did not own slaves, it was increasingly difficult to get one's foot on the first rung of the slaveholding ladder. (There is a modern parallel in the increasing property value for the homeowner in a rising real estate market and the obstacles facing the first-time buyer in his or her attempt to break into that market.) In the slave South, such a situation brought political and social as well as economic anxieties. James Oakes stresses that "it was the promise as much as the reality of upward mobility that traditionally sustained the dreams of many nonslaveholding whites." He quotes the somewhat melodramatic warning of one slaveholder that "the minute you put it out of the power of common farmers to purchase a negro man or woman to help him on his farm, or his wife in the house, you make him an abolitionist at once."[40] Ironically, it was the success of the Southern slave economy in the 1850s which put the price of slaves beyond the reach of many farmers, and therefore denied them a share in the profits of the system.

Whatever the external pressures and the internal tensions, and whatever the calculations of profit and loss, there was little immediate sign of slavery losing or even loosening its grip. Slaveholders, and most nonslaveholders too, adhered to slavery above all because it was there, and they dreaded the consequences of its demise. "We were born under the institution and cannot now change or abolish it," said a Mississippi planter. He would have preferred to be "exterminated" rather than be forced to live in the same society as the freed slaves.[41] Behind considerations of efficiency and profitability lay something much deeper still. Slave and master were locked together in a system which the one could not escape and the other would not abandon.

NOTES

1. Gavin Wright, The Political Economy of the Cotton South: Households, Markets and Wealth in the Nineteenth Century (New York, 1978), xii.

2. The questions asked, and the distinctions made, in this and the following paragraphs, owe much to Harold D. Woodman, "The Profitability of Slavery: A Historical Perennial," Journal of Southern History 29 (1963): 303–25.

3. Stampp, The Peculiar Institution, 390, and, more generally, 383–90. See also Wright, Political Economy of the Cotton South, 2–3.

4. Wright, Political Economy of the Cotton South, 14–18.

5. Recent controversy has sometimes obscured the importance of the pioneering work on this subject of Alfred H. Conrad and John R. Meyer, "The Eco-

nomics of Slavery in the Ante-Bellum South," *Journal of Political Economy* 66 (1958): 95–130, and *The Economics of Slavery and Other Studies in Econometric History* (Chicago, 1964).

6. Fogel and Engerman, *Time on the Cross*, volume I, 192–6.

7. Wright, *Political Economy of the Cotton South*, 90–7.

8. Ibid., 55. For Wright's full argument on this point see 55–6, 74–87.

9. Ibid., 57–61.

10. Ibid., 64.

11. Ibid., 71. On the broader question of the crop-mix and the balance between self-sufficiency and risk on farms of varying sizes, see 62–74.

12. J. William Harris, *Plain Folk and Gentry in a Slave Society: White Liberty and Black Slavery in Augusta's Hinterlands* (Middletown, Ct., 1985), 22–32.

13. Wright, *Political Economy of the Cotton South*, xii, 43–55.

14. Ibid. 5–6, 87–8.

15. Eugene D. Genovese, "The Slave South: An Interpretation," in Allen Weinstein and Frank O. Gatell, eds., *American Negro Slavery: A Modern Reader*, second ed. (New York, 1973), 272. This essay first appeared in *Science and Society* 25 (1961): 320–37. In a considerably revised form, it also formed the first chapter of Genovese, *The Political Economy of Slavery: Studies in the Economy and Society of the Slave South* (New York, 1965), 13–39.

16. The above quotation from one of Genovese's early essays was deliberately chosen as an example of a particular point of view in its most direct and unequivocal form. However, Professor Genovese's views have been developed, elaborated and refined in extensive writings over the last three decades. For the evolution of his views on slaveholding paternalism and its impact on the character of Southern slave society, see *The World the Slaveholders Made: Two Essays in Interpretation* (New York, 1969), especially 95–102, 118–28; *Roll, Jordan, Roll,* 3–158; and Elizabeth Fox-Genovese and Eugene D. Genovese, *Fruits of Merchant Capital,* passim.

17. Oakes, *The Ruling Race,* 191. See also xi–xii, 69–73.

18. Genovese, *Political Economy of Slavery,* 28–36; Oakes, *The Ruling Race,* x, 37–68, 192–220.

19. Oakes, *The Ruling Race,* 37–68.

20. Ibid., 102–3.

21. Steven Hahn, "Capitalists All," *Reviews in American History* 11 (1983): 222.

22. Stanley L. Engerman, "The Southern Slave Economy," in Owens, ed., *Perspectives and Irony in American Slavery,* 86.

23. Faust, *Hammond,* 72–3.

24. Thomas H. Bender, *Community and Social Change in America* (Baltimore, 1982), especially 86–108.

25. Oakes, *The Ruling Race, xii,* 192–6; Genovese, "Slavery: The World's Burden," in Owens, ed., *Perspectives and Irony,* 27–50.

26. Willie Lee Rose, "The Domestication of Domestic Slavery," in *Slavery and Freedom,* 18–36. The quotation appears on page 25.

27. Oakes, *The Ruling Race,* 37–51, 67–8.

28. Wright, *Political Economy of the Cotton South,* 24–40, especially 39–40. See also Lee Soltow, *Men and Wealth in the United States, 1850–1870* (New Haven, 1975).

29. Freehling, "The Founding Fathers and Slavery," 89–91. See also Barbara Jeanne Fields, *Slavery and Freedom on the Middle Ground,* 1–89.

30. Conrad and Meyer, "The Economics of Slavery in the Ante-Bellum South," 95–130, especially 112–5, 119, 121; Fogel and Engerman, *Time on the Cross,* volume I, 44–58, 78–86; Gutman and Sutch, in Paul A. David et al., eds., *Reckoning with Slavery,* 99–110, 154–61. See also William Calderhead, "How Extensive Was the Border State Slave Trade? A New Look," *Civil War History* 18 (1972): 42–55; Michael Tadman, "Slave Trading in the Ante-Bellum South: An Estimate of the Extent of the Inter-Regional Slave Trade," *Journal of American Studies* 13 (1979): 195–220.

31. See below, 86–7.

32. Wendell H. Stephenson, *Isaac Franklin: Slave Trader and Planter of the Old South* (Baton Rouge, La., 1938). See also William Calderhead, "The Role of the Professional Slave Trader in a Slave Economy: Austin Woolfolk, a Case Study," *Civil War History* 23 (1977): 195–211.

33. For various points of view on this subject, see Richard Sutch, "The Breeding of Slaves for Sale and the Westward Expansion of Slavery, 1850–1860," in Stanley L. Engerman and Eugene D. Genovese, eds., *Race and Slavery in the Western Hemisphere: Quantitative Studies* (Princeton, N.J., 1975), 173–210, and Engerman's comments, ibid., 511–14, 527–30; Richard G. Lowe and Randolph B. Campbell, "The Slave-Breeding Hypothesis: A Demographic Comment on the 'Buying' and 'Selling' States," *Journal of Southern History* 42 (1976): 401–12.

34. Wright, *Political Economy of the Cotton South,* 107. For further discussion of slavery, cotton, and the performance of the antebellum Southern economy, see 4, 8, 90–127.

35. Harris, *Plain Folk and Gentry in a Slave Society,* 27–31.

36. Claudia D. Goldin, *Urban Slavery in the American South: A Quantitative History* (Chicago, 1976), 51–128.

37. Lewis C. Gray, *History of Agriculture in the Southern United States to 1860,* volume II (Washington, 1933–41), 942.

38. Fogel and Engerman, *Time on the Cross,* volume I, 247–51.

39. Wright, *Political Economy of the Cotton South,* 34–7, 42.

40. Oakes, *The Ruling Race,* 230.

41. Quoted in James L. Roark, *Masters without Slaves: Southern Planters in the Civil War and Reconstruction* (New York, 1977), 10.

5

The Lives of the Slaves

Phrases such as "the slave experience," "the slave personality," and "the slave culture" have now become part of the common currency of all discussion of the subject. They are signs of the massive shift of focus in the historiography of slavery over the last generation toward the lives of the slaves themselves. The attempt to arrive at a slave's-eye view of slavery lies behind much recent work, but it is fraught with dangers and difficulties. It becomes all too easily entangled in contemporary political and ideological controversy. It also faces, to an unusually high degree, all the problems involved in writing history "from the bottom up"—that is, the attempt to see and understand the past through the eyes of the poor, the underprivileged, the deprived, or the illiterate. Whatever the problems, the search for a fuller understanding of slave life has yielded some remarkable results during the last two decades.

Inevitably, such terms as "the slave personality" or "slave culture" mean different things to different people, and their free and easy use (even in the hands of able and sympathetic historians) comes close at times to denying to slaves even a share of the varieties of experience, the vagaries of personality, and the diversity of culture other people are assumed to have. The search for some understanding of slave life involves digging through several layers of formative influences: material living conditions, the physical environment, the psychological impact of generations of bondage, the personal factors in the master-slave relationship, the survival of an African heritage, the pervading influence of white American society, and the shared experience of the slave community.

The material standards of slave life were modest, sometimes stark, but generally above the standard of bare survival. Much depended on the character of the master and on his circumstances. It was obviously in the master's interest to maintain at least a very basic level of care and provision. Failure to do so in some cases may have indicated ignorance or incompetence or indigence rather than ill will. Masters and slaves lived in an age of low standards in diet, hygiene, public health, and medical skill. Planters did quite often call in doctors to treat ailing slaves, but it may be doubted whether the slaves who received such ministrations fared better than those who did not. Slaves had a lower life expectancy than Southern whites, but the difference was not large. According to the 1860 census, 3.5 percent of the slave population was over sixty years of age, compared with 4.4 percent of the whites.

Pregnancy, childbirth, and infancy were times of great health hazards—even more for slaves than for the population at large. There is ample evidence that, although there was a high birth rate among slaves, infant mortality was also very high—perhaps even twice the rate for whites. The high incidence of "smothering" recorded among infant deaths is now thought to show the frequency of "crib" or "cot" deaths among slave children. The exact cause of this tragic problem is still not established, but modern investigations do show that it occurs more often in low-income families. It seems likely that, in the case of slave infants, it reflects inadequacies in the mother's diet, and particularly the practice of requiring expectant mothers to continue work in the fields until an advanced stage of pregnancy.

In other ways, too, the pattern of health and sickness among slaves shows some distinctive features. The folk wisdom of the time spread the belief that slaves were less vulnerable to malaria and yellow fever—two of the scourges of the South—than their white contemporaries. Modern science confirms that, for genetic reasons or because of immunity developed from their African experience, this was broadly true. In particular, the sickle-cell trait in the blood of many slaves did provide immunity against some forms of malaria. But it could also lead to sickle-cell anemia and leave slaves vulnerable to many other illnesses. Slaves suffered badly from pneumonia and other respiratory diseases, as well as many of the infectious diseases of childhood, and they were severely hit by the cholera epidemics that swept the South from time to time. Living close together in small cabins and in tightly knit communities—and often in crude and unhygienic conditions—slaves were habitually exposed to risks of this kind.[1]

The diet of slaves was in most cases adequate, even bulky, but dull and, with the wisdom of hindsight, nutritionally deficient in some respects. In this, as in its emphasis on "hogs and hominy," it resembled the diet of many Southern whites. There were slaves who sometimes went short of food, and there were local and seasonal variations; the difficulties of keeping food for any length of time in a warm climate meant that there could be very lean times of the year. On the other hand, many slaves were able to supplement their basic rations with the products of their own garden plots or hunting or fishing expeditions—or raids upon the master's smokehouse or poultry yard.

There is a danger that excessive scrutiny of the quantity and the composition of the slave diet may miss two vital points. On one hand, the preparation of meals and their actual consumption provided focal points in the life of the slave family and the slave community; they also reveal a distinctive mixture of African, European, and Native American traditions. On the other hand, there was no more regular reminder to slaves of the deprivation of freedom which was the essence of their condition; they were not free even to decide for themselves much of what they and their families were to eat.[2]

Much the same can be said of their clothing and their shelter. Slave housing varied considerably in quality and character between small farms and larger plantations—and between one owner and another. On plantations it normally consisted of small wooden cabins, averaging about fifteen feet square, arranged along a "street" not far from the master's house. While one family to a cabin was the general rule, not all slaves enjoyed even this modest luxury. Slaves belonging to smaller owners often lived in attics or in sheds attached to the master's house—and their living conditions depended very directly on the personality and the prosperity of their owner. In *Time on the Cross,* an attempted comparison between the living quarters, and specifically the living space, of Southern slaves and working-class housing (actually slum housing) in New York in 1893 purported to show the superiority of the former. However, Richard Sutch subjected these calculations to devastating scrutiny and produced an entirely different picture.[3] The attempt to measure living conditions with apparent mathematical precision created not certainty, but confusion and controversy. Charles Joyner has even suggested that African tradition favored small, intimate interiors and that slaves would not have welcomed a more generous allocation of space![4]

Unless and until the statistical evidence becomes more trustworthy, more conventional sources must be relied upon to piece together a picture based on the harsh realities of rickety, unpainted, cramped slave quarters, with earth floors and windows without glass, swept by drafts in winter, stifling in the summer heat, choking with smoke, or swarming with insects. For all that, the humble slave cabin occupied a position of prime importance. It was the place where the slaves could shut the door on the master—though never with complete assurance of freedom from intrusion—and where their family and communal life could take root and take shape.

Charles Joyner has argued that an appreciation of the material environment and the material culture of the slaves is indispensable to an understanding of other aspects of the slave experience.[5] This is a point which needs to be made; however, it is not the physical environment but the psychological impact of slavery which has become the great historiographical battlefield in the three decades since the publication of Stanley Elkins's *Slavery* in 1959. Elkins argued that the severity of the slave regime in the Southern states crippled the slave personality, but he emphasized that it was not material deprivation but the overall impact of a tightly closed system that inflicted the damage. In his view it created Sambo—docile but irresponsible, loyal but lazy, humble but deceitful—the stereotype of the American slave. In effect, the Elkins thesis replaced the old concept of the racial inferiority of the black slave with the alternative concept of psychological handicap or damage, inflicted by the total institution of slavery. The first explained the personality problems of the Negro slave by his negritude, the second by his servitude. The vigorous reaction against Elkins in the years and decades after publication of his book has encouraged a third view of a distinct African-American slave personality, in no way inferior, but forged and tempered in the furnace of generations of bondage.

The Elkins thesis has a certain coherence and logic which remains impressive, though not persuasive. The shock of enslavement detached the slaves from their old society and their old selves; the total institution of slavery fastened new standards and a new personality upon them. The authority of the master was so massive as to induce childlike dependence and conformity in the slaves. Using the insights of interpersonal theory and role psychology, Elkins argued that all lines led back to the master because of the lack of "significant others"—other people with the authority or influence to affect the slave personality. The slave therefore internalized the attitudes and standards of this sole significant other. Similarly, according to role psychology, the human personality normally develops through the playing of a number of different social roles as child, parent, spouse, friend, worker, learner, patient, customer, and many others. However, under slavery there was simply one all-pervading role which produced complete dependence and submissiveness.

The whole Elkins argument rests upon the psychological impact of "closed systems" or total institutions. It was in this context that he introduced the highly controversial analogy between the Southern slave plantation and the Nazi concentration camp. In the 1950s, when Elkins wrote his book, studies of the impact of the camps upon their inmates seemed to show in the starkest possible form the capacity of a total institution to produce drastic personality change. What such camps could do in a few years, Elkins suggested, slavery could surely do in a few generations.[6]

Elkins's thesis was vulnerable at many points, not least because the elegance and ingenuity of his theoretical model was not matched by detailed investigation of the realities of slavery as it actually existed. His greatest success and his most enduring influence have been in the quality of the response his work has evoked. The incisiveness and daring—perhaps the outrageousness—of his argument stimulated a wealth of new insights and ideas, most of them sharply critical.[7] The concentration camp analogy was a virtual invitation to counterattack, as well as misrepresentation. While the notion of a closed system offers valuable insights into slavery, it must surely be recognized that, on any scale of "total institutions," the concentration camp and the slave plantation would stand at opposite ends. (Some are more total than others!) For all its cruelties and inhumanities, the plantation was a place of life and work, the camp a systematic instrument of death, with a mortality rate sometimes running at 20 percent per month. There is evidence, too, that even amid the unimaginable horrors of the concentration camp there were some inmates who did not totally submit or collapse, who did not conform to the model. In the words of John Blassingame:

While the concentration camp differed significantly from the plantation, it illustrates how, even under the most extreme conditions, persecuted individuals can maintain their psychical balance. . . . If some men could escape infantilism in a murderous institution like the concentration camp, it may have been possible for the slave to avoid becoming abjectly docile in a much more benign institution like the plantation.[8]

This in turn raises questions about the Sambo stereotype itself. It may be hard to distinguish, as Elkins himself admits, where the true personality ends and the playacting begins, but it seems clear that, if slaves adopted the Sambo role at all, they often did so to avoid either work or trouble, or to conform to what was expected or demanded of them. Blassingame speaks of "ritual deference,"[9] particularly among domestic slaves, but among others, too. It became so habitual in the presence of the master that they thought little about it, and did not regard such routine deference as evidence of their degradation. On the other hand, Sambo was a convenient and often comforting stereotype in the minds of white Southerners, which reflected their belief in the racial inferiority of the blacks and relieved them of the need to think of their slaves as men and women.[10]

Blassingame suggests that Sambo was in fact only one of at least three white stereotypes of the Negro slave. The others were Nat, the truculent and rebellious slave; and Jack, the least clearly defined of the three, who was sullen and uncooperative when he could afford to be, deferential when he could not, and who was cautious and calculating in his efforts to make the best of his situation. Blassingame's willingness to recognize such stereotypes has been criticized by some other historians. However, he makes it quite clear that he is using them only as guides to whites' perceptions of their slaves, and not as reliable indicators of the actual personalities of the slaves themselves.[11] In short, one might suggest that Sambo was what whites would like their slaves to have been, Nat was what they dreaded their slaves might be. Jack was not so much a stereotype himself, but represented the broad middle ground between the other two.

Sambo, then, was partly a black performance, partly a white invention. Insofar as some totally submissive slaves of this type did actually exist, they represented only one possible response among many to the stresses and strains of bondage. Different slaves responded in diverse ways, and the same slave responded differently as situations changed—and as masters changed, too. Slaves commonly had experience of more than one owner, and this comparative dimension helped to broaden the range of responses and tactics they might use. Blassingame describes the typical field hand as "sullenly obedient and hostilely submissive,"[12] a characterization less tidy but much more plausible than the out-and-out Sambo. The slave personality and slave behavior were not set in any one mold. The variety of approaches, mixing persuasion and coercion, which were pursued in the practical management of slaves suggests some measure of white recognition of variations in slave personality. Ironically, the rewards and encouragements offered to slaves, which Fogel and Engerman saw as part of an elaborate scheme of work incentives,[13] may have been devices to relieve some of the inner tensions of slavery rather than to increase slave work rate. They were often tranquilizers rather than stimuli, safety valves rather than incentives.

Elkins also exaggerated the picture of the master as the only "significant other" in the life of the slave. In most cases, there were many "others" of varying significance, from members of the owner's family and other nearby whites to members of the slave's own family and neighbors in the slave quarters. Elkins badly underestimated the separate life of the slave community because he overestimated the totality of the closed system of slavery. In fact it left significant spaces which the slaves were able to fill themselves. In this, the plantation may resemble the prison, the hospital, or the army camp much more closely than the concentration camp. Elkins has admitted the force of the criticisms of Fredrickson and Lasch, Bryce-Laporte, and others, and has retreated a little from what appeared to many to be his original all-or-nothing position. If the closed system is not quite so closed after all, the way is open to recognition of a different, more complex master-slave relationship, and a richer life within the slave community itself. "Something less than absolute power," he has written, "produces something less than absolute dependency."[14]

On the whole, slaves did not come to terms with their situation in one big final decision to accept or reject the system. Abject submission was one extreme, violent rebellion the other, and the overwhelming majority of slaves established a pattern of behavior in the broad area between the two. Some historians, notably Herbert Aptheker,[15] have struggled hard to establish the existence of a revolutionary tradition among Southern slaves, but the historical record is against them. Rebellions were rare, though plots and conspiracies, real or alleged, were rather more frequent. When rebellions did occur, from the Stono uprising in South Carolina in 1739 to Nat Turner's revolt in Southampton County, Virginia, in 1831, they were localized and short-lived and, in comparison with slave revolts elsewhere in the Americas, on a very small scale.[16] There was no significant revolt in the thirty years between Nat Turner and the outbreak of the Civil War, although the fear of such rebellion remained very powerful in the white community. In the 1850s, whites in Tennessee and Kentucky responded to news of a revolt among slave ironworkers—which was probably a figment of their imagination—with ruthless and savage countermeasures.[17] After John Brown's raid on Harper's Ferry in 1859, the South was swept by fears of slave insurrections.[18]

The infrequency of armed slave insurrections in the South testified not to the docility of the slaves, but to their realism and their endurance—and to the particular kind of courage which goes with those qualities.[19] They understood that the odds were heavily stacked against a successful rebellion. Many of the conditions which encouraged revolts elsewhere—a large slave majority in the population, a concentration of the slaves on very large plantations, a preponderance of African-born or of young males in the slave population—were not present in the South. All the instruments of power were in white hands, and the problems of communication and coordination involved in planning a major revolt were immense. Particularly after the abolition of the external slave trade in 1808, slaveholders responded to the economic incentive to meet at least the basic requirements of food and shelter for their slaves. Southern slaves did not experience the consequences of economic and social collapse or the desperation born of hunger which often triggered rebellions elsewhere. Moreover, the evolving life of the slave community and the slave family created ties and responsibilities which inhibited thoughts of outright rebellion and obliged the slaves to consider what they had to lose.[20]

Genovese identifies what he regards as a change in the character of slave uprisings in the Americas as a result of the "age of revolutions" in the Atlantic world of the late eighteenth and early nineteenth centuries. Earlier revolts, he says, had aimed at escape from the system; now they increasingly represented a challenge to the system itself. If this was so—and evidence from the South is scanty—it could surely only have diminished still further the prospects, in the South at least, of success in anything but the very long term. This is not to say that failed revolts or threatened revolts had no effect at all; as Genovese has himself argued, the persistent fear of slave rebellion was one of the forces which drove the South toward the suicidal act of secession.[21]

Some of the factors which inhibited thoughts of rebellion also restrained, but did not stop, individual flight from slavery. The power at the disposal of the slaveholder and the white community, the daunting problems of coping with a strange and hostile world beyond the plantation, and the pull of family and community ties gave would-be escapers ample pause for thought. It was not the act of running away which was so difficult but the problem of evading recapture. The odds against a successful escape to the North were great—almost overwhelming for slaves in the Deep South—and most fugitives were caught within days. However, a great many runaways had no such ambitious objective in mind; they took flight for a few days or even weeks, as a ritual gesture of defiance, or as a reaction to punishment, or simply as a temporary respite from a life of servitude. Some slaves were habitual runaways and accepted the painful consequences when they either came back or were forced back into the fold. Fugitives were often fed and supported by slaves from their own or nearby plantations—one small indication that the sense of the slave community extended beyond one slaveholding.[22]

Flight was usually an act of individual resistance or defiance, although there were occasionally group escapes. The so-called "maroon" communities of runaways were rare in the South, in contrast to the Caribbean and South American experience. But they did exist, and the largest and most enduring was the group which joined the Seminole Indians in Florida. There may have been some twelve hundred maroons in Florida in the mid-1830s, and the Seminole Wars, which cost the U.S. Army hundreds of lives, came to an end only when both the Indians and the blacks were removed to the Southwest in the 1840s.[23]

Less dramatic than rebellion or flight, but also, in the main, the work of individuals or small groups, were the various forms of sabotage, disruption, obstruction, noncooperation, and malingering which were woven into the pattern of slave life. Slaves feigned ignorance or illness, worked carelessly, broke tools, damaged or set fire to property, and stole from their masters. It is difficult to draw a sharp line between, on one hand, a natural desire to avoid hard work or a quick reaction in the heat of the moment to some act of cruelty or injustice, and on the other hand, a more conscious and deliberate decision to protest or resist.

George M. Fredrickson and Christopher Lasch have cast doubt on whether most such actions can be called resistance; in their eyes, resistance is a political concept which implies some planned action, involving actual or potential violence. They prefer the term noncooperation. Similarly, Lawrence Levine observes that the slaves did not oppose slavery "politically" because they were a "pre-political" people who did not think in terms of political institutions or organized, concerted action as vehicles for protest and opposition. Rather, they resisted in other ways, whether through various forms of passive resistance or through drawing upon spiritual resources which enabled them to transcend the temporal bonds of slavery. Genovese explores similar ideas in Roll, Jordan, Roll. The combination of paternalism and racism, he says, kept the slaves from full appreciation of their individual and, more important, their collective strength. They had not learned to act like political people.[24]

Twentieth-century minds may well find difficulty in appreciating the slave's-eye view of slavery and the perceptions and priorities which flowed from it. Notions of security and insecurity, for example, were inevitably reshaped by the experience of slavery. In some respects, slaves lived in an unusually secure environment— even if it was an unwelcome kind of security, bought at appalling cost. Slaves did not have the responsibility and worry of making basic provision for the food, shelter, and clothing for themselves or their families; of providing for old age; or of searching for employment and living under the shadow of unemployment. There was a peculiar, if cheerless, sense of security and order in being enveloped in a system which governed all such aspects of life and which made decisions upon them. On the other hand, the slaves suffered the terrible insecurity of the threat of sale, which might break up the family, or of punishment and harsh treatment, which could humiliate and degrade them. Their personal and domestic lives were at the mercy of their master's whim. The fundamental fact of deprivation of liberty created a topsy-turvy world in which the slaves had to balance the urge to resist against the demands of simple survival.

If the slaves were constantly reminded of their dependence on their owners, it was also true that slaveholders were dependent upon their slaves. If slaves lived in fear of the whip and of the threat of sale, masters lived in fear not only of servile insurrection but also of slowdowns, escapes, and acts of vandalism, which would disrupt the work and the order of the plantation. In such a climate of interdependence (however unequal it was between the parties concerned), there was scope for bargaining, compromise, and tacit understandings. There was a delicate and constantly shifting balance between masters and slaves. Eugene Genovese has presented the most vivid three-dimensional picture of the master-slave relationship which emerged. "The slaves," he says, "had turned the dependency relationship to their own limited advantage. . . . Out of necessity they had made an uneven agreement but it was nonetheless an agreement." Breakdowns or betrayals of that agreement could lead to eruptions of violence, but in general "the slaves' acceptance of paternalism . . . signaled acceptance of an imposed white domination within which they drew their own lines, asserted rights and preserved their self-respect."[25] In the words of an ex-slave, "white folks do as they please, and the darkies do as they can."[26]

At times, this may all sound a little too cut-and-dried, too much like a game conducted scrupulously according to clearly defined rules. Curiously enough, however, James Oakes, who disagrees fundamentally with Genovese on many aspects of slavery, paints a very similar picture of this kind of master-slave relationship. According to Oakes, masters recognized that they relied on the labor and the skills of their slaves and understood that economic success depended on their good will. The established slave owner could not in Oakes's view "entirely disregard the will of the bondsmen without jeopardizing the plantation's efficiency, not to mention security." Oakes cites Frederick Law Olmstead's comment that the most productive plantations were those where the slaves had the most autonomy. This principle could of course be carried too far, and Oakes also refers to a plantation reduced to near-anarchy when a weak master was exploited by his slaves. "In various ways," says Oakes, "the slaves frustrated, infuriated and manipulated their owners. The bondsmen never took control of the farms on which they worked, but neither did they permit their masters to take complete control."[27] With her customary sensitivity and insight, Willie Lee Rose has perhaps summed up this relationship best of all:

> There is a certain kind of strength that goes with weakness, and a certain weakness that goes with strength, as the diaries of courtesans will demonstrate, and as children have always known. This is because power likes approval, and there are means that power dislikes to employ. The slave who learned to exploit these techniques for survival on the precarious raft of another man's good will has been called "Sambo," an inglorious sobriquet indeed, with cowardly connotations. But it is presumptuous in posterity to dismiss contemptuously the methods that enabled generations of slaves to endure their harsh lot in life, and to snatch from it a few human satisfactions.[28]

It might seem reasonable to draw from the picture presented by Genovese, and largely corroborated by Oakes, certain broader conclusions about the life-style of the slaves. It is tempting to assume that this subtle master-slave relationship, and the opportunities and the "space" it offered, must have provided fertile soil for the growth of slave community life and slave culture. However, to succumb to this temptation is to plunge headlong into another historiographical hornet's nest—a wide-ranging controversy which extends beyond scholarship into questions of ideology, social theory, political belief, racial pride, and real or alleged racial prejudice.

For all that, the protagonists do not line up neatly as left against right, or black historians against white. One might take as examples the views of two white historians, one Southern and one Northern, who have both written sensitively and sympathetically on black history. Joel Williamson restated the conventional, affirmative answer to the question of whether slave culture was largely a response to the impact of slavery itself. "Most of what constituted black culture," he has written, "was a survival response to the world the white man made; most blacks had to shape their lives largely within the round of possibilities generated by whites."[29] In sharp contrast, Herbert Gutman vigorously dissented from such a view and charged most of the leading historians of slavery with complicity in its propagation. He emphasized the way in which slave culture developed through the cumulative experience of generations and from the inner resources of the slave community. It was to some extent an adaptive process to the rigors of slavery, but the form of that adaptation was shaped from within. He agreed with Sidney Mintz and Richard Price that African-American slave institutions "took on their characteristic shape *within* the parameters of the master's monopoly of power, but *separate* from the master's institutions." Gutman criticized Genovese for his emphasis on the "paternalist compromise" at the expense of "the long and painful process by which Africans became Afro-Americans."[30] But in his eagerness to shift the emphasis away from slave "treatment," Gutman came dangerously close at times to writing the slaveholders out of the story completely.

Black historian John Blassingame drew a distinction between the slaves' primary environment, which they found in the social organization of their quarters, and their secondary environment, which centered on their work experience and the contact with whites that involved. It was the former, he insisted, which gave the slaves ethical rules, fostered cooperation, and promoted black solidarity.[31] The large slice of the slaves' waking hours which were taken up by their work may lead to speculation on how "secondary" the work environment actually was. Indeed, earlier in his book, Blassingame offered a much more comprehensive explanation of the evolution of slave culture. It was not, he says, the contrast between the slave's African past and his dependency on the plantation which determined his behavior, "but rather the interaction between certain universal elements of West African culture, the institutionalized demands of plantation life, the process of enslavement, and his creative response to bondage."[32]

Other scholars adopt a much more emphatic black nationalist position. In a volume of essays evaluating Blassingame's pioneering work, George Rawick has provided a forthright summary of this point of view:

> It asserts that the source of black culture and black struggle is the black community itself. The autonomous development within American society of a black community was made possible by the actions in their own behalf of those who were slaves. Black culture and struggle under slavery come not out of imitating or twisting or turning or internalizing the world made by the slaveholders. They come from the slaves themselves. . . .[33]

An eloquent and impassioned statement of the black nationalist interpretation appeared in Sterling Stuckey's *Slave Culture: Nationalist Theory and the Foundations of Black America*. The subtitle indicates the main thrust of the book, which is more concerned with the development of a black nationalist tradition than with slave life per se. However, in a very long first chapter, Stuckey uses a mixture of conventional historical sources and evidence from folklore to spell out his view that "the nationalism of the slave community was essentially African nationalism, consisting of values that bound slaves together and sustained them under brutal conditions of oppression." The organizing principle of his study is defined as "the centrality of the ancestral past to the African in America." Stuckey draws on material from slave songs, tales, rituals and ceremonies, and above all religion to build up his picture of the essentially African character of slave culture and to describe the process by which, as he sees it, people of diverse ethnic origins in Africa were fused in the New World into one African people.

There is unusual power and richness in Stuckey's account of slave culture, but in its passionate commitment it does not accommodate the full range of historical evidence. It is surely not possible to read completely out of the story the various influences of the American environment and the process of "creolization." Stuckey himself has to admit the important role of the English language in bringing together slaves of diverse African backgrounds; he also acknowledges that some slaves were exposed to considerable white influence, but asserts that they appropriated only those values which could be absorbed into their "Africanity."[34] It is a matter for regret that such a stimulating account of slave culture should narrow its focus so unnecessarily. In an earlier essay, Stuckey himself painted a more rounded picture. "The slaves," he says, "were able to fashion a life style and set of values—an ethos—which prevented them from being imprisoned altogether by the definitions which the larger society sought to impose."[35]

In an essay written many years before the appearance of Stuckey's book, Genovese made some characteristically blunt observations on the dangers of taking to extremes the case for the separateness of slave culture. Pleading that, for all its distinctiveness, it was "a vital variant of the larger Southern culture to which blacks contributed so much," he went on:

> To pretend that the discretely black cultural development may be
> understood as an autonomous process—that whites in general and
> slaveholders in particular made no great positive impact on black
> culture—is to descend into mystification, not to say nonsense.

Such claims, Genovese argues, fly in the face of elementary logic and
solid evidence about the harsh realities of slavery. As he also points
out, excessive claims for the "autonomy" of slave culture deny or
belittle remarkable black achievements, both in forging a distinctive
culture and community life in the face of all the handicaps imposed
by slavery, and in contributing so much to the development of
Southern and indeed U.S. culture.[36] In other words, cultural pene-
tration was a two-way street. Surely, the distinctive life of the slave
community and the evolution of slave culture demand a broad and
inclusive interpretation, rather than an exclusive or monocausal
explanation.

A modest but useful first step toward reducing these large questions
to manageable proportions may be to turn to the day-to-day realities
of the relationship between master and slave. How much direct
personal contact was there? How well did the masters know their
individual slaves? Did they always exert authority to the full or did
they relax their grip for much of the time? How much space and time
was left to the slaves in which they might develop a separate life of
their own? How much interest did the masters and their families take
in what the slaves did outside their working hours, as long as it
stopped short of riot and disorder?

Peter Kolchin, author of a major comparative study of Southern
slavery and Russian serfdom, has suggested intriguing answers to
some of these questions. In comparison with Russian serfs or slaves in
most parts of the Americas, Southern slaves were dispersed over
relatively small holdings. They were a minority of the population,
whereas there were ten blacks for every white in Jamaica in the early
nineteenth century and twenty-five serfs for every nobleman in Russia
in 1858. The Southern slaveholders normally lived on the farm or
plantation, and slaves lived their daily lives surrounded by whites.
The less acceptable face of the much discussed paternalism of the
Southern slave system was its interventionism and constant intrusiveness. The consequence, Kolchin suggests, was a drastic reduction of
the level of independence in the antebellum slave community in such

basic matters as raising its own food or offering organized resistance in anything like a strike against the authority of the master.[37]

Kolchin offers a healthy corrective to the excesses of those who, in their enthusiasm to demonstrate the vigor and autonomy of slave life, have portrayed what he calls the "idyllic" slave community. Nevertheless, he sometimes shows the strain of trying to link two such disparate societies as the United States and Russia—and this can occasionally have a distorting effect. For example, the dispersal of Southern slaves over relatively small holdings obviously affected the structure of the slave community but did not necessarily undermine it. In her study of slavery in Maryland, Barbara Jeanne Fields explains that the unusually wide dispersal of slaves in ones and twos among various owners virtually forced the development of a social life beyond the individual holding. J. William Harris shows how, in an area of smaller farms in the Deep South where slaves were in close daily contact with their owners, the slave community "spilled over farm and plantation boundaries to become a kind of wider, underground spiritual and social community." That broader community was nourished by religious services and the influence of itinerant preachers, by marriages between slaves of different owners, by the owners' practice of lending their slaves to one another, and by an underground network of social contacts and activities which the slave patrols were powerless to prevent, and to which masters often turned a blind eye.[38]

This leads to a further question raised by the Kolchin thesis. Simply by counting heads and emphasizing the physical presence of many whites alongside the slave population, one may exaggerate the degree, frequency, and directness of personal contact between owner and owned. Even on a small or medium-sized plantation, with fifteen or twenty or thirty slaves, the master may not always have known the slaves well as individuals or taken much personal interest in them. Obviously, the master saw a great deal of the domestic servants—although, like all classes who are accustomed to the presence of servants, owners and their families developed the ability to talk and act as if the servants were not there. However, the paths of the field hands and their masters—at least on the larger plantations—may only infrequently have crossed. James Oakes insists that, while blacks and whites shaped each other's destiny, they did not do so through close personal contact or mutual understanding. Oakes does not support this claim with detailed evidence, but Blassingame has described the "hands-off" policy pursued by one Florida slave owner, and according to Theodore Rosengarten, one South Carolina planter, Thomas B. Chaplin, took little interest in his slaves as individuals or in their family arrangements. In his journal, he registered the births of slave children and also of his colts. The only difference was that he named the horses' sires but not the slaves' fathers.[39] Obviously, this point must not be overstated; there was an enormous amount of daily interaction between masters and slaves, and some of it was direct and even intimate. But the degree of personal involvement was not always great, and there was much in slave life the master did not see or did not choose to see.

For their own good reasons, masters often preferred neither to apply their authority to the full, nor to interfere as constantly as they might have done. As a result, some room was left in which slaves could develop their own pattern of life. Blassingame refers time and again to the "low level of surveillance" of the activities of many slaves. "Since more than half of the slaves in 1860 lived on plantations containing twenty or more slaves, it is obvious that only a small minority of planters could personally supervise every detail of the work"—let alone, one might add, the rest of the slave's life. As long as their work was not unsatisfactory and they refrained from serious misdemeanors, many slaves had little personal contact with whites and only occasionally had to act out the rituals of deference.[40] Once again, its must be emphasized that the situation on smaller farms and the relationship between small owners and their slaves were rather different.

No single statement can cover the range of personal contacts between master and slave, which varied according to personal inclination, size of holding, and many other circumstances. However, it does seem that, while it is unrealistic and unhistorical to portray an autonomous slave community where the master and the white community were pushed to the margins, it is also true that "space" was usually left by the master which enabled the slaves to develop a separate, but not totally self-contained, community life of their own. This life existed within limits and was vulnerable to intrusion, sometimes of the harshest and most inhuman kind. But it also provided a barrier behind which slave culture could grow and flourish.

The nature and the limits of personal contact between masters and slaves also cast further doubt on any idea that slaves internalized the values of the master or their own submissive role. There may also be questions about whether the networks or mechanisms of paternalism were quite so all-embracing as Genovese describes them, and whether a paternalist system operated quite so explicitly and elaborately as he suggests. The basic element of fear on both sides of the master-slave relationship must never be forgotten. Whatever the paternalist impulses on the one side and the success in building a distinct slave community on the other, there remained an awareness on both sides that masters ultimately held sway over their slaves by force or the threat of force. It was this which set the limits within which everything else happened in slave society. For their part, masters were not unaware of the ways in which slaves were filling the spaces and cracks left open to them—and those masters often felt insecure and uneasy as a result.[41] Fear was the binding agent of the master-slave relationship.

Much of that relationship and its effect on the slave community is encapsulated by J. William Harris: "In some respects, especially in religion and family affairs, slavery was a kind of unacknowledged, negotiated agreement, under which a partly autonomous slave community emerged."[42] In that sentence, "unacknowledged" and "partly autonomous" are key words—but so too are "religion" and "family." These were probably the two most influential elements in the development of the slave community, and appropriately, both exemplify the ambivalence and the delicate balance which exist between the assertion of slave autonomy on one hand and the exercise of the master's power on the other. In traditional accounts of slavery, religion and family life were long regarded predominantly as instruments of slave control in the hands of the slaveholders. Certainly, in the pre–Civil War decades slave owners made considerable efforts, with the aid of white preachers, to inculcate spiritual and moral values which would lend safety and stability to the peculiar institution. Similarly, masters saw the family as an agent of discipline and order, as well as of population increase. However, whatever the designs and the vested interests of the masters, the slave community attached its own special significance to both institutions.

Eugene Genovese places religion at the center of "the world the slaves made." He shows Christianity as a double-edged sword which could either sanction accommodation or justify resistance. In the everyday routine of plantation life, it brought spiritual comfort and relief to the individual slave and sustaining power to the slave community. An emotional brand of Christianity, spiced with elements of the African religious legacy, developed into a distinctive African-American religion. Conjurers and magicians as well as Christian preachers wielded influence within the community. Emotional fervor and active participation—for example, in the characteristic call-and-response style—were features of slave prayer meetings, which were often held away from the eyes and ears of the whites, and which were quite separate from the "official" religious services provided by the master. The emphasis of slave religion was on faith and love, not on rigid doctrine or formal structure; the most constantly reiterated theme was deliverance and the coming of the promised land, in which the spiritual and the temporal were inextricably mixed. This was a religion of joy and solace, not of shame or guilt.[43]

The work of Albert Raboteau and others[44] has reinforced this view of a slave religion which inspired a powerful sense of community and offered leaders and spokespersons for that community. But it did more still. Lawrence Levine has shown how it helped to provide alternative standards and alternative possibilities, especially in the area of relations between slaves, left largely untouched by the master's authority. The entire sacred world of the slaves, he says:

> created the necessary space between the slaves and their owners and . . . the means of preventing legal slavery from becoming spiritual slavery. In addition to the world of the masters which the slaves inhabited and accommodated to, as they had to, they created a world apart which they shared with each other and which remained their own domain, free of control of those who ruled the earth.

Evidence from some recent local studies of slave communities lends support to the views of Genovese and Levine—particularly if the locality under the microscope is one where there were large plantations and heavy concentrations of slaves. (The picture was surely rather different in areas dominated by smaller farms.) In his study of the Waccamaw rice plantations in South Carolina, Charles Joyner comments on the religious fervor of a large slave community, although he acknowledges that such enthusiasm was not shared by all the slaves. On one hand, masters and white preachers made great efforts to proselytize the slaves. On the other hand, African influences themselves very diverse, were still strong; voodoo was still widely practiced and conjurers exercised considerable influence within the slave community. What emerged from these diverse traditions and the slaves' adaptation to the American environment was a distinct, syncretic African-Christianity—and this development is traced more broadly by Blassingame and other historians.[46]

In a study of a very different South Carolina community, Orville Burton offers a rather different picture of the role of slave religion. He points to the revolutionary potential of some aspects of slave Christianity, notably in its emphasis on the theme of deliverance. But he also stresses the role of religion as an instrument of racial control in the hands of the whites. In his early efforts to assert his authority as a slaveholder, James Henry Hammond set out to break up black churches and stop black preaching, and urged his neighbors to do the same. He replaced the slaves' own meetings with regular white-controlled services, conducted by itinerant white preachers. But this was another battle where Hammond was unable to win a complete victory over his slaves; they continued to hold their own meetings, and Hammond remained fearful of the leadership and organization they provided in the slave community and of their potential challenge to his power.[47]

The transformation in our understanding of slave religion achieved by Genovese, Raboteau, Levine, and others—like all such major reinterpretations—has aroused anxiety in those who fear that it may be pushed too far, and frustration in those who are anxious to press on still further. A leading member of the first school of thought is John Boles, an acknowledged authority on the religious history of the South, who examines slave religion in this broader context.[48] In his view, the underground church with its worship conducted away from the masters has been "insufficiently understood and greatly exaggerated." Boles does not deny the existence of the importance of religious activity within the slave quarters and among the slaves themselves, but sees it as an extension or supplement to more public worship. According to Boles, many more slaves participated in the worship of white or mixed churches than in their own private gatherings. The emotionalism, the style of preaching, and the active participation of the congregation, typical of black services had their parallels in Southern white churches. The services in a white rural Baptist or Methodist church, says Boles, had more in common with black worship than with the dignified calm of a white Episcopalian service. With the exception of a few atypical areas with a very high percentage of blacks to whites, Boles thinks it likely that "in no other aspect of black cultural life than religion had the values and practices of whites so deeply penetrated." In a comparable observation, Blassingame estimates that "the church was the single most important institution for the 'Americanization' of the bondsman."[49]

For much of the colonial period, slave owners had serious doubts about attempts to convert the slaves to Christianity. However, the coincidence in the eighteenth century of the rapid growth of the slave population and community and the development of the Southern evangelical churches led to a major change. In the nineteenth century, slaves became active members of Baptist and Methodist churches, sometimes representing a third or even half of the congregation. Boles claims that the churches were by far the most significant biracial institutions in the Old South, though he acknowledges that the races sat apart in church, and that whites dominated the churches in every way that really mattered.

It is clear, too, that slaves took what they wanted and needed from their Christian faith and worship in its various forms. The emotional and psychological strength which enabled slaves to withstand the dehumanizing aspects of their condition came in large measure from their faith. For most slaves, says Boles, Christianity provided "both spiritual release and spiritual victory. They could inwardly repudiate the system and thus steel themselves to survive it. This subtle and profound spiritual freedom made their Christianity the most significant aspect of slave culture and defused much of the potential for insurrection." But surely the faith of the slaves also kept alive the possibility of challenge to the system and the hope of deliverance.

In complete contrast to Boles, and even to Genovese, Sterling Stuckey assigns religion a central role in the essential and virtually exclusive "Africanity" of slave culture. He expresses reasonable doubts about the proportion of slaves who ever actually took part in Christian worship, but then commits himself to the extraordinary statement that "the great bulk of the slaves were scarcely touched by Christianity." Elsewhere, however, he takes a somewhat less rigid view and speaks of "the Africanization of Christianity," or a "Christianity shot through with African values." These would seem to be steps along the road to recognition of a genuinely African-American religion in which Christian and African influences interacted with each other or existed side by side. Indeed, he has some intriguing suggestions to offer about how the two traditions interrelated in practice, although he always insists on the primacy of the African influence. In a typical passage, he discusses a ceremony common to Christianity and many West African religions: water immersion or baptism. He concludes that, as in most ostensibly Christian ceremonies on slave plantations:

> Christianity provided a protective exterior beneath which more complex, less familiar (to outsiders) religious principles and practices were operative. The very features of Christianity peculiar to slaves were often outward manifestations of deeper African religious concerns, products of a religious outlook toward which the master class might otherwise be hostile. By operating under cover of Christianity, vital aspects of Africanity, which were considered eccentric in movement, sound and symbolism, could more easily be practiced openly. Slaves therefore had readily available the prospect of practicing, without being scorned, essential features of African faith together with those of the new faith.[50]

Clearly, not all the differences between the recent historians of slave religion are reconcilable, but such an analysis, and especially its last sentence, could form the basis of a widely shared understanding of the interaction of two religious traditions, if only one could dispense with the insistence that the influence of one must always be subordinate to the influence of the other.

If religion supplied the inspiration, the family provided the environment in which slaves sought to create their own domain. Until quite recently, the idea that the slave family was a bastion of the slaves' own life-style would have seemed palpably absurd. The overwhelming power of the master, the lack of any legal status for slave marriage, the denial to the father of much of the normal parental role, the constant disruption of family life by slave sales, and the sexual exploitation of slave women by white men were generally assumed to have wrecked the chances of survival of anything remotely recognizable as family life.

A new and very different picture has emerged from the work of Herbert Gutman, and from the vigorous response to Gutman's work.[51] There was no legal marriage for slaves, but "marriages" were widely recognized and served important functions for the slave community, as well as for the plantation. One-parent families existed in numbers and the maternal influence was everywhere strong, but the two-parent family predominated—even if it often included the offspring of earlier liaisons of one or both partners—and slave fathers carved out a recognizable role, despite all the difficulties. Sexual interference with slave women by white men was always a threat and often a fact. Such liaisons were occasionally voluntary, more often forced, usually casual, but sometimes enduring; there were rare instances of slave mistresses who virtually assumed the role of the planter's wife. The double standards of a slave society were nowhere more apparent. Mary Boykin Chesnut, wife of a South Carolina planter, wrote mockingly that:

> Like the patriarchs of old our men live all in one house with their wives and their concubines, and the mulattoes one sees in every family exactly resemble the white children—and every lady tells you who is the father of all the mulatto children in everybody's household, but those in her own she seems to think drop from the clouds, or pretends so to think.[52]

Revealingly, she does not mention that slave families, too, had to live with the consequences of such liaisons. The situation on another South Carolina plantation, that of James Henry Hammond, seems to have been quite bizarre. In an astonishing letter to his legitimate son, Hammond seeks to ensure that, after his death, good care be taken of two female slaves, mother and daughter, and their children. It emerges from the letter that both women had been the mistresses of both the senior and junior Hammond, and there was more than a little uncertainty about which Hammond had sired which children![53]

The slave trade was the chief cause of broken marriages and divided families among the slaves, but it did not break the institution of marriage and the family, or the belief in it. Perhaps as many as one-quarter or one-third of slave marriages were broken by such forced separation.[54] Not all slave sales were a matter of unfettered choice or callous indifference on the part of the owner. Many resulted from debts, bankruptcy, and particularly the owner's death, when his estate was often divided. The frequent movement of owners from one place to another was another common cause. Gutman's extensive researches showed a curious pattern of stability and instability in marriage and family life. A stable marriage lasting many years could be broken by the sale of one partner, and the separated husband and wife were unlikely ever to meet again. After such forced separations, each would commonly take a new partner—and might be required to do so—and perhaps start a new family.[55] It is this pattern which Genovese labels "sequential polygamy."[56] Separation of parents and children was common, especially so because adolescent, single slaves were always among the most salable. On the other hand, a sale occasionally united marriage partners belonging to different owners.

Because of the appalling stresses and strains they faced, slave marriage and family life—and slave sexual mores—developed their own distinct character. Fogel and Engerman attempted to show what they called the Victorian "prudishness" of slave sexual morality, but to support their assertion, they rely almost entirely upon the claim that the average age at which women gave birth to their first child was surprisingly late.[57] In a noncontraceptive society this might well be significant, but their evidence has been hotly disputed. Gutman concludes that premarital sex was commonplace and incurred little disapproval, but that pregnancy or the birth of the first child normally marked a clear turning point. The mother was expected to "marry" thereafter—though not necessarily to marry the father of the first child. One child by one father and then a large family by a settled partner was a not uncommon pattern. Premarital promiscuity was followed by marital respectability—although no set of sexual mores has ever guaranteed the latter. Slave marriage, says Gutman, was a license for parenthood, not a license for sex.[58]

Lacking legal sanction, slave marriage developed its own wedding rituals, often including a religious service. Churches seriously debated the extent to which they could sanction "remarriage" after forced separation had ended the first marriage. Lacking wide choice, slaves, particularly those belonging to small owners, often found partners from neighboring farms or plantations, and this often restricted married life to weekend conjugal visits. Some even preferred this arrangement, as husbands and wives belonging to the same owner could not avoid witnessing harsh or humiliating treatment meted out to their spouses. Lacking control over their own lives, slaves set their own standards and accepted the consequences of forced separation by tolerating sequential "marriages." Lacking a sense of enduring security within the nuclear family, slaves established extended kin networks not merely in their own locality, but spreading through sale and forced migration, far and wide across the South.

The slave family was the victim of adversity but also a positive response to it. Astonishment at its persistence under severe stress and enormous handicap may reflect an erroneous assumption that the institutions of marriage and family flourish only in a free society. Their long history in many different societies surely suggests otherwise. On the other hand, slave attitudes toward sex and marriage also have a curiously modern ring—for example in the relaxed view of prenuptial sex, the pattern of accepting several marriages, the normal presence of two working partners in a marriage, and an approach toward something resembling equality between the sexes.[59] The parallel is of course far from exact or complete; slave mothers, after all, commonly produced six, eight, or ten children.

Herbert Gutman overstated his case that the slave family grew almost entirely from within the slave community. It existed after all on the sufferance of the owner, and it was often shattered at his whim. Much of Gutman's own evidence—whether on the forced breakup of marriages or the interference of masters with the domestic arrangements of their slaves—serves to emphasize this fundamental point. James Henry Hammond interfered in the family life of his slaves at every point, from the naming of babies and the care and upbringing of young children to the encouragement of large families and the punishment of marital infidelity—though he did not lead by example in this latter respect. Like most masters, Hammond had a vested interest in the slave family as a means to the achievement of an enlarged work force, peace and order in the slave quarters, and a deterrent to escape or violent protest.[60]

To some extent, Gutman was the victim of his own eagerness to demolish the arguments of other scholars and commentators, and in particular the claim that the instability of the modern urban black family was somehow the legacy of the slave experience. He was overanxious to demonstrate the autonomy and the "independence" of slave culture in general and the slave family in particular. For all that, he established that the family was probably the most solid cement the slave community had. It was also uniquely important in that the family linked generations of slaves and their cumulative experience. It was the most powerful transmitter of slave culture.[61]

The culture (in the more specialized use of the term) which the family helped to transmit has itself been the subject of much discussion among recent historians. This has taken place in the shadow of the long-running debate about African survivals in black American culture.[62] The once widely held view that traces of the African heritage had been virtually extinguished in the Southern colonies and states has now been generally discarded. Instead, attention has increasingly focused on the contributions of diverse African cultures to the evolution of a distinctive African-American culture. Indeed, the black nationalist school of thought, typified by the work of Sterling Stuckey, which has already been discussed, has carried this line of argument a stage further by insisting on the fundamental "Africanity" of that culture.[63]

Other historians have focused more on the interplay between African and American influences and have described it very much as a two-way process. John Blassingame devotes the first third of his study *The Slave Community* to two long chapters, titled "Enslavement, Acculturation and African Survivals" and "The Americanization of the Slave and the Africanization of the South," which deal with music, dance, folk tales, religion, and magic.[64] He examines the interaction between the African heritage and the American environment and compares the African-American experience with the process of acculturation undergone by slaves in other societies and other ages. Blassingame and other historians have also pointed to the African influence on various artifacts, and the skills associated with them, in the South—for example, basket weaving, wood carving, pottery, the making of musical instruments, some architectural features, and many agricultural practices.[65]

In his study of the Waccamaw rice plantations in South Carolina, Charles Joyner takes as one of his central themes the process of what he calls "cultural creolization," through which American ways were necessarily absorbed, but adapted, articulated, and understood with the aid of "African cultural grammars." Joyner was writing of an area of great plantations, with perhaps the highest density of slave population on the North American mainland, where African influence was at its strongest. These special circumstances bred a distinct creole language, Gullah, the result of the convergence of a number of African languages with English.[66] Clearly, many of the conditions of cultural creolization on the South Carolina sea islands were not replicated elsewhere.

The broader evolution of African-American culture has been brilliantly explored by Lawrence Levine in his *Black Culture and Black Consciousness*. To search insistently for survivals of African culture is misleading, he says, for aspects of old cultures—African and European—continued in the New World not as vestiges or relics but as dynamic contributions to a new group life. Resistance to change may suggest weakness in a culture; ability to respond may suggest creativity and strength. The question is not one of survival but of interaction and transformation.

He sees in music and dance, song and story, rich evidence of the separate, independent life slaves lived alongside their existence of dependence upon their owners. These elements of culture fostered a sense of community, and in songs and spirituals in particular it was possible to voice criticism as well as to uphold cherished values. Slave music was a distinct cultural form, created and constantly recreated through a blending of individual and communal expression—as, for example, in the call-and-response pattern of many songs. The most persistent image of the spirituals is that of a chosen people on its way to the promised land. The spirituals are typical of slave religion in their sense of immediate personal contact with God; figures like Jesus and Moses were "significant others" in the lives of many slaves. The sacred world of the slaves fused "the precedents of the past, the conditions of the present, and the promise of the future into one connected reality." This sense of the oneness of things was reinforced by a firm belief, inherited from Africa, in a universe filled with spirits who could be invoked, or for that matter provoked. Belief in magic and luck were valuable supports in a way of life as unpredictable and uncontrollable as that of the slave.

Slave tales also helped provide hope for the future and served as a survival kit for the present. Some were obviously tales with a moral, reinforcing religious beliefs and preaching the virtues of kindness, humility, family loyalty, and obedience to parents, and sometimes submissiveness, or at least resignation, in the relationship with the master. However, even such moral tales also offered advice which was essentially practical, and this was much more true of the so-called trickster tales of the Brer Rabbit type. Such tales often had several layers of meaning and offered different lessons at different levels. (They may also tempt modern commentators to be overconfident or overambitious in their interpretation.) Obviously, the trickster tales suggested how the weak might outwit, deceive, or manipulate the strong. More broadly, they outlined the tactics and attributes necessary to cope with an irrational world where the good and the right did not generally prevail. They may have been escape valves for the pent-up frustration and bitterness of the slaves but they could also serve as cruel parodies of white society, exposing its pretension, hypocrisy, and injustice to ridicule. There was an inevitable contradiction between the amoral strategy for survival recommended by the trickster tales and the standards and values taught by the moral tales or the spirituals. However, slaves learned to live with this contradiction because it reflected the tension in their daily lives. The two sets of lessons served different functions, helping the slaves live in the real world of the present while keeping alive their hope for the future.[67] Sterling Stuckey has drawn particular attention to the importance of storytelling in the transmission of slave culture to each succeeding generation, and to the powerful African influence in many of the tales.[68]

Religion, magic, folk beliefs, songs and spirituals, moral fables, and trickster tales were all part of the distinctive cultural style of the slaves. Their supreme importance was to give the slaves something which was unmistakably their own. In particular, religion, family, and popular culture have been the focal points of the great outpouring of new work on the slave community since the 1970s. Now other promising areas of exploration of the interior life and the internal structure of the slave community are being opened.

Blassingame has offered some intriguing speculations on status within the community. Those who were accorded higher status by the outside world—house servants, slave drivers, mulattoes—were often assigned a much humbler place by the inhabitants of the slave quarters. The slave community set its own standards, prizing above all loyalty and services performed for other slaves by, for example, preachers, conjurers, midwives, teachers, and in a different way, rebels. Occupations which took slaves away from the plantation or enabled them to earn money carried a certain prestige, and some special strength or skill—not least the cunning and resourcefulness to outwit the master or escape trouble—commanded a measure of respect in the community.[69]

Deborah Gray White has focused attention on the lives of female slaves, including their special vulnerability and the special burdens they carried. Slavery was not necessarily worse for them than for men, but it was different. Their work and their childbearing and child care responsibilities tied them more closely to the plantation or farm. On the other hand, White shows that what she calls "the female slave network" provided yet another support system for the slave community.[70] Various scholars, including Thomas L. Webber in his study of education in the slave community, have touched on the life of slave children. Stuckey refers to the process by which children absorbed much of their African cultural heritage in their early years. In her essay "Childhood in Bondage," Willie Lee Rose discusses the early lessons in survival, and the techniques of accommodation and resistance, which children learned from their parents.[71] She describes the traumatic moment when, after the relatively carefree years of childhood, the young slave was confronted with the hard truths of slavery—toil in the fields, the discipline of the whip, constant reminders of the intrusive power of the master—which compelled the stark realization of what it meant to be a slave.[72]

The great achievement of the recent historiography of slavery lies in the depth and substance and insight which it has added to our picture of the life of the slaves themselves. The great problem of that same historiography has been to reconcile a recognition of the severity and basic inhumanity of slavery with a conviction that the slave personality was not shattered by the experience, and that slave culture not merely survived but prospered.[73] Now it can be generally accepted that the total institution was not total, the closed society not completely closed, and the victims of the system not entirely helpless. They had enough strength to exploit their weakness and their dependence, and enough courage and endurance to triumph over their servitude. Their masters had enough human weakness not to act fully on the strength of the principle that slaves were merely property. Compromise, contradiction, and compartmentalization filled the gap left between the extremes of total mastery and total surrender.

If that is so, the main debate can then shift—and has shifted—to the question of the relative strength and influence of on one hand the master, with all the power of white society behind him, and on the other hand the slave community, with all its personal, spiritual, familial, and cultural resources. Slavery inflicted terrible wounds and left permanent scars, but adversity can encourage as well as inhibit a powerful response. The response of slaves was powerful enough to keep alive the idea and the perception of freedom until freedom came.

NOTES

1. For good brief discussions of health and ill-health among slaves, see Boles, *Black Southerners*, 94–104; Leslie H. Owens, *This Species of Property: Slave Life and Culture in the Old South* (New York, 1976), 27–49; and, for one local example, Rosengarten, *Tombee*, 181–5, 187. The most authoritative study is Todd L. Savitt, *Medicine and Slavery: The Diseases and Health Care of Blacks in Antebellum Virginia* (Urbana, Ill., 1978), but see also Kenneth F. Kiple and Virginia H. King, *Another Dimension to the Black Diaspora: Diet, Disease and Racism* (Cambridge, 1981).

2. Boles, *Black Southerners*, 88–94; Owens, *This Species of Property*, 50–69.

3. Fogel and Engerman, *Time on the Cross*, volume I, 115–6; Sutch, "The Care and Feeding of Slaves," in David et al., eds., *Reckoning with Slavery*, 292–8. As with so many other topics, Fogel and Engerman opened up a new chapter in the debate on slave living conditions and standard of living by suggesting that they compared favorably with the diet, housing, and health of workers elsewhere. See *Time on the Cross*, volume I, 109–26. Their conclusions are called into question by Sutch, "The Care and Feeding of Slaves," 233–301.

4. Joyner, *Down by the Riverside*, 119–20.

5. Ibid., 90. Joyner provides valuable evidence from one locality about slave food, clothing, and housing. See 90–126.

6. Elkins, *Slavery*, third ed., 81–139.

7. A good cross section of critical responses to Elkins may be found in Ann J. Lane, ed., *The Debate over Slavery: Stanley Elkins and His Critics* (Urbana, Ill., 1971).

8. John W. Blassingame, *The Slave Community: Plantation Life in the Antebellum South*, revised and enlarged edition (New York, 1979), 331 and more generally 323–31. (All subsequent references to *The Slave Community* are to the revised and enlarged edition.)

9. Ibid., 288, 308, 321.

10. Ibid., 230.

11. Ibid., 223–6, 238, 248. For examples of Blassingame's critics, see George P. Rawick, "Some Notes on a Social Analysis of Slavery: A Critique and Assessment of *The Slave Community*," in Al-Tony Gilmore, ed., *Revisiting Blassingame's "The Slave Community:" The Scholars Respond* (Westport, Ct., 1978), 19–20, 34–5; Leslie H. Owens, "Blacks in the Slave Community," ibid., 65–8.

12. Blassingame, *The Slave Community*, 305. On 322, Blassingame amplifies his description of the typical slave as "hostilely submissive and occasionally obstinate, ungovernable and rebellious."

13. Fogel and Engerman, *Time on the Cross*, volume I, 148–52, 238–42.

14. Lane, ed., *The Debate over Slavery*, 350. See also the essays by Roy S. Bryce-Laporte and by George M. Fredrickson and Christopher Lasch, ibid., 269–92 and 223–44.

15. Herbert Aptheker, *American Negro Slave Revolts* (New York, 1943).

16. Stephen B. Oates, *The Fires of Jubilee: Nat Turner's Fierce Rebellion* (New York, 1975) is a good account of the most notable slave uprising in the antebellum decades.

17. Charles B. Dew, "Black Ironworkers and the Slave Insurrection Panic of 1856," *Journal of Southern History* 41 (1975): 321–38.

18. C. Vann Woodward, "John Brown's Private War" in *The Burden of Southern History* (Baton Rouge, La., 1960), 61–8; Steven A. Channing, *Crisis of Fear: Secession in South Carolina* (New York, 1970) especially 18–30, 47–57, 83–101.

19. Two influential essays by leading historians dealing with the slave personality and slave resistance are: Kenneth M. Stampp, "Rebels and Sambos: The Search for the Negro's Personality in Slavery," *Journal of Southern History* 37 (1971): 367–92, reprinted in Stampp, *The Imper-*

iled Union: Essays on the Background of the Civil War (New York, 1980), 39–71; and Eugene D. Genovese, "Rebelliousness and Docility in the Negro Slave: A Critique of Elkins' Thesis," Civil War History 13 (1966): 293–314, reprinted in Genovese, In Red and Black: Marxian Explorations in Southern and Afro-American History (New York, 1971), 73–101.

20. For a superb analysis of the greater difficulties of rebellion for Southern slaves in comparison with slaves elsewhere in the Americas, see Eugene D. Genovese, From Rebellion to Revolution: Afro-American Slave Revolts in the Making of the New World (Baton Rouge, La., 1979; paperback edition, New York, 1981), 1–50. For good brief discussions, see Boles, Black Southerners, 172–5, and Blassingame, The Slave Community, 214–6, 222.

21. Genovese, From Rebellion to Revolution, xix–xxii, 82–125.

22. For examples of this support for runaways from the local slave community, see Harris, Plain Folk and Gentry in a Slave Society, 55–6. For good, brief discussions of slave runaways, see Boles, Black Southerners, 177–9, and Genovese, Roll, Jordan, Roll, 648–57.

23. For a brief account, see Blassingame, The Slave Community, 211–14.

24. Fredrickson and Lasch, in Lane, ed., The Debate over Slavery, 225–8; Levine, Black Culture and Black Consciousness, 54–5; Genovese, Roll, Jordan, Roll, 148–9.

25. Genovese, Roll, Jordan, Roll, 146–7.

26. Herbert G. Gutman, The Black Family in Slavery and Freedom, 1750–1925 (New York, 1976), 99.

27. Oakes, The Ruling Race, 179–90. The quotations appear on pages 184, 190.

28. Rose, Slavery and Freedom, 188–9.

29. Joel R. Williamson, "Black Self-Assertion Before and After Emancipation," in Nathan I. Huggins, Martin Kilson, and Daniel M. Fox, eds., Key Issues in the Afro-American Experience, two volumes (New York, 1971), volume I, 219.

30. Gutman, The Black Family, 335, 316–8. See 309–19 for Gutman's extended critique of Genovese's emphasis on slaveholder paternalism.

31. Blassingame, The Slave Community, 105–6, 147–8.

32. Ibid., 6.

33. Rawick, "Some Notes on a Social Analysis of Slavery," 17–18.

34. Sterling Stuckey, Slave Culture: Nationalist Theory and the Foundations of Black America (New York, 1987), preface and chapter 1, especially viii, ix, 23, 35–6, 53–61.

35. Stuckey, "Through the Prism of Folklore: The Black Ethos in Slavery," The Massachusetts Review 9 (1968): 417–37, reprinted in Weinstein and Gatell, eds., American Negro Slavery, second ed., 134–52. The quotation appears on page 135.

36. Eugene D. Genovese, "Toward a Psychology of Slavery: An Assessment of the Contribution of The Slave Community," Gilmore, ed., Revisiting Blassingame's "The Slave Community," 29.

37. Peter Kolchin, "Re-Evaluating the Antebellum Slave Community: A Comparative Perspective," Journal of American History 70 (1983): 582–8.

38. Fields, Slavery and Freedom on the Middle Ground, 24–33; Harris, Plain Folk and Gentry in a Slave Society, 43–55. The quotation appears on page 43.

39. Oakes, The Ruling Race, xiv–xv; Blassingame, The Slave Community, 35; Rosengarten, Tombee, 153 and, more generally, 151–6.

40. Blassingame, The Slave Community, 271. See also 286, 307, 323. See also Engerman, "The Slave Economy," in Owens, ed., Perspectives and Irony in American Slavery, 89, and Harris, Plain Folk and Gentry in a Slave Society, 52–5.

41. Harris, ibid., 61–3.

42. Ibid., 43.

43. Genovese, Roll, Jordan, Roll, 161–255.

44. Albert J. Raboteau, Slave Religion: The "Invisible Institution" in the Antebellum South (New York, 1978). There are valu-

able observations on various aspects of slave religion in Blassingame *The Slave Community*, 71–98, 130–47.

45. Levine, *Black Culture and Black Consciousness*, 80.

46. Joyner, *Down by the Riverside*, 141–71.

47. Orville H. Burton, *In My Father's House Are Many Mansions: Family and Community in Edgefield, South Carolina* (Chapel Hill, N.C., 1985), 152–8; Faust, *Hammond*, 73–4, 90–2.

48. Boles, *Black Southerners*, 153–68. This and the following two paragraphs are largely based on Boles' searching analysis of slave religion.

49. Blassingame, *The Slave Community*, 98.

50. Stuckey, *Slave Culture*, 37–8, 54, 57, 35–6.

51. In addition to Gutman, *The Black Family*, see, for example, John Modell, Stephen Gundeman, and Warren C. Sanderson, "A Colloquium on Herbert Gutman's *The Black Family in Slavery and Freedom, 1750–1925*," *Social Science History* 3 (1979): 45–85; Burton, *In My Father's House*, 9–13, and chapter 4.

52. C. Vann Woodward, ed., *Mary Chesnut's Civil War* (New Haven, 1981), 29.

53. Faust, *Hammond*, 86–7.

54. On the disruption of slave families, see Blassingame, *The Slave Community*, 173–7; Oakes, *The Ruling Race*, 176–9; Jo Ann Manfra and Robert R. Dykstra, "Serial Marriage and the Origins of the Black Stepfamily: The Rowanty Evidence," *Journal of American History* 72 (1985): 18–44.

55. Herbert Gutman discussed at considerable length the impact of sales on slave marriage and the slave family. As he sought to emphasize the stability of slave marriage, but also recognized the intrusion of harsh slaveowners into the personal life of slaves, his detailed evidence produces a very mixed picture. See *The Black Family*, 11–28, 128–33, 145–55, 285–90, 317–9, 354–9, 418–25.

56. Eugene D. Genovese, "American Slaves and Their History," in his *In Red and Black: Marxian Explorations in Southern and Afro-American History* (New York, 1968; paperback edition, 1972), 112.

57. Fogel and Engerman, *Time on the Cross*, volume I, 135–9.

58. Gutman, *The Black Family*, 60–75.

59. Genovese, "American Slaves and Their History," 112–3.

60. Faust, *Hammond*, 83–9.

61. The whole discussion of the slave family in this and preceding paragraphs relies heavily on Gutman, *The Black Family*.

62. An earlier phase in the debate can be followed in the works of Melville Herskovits, who emphasized continuity, and E. Franklin Frazier, who saw a clear break. See Herskovits, *The Myth of the Negro Past* (New York, 1941), and Frazier, *The Negro Family in the United States* (Chicago, 1939; revised ed., 1966), and *The Negro in the United States* (New York, 1949: revised ed., 1957).

63. Stuckey, *Slave Culture*, especially chapter 1.

64. Blassingame, *The Slave Community*, 3–104.

65. See, for example, Boles, *Black Southerners*, 143–6, and Joyner, *Down by the Riverside*, 71–6.

66. Joyner, ibid., xix–xxii, 88–9, 236–9, and on Gullah, 196–224.

67. Levine, *Black Culture and Black Consciousness*, 3–135. The quotation appears on page 51.

68. Stuckey, *Slave Culture*, 3–10, 17–19. See also Joyner, *Down by the Riverside*, 172–95, for an excellent discussion of the role of stories and storytelling in the slave community.

69. John W. Blassingame, "Status and Social Structure in the Slave Community: Evidence from New Sources," in Owens, ed., *Perspectives and Irony in American Slavery*, 137–51. See also Blassingame, *The Slave Community*, 311–13.

70. Deborah Gray White, *Ar'n't I a Woman? Female Slaves in the Plantation South* (New York, 1985), especially 119–41.

71. Thomas L. Webber, *Deep Like the*

Rivers: *Education in the Slave Quarter Community, 1831–1865* (New York, 1978), especially 257–62; Stuckey, *Slave Culture,* 31, 86, 88–9; Rose, "Children in Bondage" in *Slavery and Freedom,* 37–48.

72. Rose, ibid., 37–8, 47–8.

73. For some cautionary words on the dangers of emphasizing the supportive role of the slave community at the expense of the harsh realities of slavery itself, see Peter Kolchin "American Historians and Antebellum Southern Slavery," in Cooper, Holt, and McCardell, eds., *A Master's Due,* 92–5.

6

Variations, Exceptions, and Comparisons

Any brief survey of the slave system is almost bound to convey a spurious impression of uniformity, at odds with the untidy historical reality. The balance may be restored a little by a reminder of some of the variants and the exceptions—the edges of slavery—where its dividing lines, so often very sharp and clear, become blurred and uncertain. There is a more positive reason, too, for devoting attention to these areas of the slave system. Much of the character of an institution may be revealed by its margins and its abnormalities. Exceptions may not prove rules but they can put them into clearer perspective. Inevitably, the key books which have transformed the history of slavery during the last generation have been comprehensive, panoramic, or synoptic in their approach. In attempting to treat the subject at large, Stampp, Elkins, Blassingame, Genovese, Fogel and Engerman, and several others, all tend to flatten out differences and variations (whether of time or space, or social context or individual personality) and to pay inadequate attention to slavery in its more unusual forms.

At the same time, there have been excellent studies of particular aspects of slavery. It may be helpful to examine briefly four examples from the exceptions to the rule, the edges of Southern slavery: slaves in the towns and cities, slaves in industry, slaves hired out to employers other than their owner, and the free blacks living in slave states. Each of these four groups represented only a very small minority of the total black population of the South in the antebellum decades—seldom if ever more than 5 percent—and there was some overlap between one group and another. Nevertheless, the history of these deviants from the pattern of Southern slave society raises important questions about the clear lines of division and the rigid structure normally associated with Southern slavery, about the nature of the master-slave relationship, about the economics of slavery, and about the conventional picture of an agrarian society at the apex of which stood an elite of slave-owning planters.

Many of these concerns can be subsumed into one basic question: Were the exceptions to the norms of the slave South signs of flexibility, adaptability, and potential for growth and development—or at least useful safety valves for a tension-ridden society—or did they constitute a series of threats to both the efficiency and the stability of the system? In other words, were they a sign of weakness or a source of strength? On one hand, the city, the factory or mine, the system of slave hire, and the free black community appeared to threaten the safeguards, if not indeed the foundations, of the Southern slave system. On the other hand, these same exceptions to the general rule could be interpreted as offering the promise of a healthy and prosperous future for the South, whether through a more balanced and diversified economy within the national framework of the United States or through greater self-sufficiency and adaptability in an independent South. At the edges of slavery, as well as at its core, there were difficult choices between economic calculation and racial control—the maximization of profit or the preservation of a particular way of life.[1]

Urban slavery was perhaps the most conspicuous of all the exceptions to the Southern rule. The Southern way of life was ill at ease with the city. In 1860 there were only thirteen Southern towns with a population of ten thousand or more. Most of those were on the periphery of the South—either on the coast or in the border states. States like Mississippi, North Carolina, Arkansas, and Florida could not muster a single town of ten thousand souls. With its population of 145,000, New Orleans was the only urban center in the Southern heartland on the eve of the Civil War which would be even vaguely recognizable as a modern city. The other leading cities of the Old South—Charleston, Savannah, Richmond, Memphis—each had between twenty and fifty thousand inhabitants.

The urban slave population grew steadily until the 1830s and then declined relatively, and in some cities absolutely, in the two decades before the Civil War. The slave proportion of the total population varied enormously, from a very small minority in Baltimore to more than half the total in Charleston in 1840.[2] There was much coming and going among the black population of most towns, as owners commuted between their plantations and their town houses, as slaves were shifted between agriculture and other employment, or hired to another employer, or as drifters and runaways sought shelter and unofficial freedom in the anonymity of urban life.

Slave ownership in the cities was widely diffused, mainly because much of the largest occupational group consisted of domestic servants, distributed in ones, twos, and threes throughout the larger houses of the town. Other urban slaves were employed as drivers, porters, roadmen, handymen, and shop assistants, and in various other occupations. Some worked in industry, although in the South, as in many essentially preindustrial societies, manufacturing was commonly carried out in the countryside or in villages and very small towns. The larger towns were commercial, transport, social, and political centers rather than hives of industry.

The urban environment was almost bound to have a relaxing effect upon the institution of slavery and the day-to-day lives of the slaves. However hard owners tried to control their slaves, the slaves' situation and daily working routine took them out and about, onto the streets and into the shops, into churches, and into drinking dens. They had frequent opportunities to mix with other blacks—slave, free, or runaways—and also with whites of various backgrounds. Urban slaves were more mobile and less restricted, and had higher levels of literacy and more opportunity for adventure and initiative than their rural counterparts. There were obvious implications for law and order, and for normal standards of slave discipline. Quite simply, the power of the owner was less assured in the town than in the country. The lines of authority did not run in a short straight line from owner to owned, particularly in cases where the slave had been hired out, and often also lived out. The law was therefore invoked much more often and interposed itself more frequently between master and slave. In the urban setting, the law became a constant, and not just a last, resort. Countless city ordinances and bylaws were passed in attempts to control the slave population, and because law enforcement was patchy and erratic and policing totally inadequate, the master's authority was inevitably compromised.

The urban environment clearly posed searching questions about the effectiveness of slavery as a system of social and racial control. Richard Wade has made a powerful case that the explanation of the decline in the proportion of slaves among the urban population during the pre–Civil War years lies basically in fear. Whites were afraid that slavery was running out of control in the towns and cities because it was impossible to keep a safe distance, both literally and figuratively, between white and black, free and unfree. As attempts to tighten the laws proved ineffective, Southern towns began to resort increasingly to segregation in housing and discrimination in jobs. In the Southern countryside, slavery had never needed legally imposed segregation to buttress it; in the towns, slavery became unmanageable if the number of slaves became too large and their opportunities too great.[3]

Another historian of urban slavery, Claudia Goldin, has disputed Wade's explanation. Charging him with having been deceived by the propaganda of white workers who feared slave competition, she found the explanation of the ebbing tide of urban slavery not in social tension but in the laws of supply and demand, not in the push from the towns but in the pull of the plantations. During the cotton boom of the 1850s, more slave labor was needed in the fields, where there was no alternative white labor available, rather than in the towns where free white workers, whether Southerners or immigrants, were available in steadily increasing numbers.[4] Goldin's thesis is open to a number of criticisms. She tends at times to confuse or conflate urban and industrial slavery, and some of her own evidence can be used to arrive at different conclusions. The possibility of choice between slave and free labor and the competition it engendered did produce social and racial tension in Southern towns—including tension between white property owners and white wage earners. The result was to stir the very fears and anxieties which Wade sees as the root cause of declining slave population.

For all that, this is one of those happy historical controversies where both sides are probably right, at least up to a point. Goldin may well be correct about the particular economic situation in the 1850s, but Wade's case about the broader and longer-term dangers of urban slavery has the ring of truth. As he sums it up:

> On the one hand, the institution [of slavery] required a high degree
> of order, the careful regulation of Negro affairs, and a fixed status

for bondsmen. On the other hand, the city demanded fluidity, a constant re-allocation of human resources, and a large measure of social mobility.[5]

In their very different ways, Wade and Goldin both offer support for the view that urban slavery was tolerable or even useful only so long as it was limited in scale and peripheral in its role. Wade indicates the explosive potential of urban slavery if it were allowed to become more than a small exception to the rule. Goldin's argument, intentionally or not, demonstrates that slave agriculture was central, and urban slavery marginal by comparison.

Indeed, such conclusions have been reinforced in recent years by other historians. Carl Degler has stressed that it was the hard and fast racial lines of Southern slavery which made it incompatible with the urban environment—in contrast with what happened in the different social and racial climate of Latin America.[6] In her book on Maryland, Barbara Jeanne Fields develops a much deeper and broader argument. There was, says Fields, "a much more profound basis for antagonism between slavery and urban development than the problem of controlling the behavior of the slaves." It is vital, she insists, to distinguish between slaves as individuals and slavery as a system. Individual slaves could be and were employed in the cities, but slavery as a system could not provide the basis for urban or industrial development. Increasingly, urban employers found it cheaper and more efficient to use free wage labor, often provided by immigrants. "Objective structural requirements, not subjective individual preferences, explain the prevalence of free labor in urban employments." Slavery held back urban and industrial development in the South because, "as the dominant principle of social organization, [it] confined them to exceptional circumstances and to the margins of Southern society."[7]

Urban and industrial slavery were distinct but related phenomena, and many of the same considerations applied to both. The distinction made by Barbara Jeanne Fields between slaves as individuals and slavery as a system can certainly be applied to the employment of slaves in manufacturing and other industry. Many Southern planters invested money or slaves, or both, in manufacturing, but for them it was usually a sideshow or a spin-off from their main interest. They favored small-scale local industry to serve local needs but not major moves toward industrialization. James Henry Hammond had no doubt about the deleterious effects of industrial employment upon slaves: "Whenever a slave is made a mechanic," he declared in 1849, "he is more than half freed, and soon becomes, as we too well know, and all history attests, with rare exceptions, the most corrupt and turbulent of his class."[8]

For all that, slaves were extensively used in Southern industry—which was itself on a very small scale in comparison with the North. In the 1850s, there were up to two hundred thousand slaves working in industry out of a total slave population approaching four million. They were employed in iron works and coal mines, in transport and construction, as well as in industries directly related to the products of the fields and forests of the South—cotton mills, tobacco factories, sugar refineries, sawmills, and turpentine extraction.[9]

Despite long hours and tough and often hazardous working conditions, many slaves seemed to have preferred jobs in industry rather than agriculture. The attraction probably sprang from the same causes as in the case of urban slavery—a relaxation of the discipline and close supervision of the plantation, the opportunity to lead more of a life of one's own, and even the possibility of earning a little money. It was quite common for slaves in industry to receive money payments for extra work, usually called "overwork." Some slaves regularly received such payment for undertaking supervisory duties or for practicing a particular skill or craft. Amounts were seldom large, but one slave skilled in ironwork, for example, averaged between $50 and $100 per year in the 1850s—no mean income in the mid–nineteenth century. That particular slave used his income to buy coffee and sugar for his family, dress material for his wife, and furniture for his home. He—and his wife—had savings accounts at a bank in the nearby town. So aware did he become of his importance to his owner that he felt able to take four weeks off from his work at the forge during one hot summer, without any apparent fear that his master might punish him or get rid of him.[10] Not all slaves were so prudent, and drink was sometimes a temptation to those with a little money in their pockets.

Clearly, industrial slavery, like urban slavery, had the potential to undermine the normal routines and disciplines established by plantation slavery. But it was also related to a wider issue with serious implications for Southern society. If industry was to have any significant role in Southern life, should its labor force be composed of slaves or free white workers—or both? The issue was hotly debated because the industrial environment offered a real choice between slave and free labor, whereas the plantation did not. As industry was underdeveloped in the South, experience offered only limited and uncertain guidance. A few factories and mines had work forces which were in effect racially integrated. An English visitor to Athens, Georgia, in 1842 was surprised to find that three local cotton mills employed roughly equal numbers of black and white workers, some of the former owned by the mill owners, others hired for monthly wages from neighboring planters. He goes on:

> There is no difficulty among them on account of colour, the white girls working in the same room and at the same loom with the black girls, and boys of each colour, as well as men and women, working together without apparent repugnance or objection.[11]

On the other hand, racial tensions did clearly exist in Southern industry. White workers resented the effect of slave labor in depressing their wage levels and, in some places, the resort to slaves as strikebreakers. In the 1840s and 1850s, white artisans and craftspersons, and sometimes unskilled workers too, increasingly petitioned city and state governments to exclude slaves from particular occupations. Conversely, masters who had invested heavily in their slave property were scarcely enthusiastic about the encouragement of an alternative labor supply in the form of white immigration.

However, the issue between free and slave labor in industry was not fundamentally a financial or economic one. Employers with experience of both generally agreed that slave labor, if not more efficient, was more economical to operate, although the differential was narrowing in the 1840s and 1850s as slave prices increased and hiring rates rose. The white labor available in the South was generally of a low standard, and whether free or slave labor was used, the quality of the work force was one restraint upon technological progress and rapid industrial advance in the South.

The root question concerned the social structure and stability of the South rather than its economic progress. The protagonists of slave labor in industry argued that it would reinforce the slave system by diversifying it, mop up surplus labor in the rural areas, and maintain a clear line between the races in terms of employment and status. Opponents of industrial bondage feared that it would eventually undermine slavery throughout the South. They also argued that the resort to slave labor would degrade the status of white industrial workers. Those who favored the idea of reserving Southern industry for white labor claimed that it would provide new opportunity and a new economic role for the large class of poorer, nonproperty-owning whites. It would thus contain, and might remove, one of the potential sources of unrest and tension in the white South. The opposing argument was that it would lead to the creation of an urban working class—the very danger the South had prided itself on avoiding through the blessings of slavery. Free labor in Southern industry would recreate the evils and errors of industrial society in the North, which Southern propagandists had so gleefully condemned.[12]

The most searching modern study of the problem concludes that the explanation of the relatively slow rate of industrial growth in the South lay mainly in the economic behavior of the planter class. However, as the authors themselves go on to explain, the economic behavior of the planters was dictated largely by their social priorities, racial preoccupations, and cultural conditioning. They preferred to adhere to familiar agricultural activities rather than risk their capital in unfamiliar industrial enterprises, but their caution sprang in large measure from noneconomic concerns. In the strangely impersonal language of today's economic historians, the planters are said to have "attached unagreeably high social costs to industrial diversification." Fred Bateman and Thomas Weiss make the excellent point that, while a generalized concern for the effects of industrialization upon the whole of Southern slave society might not have dissuaded all would-be investors, many individual planters may well have been deterred by fear of loss of status, and even social ostracism, in a community which rated investment in land and slaves much more highly in the social scale than investment in industry.[13]

Any attempt, based on hindsight, at objective assessment of the capability of slaves as industrial workers largely misses the point. The crucial question was how many more industrial slaves could or would the white South have tolerated before anxiety about their impact upon the prevailing social and racial order led to an irresistible cry of "so far and no further." As with urban slavery, industrial slavery was tolerable and in some ways beneficial, provided that it was very limited in extent and clearly secondary to the employment of slaves in agriculture. But when industry—and industrial slave labor—were subject to these severe constraints, they could not trigger the kind of economic growth industrial development had stimulated in the Northern states or in Britain. Industrialization on that pattern, and on that scale, required the release of a substantial part of the rural population to become factory workers and urban consumers. But for social and racial reasons, the planter class preferred to keep the bulk of the South's rural workers down on the farm. They believed that. there was a point at which slavery and industrialization would become incompatible, and they were prepared to live with the exceptional case of industrial slavery only so long as it stopped well short of that point. Even Claudia Goldin conceded that "few can imagine American black slavery surviving in an advanced industrial economy. Modern transportation networks, increased education, and industrial growth would all have led to its downfall."[15]

Urban and industrial slavery were the main, though not the only, breeding grounds of another remarkable exception to the rules of Southern slave society—the practice of slave hiring. This became a highly organized business, sometimes conducted through agencies, more often directly between the parties concerned. Often, contracts ran for a period of a year, but much shorter periods of hire—a few weeks, a few days, even a few hours—were possible, especially in the towns. Slaves learned how to manipulate the system in order to win advantages or concessions for themselves. Indeed, an unusual triangular relationship could develop between owner, hirer, and slave. Fears that hirers might abuse their slaves because they had no interest in their long-term welfare were offset by the bargaining which went on between owner and temporary employer. The market for hired slaves was often highly competitive, and a reputation for ill-treatment of slaves could soon damage the prospects of a would-be hirer.[16]

The hiring system had attractions for slave owners because it helped to mop up their surplus or seasonally unemployed labor and brought in extra income. Frederick Law Olmstead even encountered one small slave owner in Mississippi who found it profitable to employ a white worker to help him on his farm while he hired out his four male slaves to work as porters or servants in nearby Natchez.[17] Hirers liked the system because it allowed more flexible, and therefore more economical, use of labor, and it did not require the large initial investment necessary to purchase slaves. The slaves themselves liked it because it raised their status and broadened their horizons. The divorce or temporary separation of ownership from management created elbowroom, space in which slaves had more opportunity to live their own lives in their own way.

Slave hire was a great convenience but also a considerable hazard, actual or potential, to Southern society. Obviously, when a slave owner was willing to hire out slaves to another employer, another element of both flexibility and complexity—not to mention uncertainty—was added to the system. Inevitably it altered the master-slave relationship and intervened in the direct connection between owner and owned. In the eyes of some whites, it looked like a dangerous step toward freedom.[18] This was all the more true of those slaves who were allowed to hire out their own services. They were usually slaves with a particular skill, for example as carpenter, blacksmith, or mechanic. In return for either a fixed sum or a percentage of what they earned, they were allowed by their master to make their own way, earn their own living, and often find their own accommodation, usually in a town.

A skilled slave, separated from the owner, living in town on his or her own, earning a money income from his or her labors, is clearly far from the conventional picture of the oppressed slave. Reflecting on his meeting with a group of hired slaves at a Virginia iron furnace, Olmstead was taken aback by the extent to which they were left to care for themselves. It prompted some observations on the slave owners' dilemma: "I begin to suspect that the great trouble and anxiety of Southern gentlemen is: How, without quite destroying the capabilities of the negro for any work at all, to prevent him from learning to take care of himself."[19]

Slaves who were hired out and who lived away from the owner with minimum supervision have often been referred to as "free slaves." The difference between a "free slave" and a free black who was not a slave was often very hard to draw. The only other small group so far out on the margins of slavery were those described by John Hope Franklin as "slaves virtually free."[20] These were slaves whose owners wished to free them, but found it difficult or impossible to do so because of the tightening of the laws governing individual manumissions. The owners therefore treated them as free, without going through any legal process of emancipation. They were often personal favorites, or slaves of high intelligence or unusual talent—and sometimes the master's own illegitimate mulatto offspring. For "slaves virtually free," like slaves who hired themselves out, safety lay, if at all, in their small numbers. As long as they remained rare exceptions to the rule, Southern white society did not lose too much sleep over them.

Ironically, as the freedom of some slaves expanded, the liberties of free blacks came under increasing threat. The existence of a quarter of a million free blacks in the sharply defined slave society of the South was more than an exception; it was an anachronism. At a time when the South based its public defense of slavery upon the contention that it was a positive good not merely for the owners but for the slaves, it was not easy to explain the continued presence of even such a modest number of free blacks—but it was not easy to get rid of them either. In the antebellum decades, restrictions upon them were tightened, they were excluded from certain occupations, and even where they were employed in preference to slaves, the reasons could be more than slightly sinister. For example, in one mine where explosions were frequent, slaves were too valuable as property to be lightly risked; free blacks were employed because they were more expendable.[21]

The free blacks of the South have attracted much scholarly attention in recent years. In his *Slaves without Masters,* the definitive general history of the subject,[22] Ira Berlin uses the history of the free blacks to pose important questions about the character of Southern slave society. The title of his book certainly seems very appropriate. Even more than the others who were exceptions to the rule, the free blacks lived on sufferance—part nuisance, part convenience as long as they remained a small and weak minority, a menace if they became anything more. It was they above all who blurred the clear, sharp lines of a rigid system of racial slavery. Blurring was tolerable; rubbing out that line was unthinkable.

Berlin emphasizes the distinction between the great majority of the free blacks who lived in the border states and the much smaller number in the Deep South. The former lived in an area where slavery was in relative or even absolute decline. Many of the free blacks worked on the land, often alongside slave workers, and had close ties with the slave community; marriages between slaves and free blacks were quite common. The small free black population in the Deep South lived mainly in the towns, and unlike their counterparts further North, many of them were not black at all, but light-skinned mulattoes—hence the Deep South preference for the term "free people of color." Indeed, according to Ira Berlin, this community in the Deep South was closer to the whites than to the slaves and was treated by the whites as a sort of third, middle caste in a rigid caste system.

The contrast between the free blacks of the upper and lower South is borne out by the findings of two fascinating recent studies of particular groups or communities. In *Black Masters,* Michael Johnson and James Roark tell the remarkable story of William Ellison and his family, of Stateburg, South Carolina, and the Johnson family of Charleston. Freed from slavery as a young man in 1816, Ellison used his highly marketable skill as a maker of cotton gins to build up a flourishing business, to acquire a large house, to buy land (some of it from a former governor of the state who was the father of Mary Boykin Chesnut), to become the master of up to thirty slaves, and to be accepted as a neighbor and an established local figure in an area dominated by substantial planters. In order to achieve so much, Ellison had to compromise, to know how far he could go and what he could do and not do; in other words, he had to know his place. Clearly, even within the exceptional framework of the free black community, he was a truly exceptional figure. One of the merits of *Black Masters* is that Johnson and Roark use the story of this extraordinary figure to illustrate some of the difficulties and dilemmas of the life of free people of color in the Deep South. In their words:

> He [Ellison] enslaved other Afro-Americans, ignored most free people of color, dominated members of his own family, and spent his life trying to please whites. . . . As a young man he decided that the route to security lay through accommodation and sweat. His tools were calipers and files, deference and circumspection. He stood as far from the river of heroic, militant black protest as any man in his era. He did not challenge Southern society, but he did seek to defend himself from the degradation it reserved for people of color. He contradicted the basic notions white Southerners had about Negroes. In that modest, quiet way he led a life of protest. . . . His experience shows what antebellum Southern whites demanded of an Afro-American who wanted freedom and security for himself and his family.[23]

Unlike Ellison, most free blacks in the Deep South lived in the cities. The Ellison family had close connections with the Johnsons of

Charleston, who experienced both the advantages and the tensions of the urban environment. In most towns and cities, free blacks were able to develop something of a community life of their own, centered around churches, shops, clubs, or occasionally schools.[24] For many free blacks, however, the most valuable asset the city offered was anonymity, the chance to lose oneself in the crowd. As Leonard P. Curry has pointed out, "It is a measure of the degraded and subject status assigned to the Negro in antebellum America that such depersonalization and loss of visible identity were perceived as desirable."[25] (One might add that many others apart from free blacks have been pleased to share the anonymity, or privacy, of the city.) The inescapable difficulty for the free black, however, was that, in a society where skin color was the immediate and obvious indicator of free or slave status, his or her freedom was always exposed to threat or challenge. In Charleston, as in other cities, the net tightened around the free people of color during the 1850s, and the threat of enslavement came very close, as elements in the white community became increasingly unsettled by their very presence.[26]

William Ellison's wealth and standing were of course very atypical of free blacks as a whole. There were others who achieved the same kind of "success," including William Johnson, the Natchez barber who hired a white overseer to manage his slave labor force while he devoted himself to various gentlemanly pursuits. Another example was Andrew Durnford of Louisiana, who owned a large plantation with some seventy-five slaves and frequently complained about the idleness of his "rascally Negroes."[27] In sharp contrast, most free blacks lived much more humble or even dismal lives, sometimes suffering abject poverty, often performing menial tasks, and constantly harassed by authorities who were armed with more and more laws designed to crack down on this awkward minority group.

This contrast is made crystal clear in Barbara Jeanne Fields's important study, *Slavery and Freedom on the Middle Ground,* which deals with the very special case of Maryland, where by 1860 numbers of slaves and free blacks were almost equal. Here the decline of slavery bred an attitude of defensiveness and nervousness among whites which often showed in harshness toward blacks, whether slave or free. Indeed, the lives of free blacks were severely circumscribed by restrictions imposed upon slaves, and their living standards were often deplorably low. Free blacks were an anomaly but their labor was a necessity. Many slaveholders deplored the increase in the free black community, while individually they were swelling its ranks by getting rid of their slaves. Maryland could not go back to the days when slavery had flourished, and would not go forward to a completely free labor system. Fields shows how the free blacks highlighted the difficulties of a society where slavery was disintegrating but very slow to die:

> In small enough numbers they posed a manageable, if ideologically troublesome, problem. But in large numbers, and under conditions that required slaveholding society to depend as much upon them as upon the slaves, they posed an unanswerable challenge both to the material and the ideological basis of slave society.[28]

Some of the very best recent work on the history of Southern slave society has dealt with one or other of these "special cases," such as urban slavery, industrial slavery, and the free black community. What is needed now is some attempt to pull the threads together in an assessment of the cumulative effect of these different but overlapping and interacting exceptions to the Southern rule.

The starting point for any such analysis must surely be that these exceptions were important simply because they were exceptional or peripheral or strictly limited in scope. Moreover, they were tolerated, accepted, even appreciated, not in spite of their exceptionalism but because of it. If the slave system was to work in day-to-day practice without constant friction and crisis, its rigid structure and tight restraints had to be prepared to give a little. It was important to pass laws restricting the freedom and opportunities of urban slaves or hired slaves or free blacks—the laws set proper standards—but Southern whites were past masters at ignoring such laws in practice if it proved convenient or prudent to do so. The sharply stretched lines of slavery were fudged somewhat in practice, above all by the exceptional Southern tolerance of the living lie and the double standard—the ability to say one thing and do another.

The exceptions to the rules of slavery were tolerated within tacitly acknowledged limits. The existence of urban slavery or the practice of slave hiring did not betoken radical change or reveal hidden dynamism within the system. They provided a little space within which the system could breathe—enough air to avoid suffocation but not so much as to stimulate hyperactivity or overexcitement. The exceptional cases served as economic regulators, social stabilizers, racial safety valves. They did not offer a bright new future for the peculiar institution; they were slavery's thermostat, not its dynamo. But like everything else in the South, these exceptions had to know their place and accept it. If they grew too big or powerful or important, they became dangerous—hence all the legal and other devices designed to contain them, and hence the ebbing tide of urban slavery and the possible turn of the tide for industrial slavery in the 1850s, not to mention the danger of total submergence facing free blacks.

In confirming the general Southern rule, the exceptions may serve to illuminate many features of slavery and of Southern society generally—its racial attitudes and compromises, its internal pressures, its readiness sometimes to subordinate economic to racial and social priorities, its combination of inflexible rules with flexible application, and not least the ability of the slaves to exploit the weaknesses or loopholes of the system in their own interest.

The exceptions which have been discussed represent only a part of the variegated pattern which existed within the framework of Southern slavery. A different kind of variation which probably needs greater emphasis is the process of change over time.[29] Slavery was neither a static nor a uniform institution. One of the merits of James Oakes's study of slave owners is its emphasis on the mobility and expansion of slavery. If westward expansion and the settlement of the Mississippi Valley constituted the central theme of American history in the half century between the War of 1812 and the Civil War, slavery was very much a part of that remarkable story. Slavery was an institution of the frontier as well as the Old South, and thousands of masters and many thousands of slaves passed much of their lives in crude frontier conditions rather than on long-established plantations.[30] The history of slavery was a history of many kinds of movement, apart from westward expansion: for the slaveholder, from one farm or plantation or occupation to another, or indeed in and out of slaveholding itself; for the slave, from one owner to another, into and out of the towns and cities, in and out of periods of hire to another employer, and in dreams and occasionally in fact, out of slavery itself.

In the years of its pre–Civil War maturity, some of the internal contradictions of slavery intensified as the system became at once harsher and milder. On one hand, it was the established, domestic institution of the South, regarded by most whites as the guarantee of their security, the vehicle of their society's progress, and the mechanism which, with its blend of firmness and benevolence, regulated their relations with the "inferior" race in their midst. On the other hand, it is clear that, by the 1850s, a good deal of unease and anxiety surrounded this mature and domesticated institution. Some doubts focused on the prospects for further expansion, others on the apparently diminishing opportunities for nonslaveholders to join the ranks of the slaveholding classes. There were anxieties about slavery in the cities, about slave hiring, and about the "threat" posed by the free black community. The haunting fear of slave insurrection never receded for very long. Uncertainty and unease in white minds bred a double-barreled approach toward the slaves themselves. On the whole, the material conditions of slave life showed some improvement in the antebellum period, as a combination of paternalism and self-interest encouraged concern for such matters. However, at the same time, the legal codes regulating slavery were stiffened, restrictions on free blacks were tightened, and the escape hatches were battened down more securely. White Southerners faced increasing difficulties in living with some aspects of slavery, but they were as convinced as ever that they could not live without it.

The variations, exceptions, and paradoxes which abounded in Southern slavery contribute much to the difficulty of effective and illuminating comparison with other slave societies. The intense modern interest in the comparative history of slavery has yielded valuable insights into the South's peculiar institution, and has served most of all to place some of its most familiar features in a fresh perspective. If the results so far have been limited, this may be in part because Southern slavery, if it is not the exception to every rule, sits rather uncomfortably, almost as an odd man out, in any group portrait of slave systems in the New World. Those comparative studies which take as their starting point the Atlantic slave trade and its triangular relationship between three continents have to come to terms with the fact that the North American mainland was one of the smallest importers of slaves from Africa, and yet became the home of the largest slave population in the Western Hemisphere. Moreover, that slave system expanded and flourished in the midst of what was generally acknowledged as the most advanced democratic society—for whites at least—in the Atlantic world. It reached its peak in the mid–nineteenth century at a time when slavery had been abandoned virtually everywhere else in the Americas, except for Cuba and Brazil. Geographically and historically, Southern slavery lies on the margin of the broad comparative approach to the subject, but it is much too important to be ignored.[31]

The multilateral comparative approach, encompassing in its broad sweep slave societies all around the globe, tends almost by definition to emphasize what various systems have in common rather than what distinguishes one from another. In his magisterial volumes, David Brion Davis writes from the perspective of an intellectual historian and examines ideas and attitudes concerning slavery, and particularly antislavery, rather than the institutional history of slave systems. He does, however, make clear his view that "Negro bondage was a single phenomenon whose variations were less significant than underlying patterns of unity."[32]

The most ambitious and wide-ranging of modern attempts at the multilateral approach is Orlando Patterson's *Slavery and Social Death.* It is hardly surprising that, in a comparative investigation of sixty-six slaveholding societies spanning several continents and many centuries, slavery in the Southern states only occasionally occupies center stage. Patterson admits at several points that Southern slavery had unusual features, but he adds that "it shared with all slaveholding societies certain imperatives of the interaction between slaveholder and slave."[33] The common characteristics of that interaction in many different slave societies is what really interests Patterson and is also what he is most anxious to demonstrate. His bold attempt to erect an elaborate and highly schematic framework for comparative study does at least offer one possible device for placing Southern slavery in a broader context.

Patterson's preliminary definition of slavery provides the key to much of his later comparative analysis. "Slavery," he writes, "is the permanent, violent domination of natally alienated and generally dishonored persons." The concept of natal alienation is used to describe the process by which the slave is deprived of all claims or rights of birth and thus ceases to belong to any legitimate social order. Consequently, the slave may be defined as a socially dead person— hence the title of Patterson's book. In their turn, violence and natal alienation led to a condition of powerlessness and dishonor which completes his tripartite definition of slavery.[34]

The rather stark, uncompromising character of Patterson's basic approach cannot comfortably accommodate all the recent work on the Southern slave community and slave culture. In some ways it is reminiscent of Elkins's unqualified application of a particular model to a complex and multifaceted historical situation. To be fair, Patterson's encyclopedic study is very much more subtle and varied than a simple summary can convey, but Southern slavery does not fit easily even into a work of such prodigious scope.

On the whole, bilateral comparisons between the Southern states and one other slave society (or related group of societies) have proved more illuminating. Such studies are more manageable and more meaningful, less comprehensive but more comprehensible. In this, as in other aspects of the modern historiography of slavery, Stanley Elkins occupies a pivotal position. Rejecting earlier tendencies to stress similarities between slave systems in North and South America and drawing upon the work of Gilberto Freyre and Frank Tannenbaum, he suggested that Southern slavery was generally harsher than in Latin America. He offered a twofold explanation: first, slavery in the North American colonies and subsequently in the United States operated under a system of unrestrained capitalism where maximization of profit was all; and, second, in Latin American societies the harshness of slavery was mitigated by the combined influences of the Catholic church, an aristocratic tradition, and the heritage of Roman law.[35] Both parts of this explanation have now been largely undermined by Genovese and other historians, who find that Southern slave owners were not after all such uninhibited capitalists, at least where treatment of their slaves was concerned, and that in Latin America the influence of the church and the law were much weaker in practice than in theory.[36]

The debate triggered by Elkins leaves behind at least two major problems. The first concerns definition of terms. What is to be included under the heading of slave treatment? Surely it ought to embrace much more than physical condition, material provision, and methods of punishment. Genovese has suggested that such matters must form only the first layer of a three-tier definition, of which the second is slave culture and community life, including religion and the family, and the third is access to freedom and citizenship—that is, the prospect of manumission or escape from slavery.[37] If something approaching a consensus now prevails on any aspect of the subject, it would be that, on the first two counts—living conditions and community life—Southern slavery was surely milder than its counterparts elsewhere in the Americas. However, on the third count—access to freedom—it was distinctly harsher. Individual manumissions were very much less frequent, and the free black community very much smaller, than in Latin American slave societies. This was where the strict lines of racial slavery asserted themselves, with only a few exceptions. In the United States, anyone with the slightest trace of Negro blood was classified as black; this was in sharp contrast to the various subtle gradations recognized in Latin America. Southern slave society did not allow what Carl Degler calls the mulatto escape hatch.[38]

The second problem left behind by Elkins stems from the emphasis on slave treatment as a standard of comparison. Of course it remains one perfectly proper focus of such investigations, but surely it should not be the exclusive or dominant one. As Peter Kolchin has pointed out, the priority given to slave treatment in comparative studies has been increasingly at odds with the emphasis in modern studies of Southern slavery on the interior life of the slave community and the development of a distinct African-American culture.[39] (It is ironic that much of this work was sparked as part of the response to Elkins's major thesis concerning the slave personality.) Clearly there are many other topics apart from slave treatment which offer scope for revealing comparisons—or contrasts—between the Old South and other parts of the New World, and even beyond. Some of the major modern historians of Southern slavery—notably John Blassingame and Eugene Genovese—have always been at pains to place all their work in an international or comparative context. Genovese in particular excels in this grasp of the wider American or Atlantic or world perspective, whether he is discussing slave revolts, the master-slave relationship, or the economics of slavery.[40]

Understandably, many comparative studies have centered upon other slave societies in the Western Hemisphere. A few examples may suffice to illustrate some of the major themes. Despite geographical proximity, the Caribbean offers some of the most striking contrasts with Southern slave society. It is true that Herbert S. Klein has compared slavery in Virginia and Cuba in a way which broadly follows the Elkins line of argument,[41] but most historians have stressed the extreme harshness of Caribbean slavery. One of the most authoritative of such studies, Richard Dunn's *Sugar and Slaves,* explores the sharp contrast between West Indian planters and their English counterparts on the mainland of North America. Whereas the island planters plunged into the slave business, he says, the mainland colonies inched into it—and much of the divergent character of the two systems flowed from that initial distinction. Dunn concludes that slavery in the sugar islands became "one of the harshest systems of servitude in Western history."[42] The differences from the Southern pattern were enormous. Small islands with large sugar plantations, often with absentee owners; slaves being worked to exhaustion and death and then replaced by fresh imports from Africa; a slave population with a preponderance of young males—all this may have been the state of affairs only a few hundred miles from the Southern coast, but it belonged to another world.

Where Latin America is concerned, the contrasts with the Southern United States are less dramatic and the comparisons more finely drawn. Perhaps the most direct and sustained one-to-one comparison of two societies is to be found in Carl Degler's *Neither Black Nor White: Slavery and Race Relations in Brazil and the United States*. Degler underlines the importance of demographic and racial factors in his exploration of the differences between the two slave systems. Through most of the history of slavery in Brazil, whites were a small minority of the population, miscegenation was widespread, and a substantial mulatto population became a feature of Brazilian society. Manumission of slaves was quite common—not always, it should be added, for enlightened or humanitarian reasons—and free blacks and mulattoes played a key role in economic life, filling a variety of trades and occupations, and compensating for the shortage of white labor.

In contrast to the remarkable natural increase of the Southern slave population, Brazil remained dependent until the mid–nineteenth century on the external slave trade to replenish its labor force. Partly because of the imbalance of the sexes, slave family life did not develop in any way comparable with the Southern experience, birthrates were much lower, and infant mortality was appallingly high. These factors, Degler concludes, are key indicators of the much greater harshness of the Brazilian system in comparison with the Southern. On the other hand, the Southern system had its own kind of severity, resulting largely from its racial character. While noting that Brazil was by no means a society free from race consciousness, Degler makes an effective contrast with the position in the United States: "in Brazil, the slave may have been feared but the black man was not, whereas in the United States both the slave and the black were feared." It is significant that the South articulated a racial defense of slavery which had no real Brazilian counterpart.[43]

Degler has been criticized for paying too little attention to questions of culture and ideology, but he does in fact stress that the liberal ideology of the United States drew a sharp line between freedom and slavery which was all too easily transferred into another duality between white and black.[44] An additional point too often neglected by comparative historians is that, in the nineteenth century, slavery existed only in a part of the United States, that Southern slave society was engaged in a competitive process of westward expansion with the numerically stronger nonslave section, and that it was subject to mounting political and ideological attack from that section. The character of Southern slavery was surely not unaffected by its sensitivity and vulnerability to such pressures from without.

The pursuit of one-to-one comparisons between the South and other societies has now reached out beyond the Americas. George Fredrickson's White Supremacy is a wide-ranging comparative study of American and South African history, in which race relations are the major theme, but it does include some pertinent comments on slavery. Fredrickson sees some similarity in the motivation behind the resort to imported slave labor in both societies in preference to reliance on either the native population or white wage labor. Although the reasons were to a great degree economic, slave labor offered particular advantages in terms of social control and the achievement of a stable and cohesive social order. Fredrickson also shows how in both societies the use of black slave labor helped defuse class conflict within the white community. However, the contrasts between the South African situation and the American South serve to highlight distinctive features of Southern slavery. The Cape colony produced no great staple crop, like cotton, for which there was a massive world demand. Partly for this reason, there was no real plantation system and slave ownership was very widely diffused. Normally, in world terms, the Southern slave system is presented as one in which slaveholding was widely shared and a small number of great planters did not dominate; the comparison with the Cape colony puts this into a somewhat different perspective.

For all their various differences, Fredrickson is impressed above all by one highly significant similarity between South Africa and the American South. However they started out, both slave systems became essentially racial in character, and drew a clear line between freedom and slavery which was based on race and color. They became much more tightly closed systems than those in Latin America, and they both lacked a substantial intermediate group or caste of "free people of color." Fredrickson concludes that this dichotomy of white and black, running parallel to the other of free and slave, set the future pattern of race relations in both societies. "A slaveholding mentality," he writes, "remained the wellspring of white supremacist thought and action long after the institution that originally sustained it had been relegated to the dustbin of history."[45]

In contrast, the race factor is conspicuous by its absence in the society which forms the basis of the most arresting and ambitious essay yet attempted in the bilateral comparison of two slave systems. The notion of a detailed and sustained comparison between Russian serfdom and Southern slavery might seem at first sight to be justified by little more than the coincidence of their almost simultaneous abolition during the 1860s. However, Peter Kolchin has set out to make just such a comparison in his remarkable study *Unfree Labor*. Kolchin sees a basic similarity in the conditions which encouraged the development of systems of "unfree labor" in both cases: sparseness of population and particularly a severe shortage of labor in a society undergoing rapid growth and expansion. Both systems were marked, says Kolchin, "by an essential contradiction between the commercial orientation of the masters with respect to the *distribution* of their product and the noncapitalist nature of its *production*"[46]—a point which would no doubt strike a responsive chord with Genovese. From this more or less common starting point, Kolchin does not seek to stretch beyond credibility the similarities between the two systems; in fact, it is the very deep differences between them which often make his study so stimulating and illuminating. Indeed, the startling originality of his particular comparative approach will prompt a fresh look at some long-familiar features of the Southern slave landscape.

Some of the contrasts highlighted by Kolchin could scarcely be more dramatic. In round figures, there were two whites to every black in the antebellum South; in Russia in 1858, there was one male nobleman to every fifty-two male peasants. In the South, there were just over two slaves for every member of a slaveholding family; in

Russia, there were more than twenty-four male serfs for every male nobleman. Russian serfs were generally held in very much larger units than Southern slaves. To take the extreme case, the U.S. census of 1860 listed only one owner of more than one thousand slaves; the 1858 census in Russia listed 3,858 owners of over one thousand serfs. One Russian family owned more than 37,000 serfs, scattered over numerous estates.

The consequences of these enormous differences were profound. Because many Russian owners were absentees, the relationship between owner and owned was inevitably more distant, geographically as well as personally. Serfs were probably punished less often, but more brutally, than slaves. Many of them rarely saw their owners, and dealt mainly with minor officials and bureaucrats. Nothing is more salutary in Kolchin's work than his reminder of the peculiar importance of the simple fact that most Southern slaveholders were resident on their plantations or farms. The greater "paternalism" of the Southern system resulted in better material living conditions but also in much more interference in the lives of the slaves, and a more sustained effort to inculcate a sense of dependence. As already discussed in Chapter 5, Kolchin is somewhat sceptical about the degree of autonomy within the slave community and believes that serfs enjoyed a much larger measure of control over their daily lives.[47] They grew their own food, had a voice in local government, and were able to engage in organized rather than individual resistance. Moreover, unlike slaves, they were required to devote only a part of their labor to the service of their owners.

Kolchin acknowledges the fundamental difference between a system where the serfs were living in their own homeland and a system of racial servitude where black slaves had been introduced by forced migration and were treated as outsiders in a white society of European derivation. This question of what Kolchin calls geographical continuity or discontinuity has a key role in his proposed "spectrum" of systems of bondage. The other factors he includes are the presence of a large nonwhite or peasant majority in the population, as in Jamaica or Russia; the prevalence of large-scale holdings, again as in Jamaica and Russia; and a high incidence of absentee ownership, as in all the other countries apart from the United States and to some extent Brazil. These he regards as the main influences on the degree of autonomy which was possible for the slaves or serfs. In Kolchin's spectrum, Russia stands at one extreme, with Jamaica, St. Dominque, Cuba, and Brazil following in that order, while, at the other extreme the United States provided the least scope of slave autonomy. He concludes that "only antebellum American slaves constituted a heavily creole population living in relatively small units in a largely white world where a resident master class impinged on them on a daily basis."[48]

Kolchin may well have good grounds for challenging some of the bolder claims which have been made for the autonomy of Southern slaves; he is particularly severe on any idea of slave life as comfortable or even cosy—and quite rightly so. However, his argument does surely fly in the face of strong evidence of the separate life of the slave community and of a vigorous slave culture. Despite all the obstacles and deterrents he lists, it is abundantly clear that Southern slaves did create some latitude in which to conduct their own lives, and that their owners permitted them to do so—or were unable to prevent them from doing so. A strictly racial form of slavery surely encouraged the sense of a separate identity and a distinct way of life. Adversity often encourages a strong reaction, and the intrusiveness of paternalist owners may even have stimulated, rather than inhibited, the determined efforts of the slaves to assert their own autonomy whenever and wherever they could.

Finally, the huge difference between the U.S. and Russian political and social systems must have had some bearing on the matter; the "looser," more decentralized style of U.S. (including Southern) government, politics, and social organization may possibly have left some space within which the slave community could take shape. To be fair, it should be added that Kolchin does generally give more weight than most comparative historians to the political climate and the political system in the United States—its decentralization as well as its democracy—and also to the sectional character of slavery within that system.[49]

Whatever specific criticisms may be made, Kolchin's work has carried the one-to-one comparison of two different systems of bondage to a new, higher, and more productive level. Such a comparison can never again be tied simply to the question of which system resulted in milder or harsher treatment of the slaves. Comparative studies have served above all to identify clearly what was different, if not necessarily unique, about Southern slavery—the growth of the population by natural increase, the intensely racial character of the system, the emergence of a distinct African-American culture, the wide diffusion of ownership, the close but uneasy coexistence of the resident master and his slaves, and the extraordinary cohabitation of racial slavery and white democracy under the same Southern roof. Out of that unusual amalgam of forces at work (and sometimes at war) within the system there emerged a Southern society and way of life which was increasingly out of step with the rest of the United States, and which was an anachronism in the North Atlantic world of the mid–nineteenth century.

NOTES

1. There is no single book dealing with all the "exceptions" to the Southern slave rule, but see my "The Edges of Slavery in the Old South: Or, Do Exceptions Prove Rules?," *Slavery and Abolition: A Journal of Comparative Studies* 4 (1983): 106–25, on which I have drawn heavily in this chapter.

2. For detailed statistics on population, see Richard C. Wade, *Slavery in the Cities: The South, 1820–1860* (New York, 1964), 325–7. I have also relied on Wade for much of the basic information in this and the following paragraphs.

3. Ibid., 243–81.

4. Goldin, *Urban Slavery in the American South*, 51–128.

5. Wade, *Slavery in the Cities*, 262.

6. Carl N. Degler, "The Irony of American Negro Slavery," in Owens, ed., *Perspectives and Irony in American Slavery*, 20.

7. Fields, *Slavery and Freedom on the Middle Ground*, 33–5, 40–57, 62. The quotations appear on pages 54, 55. If Fields regards Wade's emphasis on law and order as too narrow an explanation, she reserves her severest criticism for the Goldin thesis and its use in Fogel and Engerman's *Time on the Cross*.

8. *DeBow's Review* 8 (1850): 518, quoted in Genovese, *Political Economy of Slavery*, 225.

9. Much of the information in this and the following paragraphs is drawn from two valuable studies: Robert S. Starobin, *Industrial Slavery in the Old South* (New York, 1970), and Ronald L. Lewis, *Coal, Iron and Slaves: Industrial Slavery in Maryland and Virginia, 1715–1865* (Westport, Ct., 1979).

10. Charles B. Dew, "Sam Williams, Forgeman: The Life of an Industrial Slave in the Old South," in J. Morgan Kousser and James M. McPherson, eds., *Race, Region and Reconstruction: Essays in Honor of C. Vann Woodward* (New York, 1982), 214–9, 222–3. See also Dew's article, "Disciplining Slave Ironworkers in the Ante-Bellum South: Coercion, Conciliation and Accommodation," *American Historical Review* 79 (1974): 393–418.

11. James Silk Buckingham, *The Slave States of America*, two volumes (London, 1842), volume II, 112.

12. This debate is discussed in Starobin, *Industrial Slavery*, 186–9, 204–14, 230–2, and Genovese, *Political Economy of Slavery*, 221–35, and, more generally, chapters 7 through 9.

13. Fred Bateman and Thomas Weiss, *A Deplorable Scarcity: The Failure of Industrialization in the Slave Economy* (Chapel Hill, N.C., 1981), especially 158, 160, 162.

14. Genovese, *Political Economy of Slavery,* 181, 183–5, 234–5; Starobin, *Industrial Slavery,* 189.

15. Goldin, *Urban Slavery,* 126.

16. Lewis, *Coal, Iron and Slaves,* 81–3.

17. Frederick Law Olmstead, *A Journey in the Back Country* (New York, 1860; reprint, 1970), 41.

18. See Clement Eaton, "Slave Hiring in the Upper South: A Step toward Freedom," *Mississippi Valley Historical Review* 46 (1959–60): 663, 669–70, 675–8, and Fields, *Slavery and Freedom on the Middle Ground,* 27–8, 47–9.

19. Quoted in Dew, "Disciplining Slave Ironworkers," 404.

20. John Hope Franklin, "Slaves Virtually Free in Ante-Bellum North Carolina," *Journal of Negro History* 28 (1943): 284–310.

21. Lewis, *Coal, Iron and Slaves,* 67.

22. Ira Berlin, *Slaves Without Masters: The Free Negro in the Antebellum South* (New York, 1974).

23. Michael P. Johnson and James L. Roark, *Black Masters: A Free Family of Color in the Old South* (New York, 1984), 150. The remarkable story of William Ellison and his family dominates the first four chapters of *Black Masters.*

24. See ibid., chapters 5 through 8, on the free black community in Charleston. James Marsh Johnson, William Ellison's son-in-law, is one of the central figures, and also the writer of many of the letters published in a companion volume: Johnson and Roark, eds., *No Chariot Let Down: Charleston's Free People of Color on the Eve of the Civil War* (Chapel Hill, N.C., 1984).

25. Leonard P. Curry, *The Free Black in Urban America, 1800–1850: The Shadow of the Dream* (Chicago, 1981), 239.

26. Johnson and Roark, *Black Masters,* 153–94. See also Fields, *Slavery and Freedom on the Middle Ground,* 68–86, for an excellent account of similar problems and tensions in a border slave state.

27. Berlin, *Slaves Without Masters,* 253–4, 273–4, 274–5. For further infor-

mation on the remarkable career of William Johnson, see William R. Hogan and Edwin A. Davis, eds., *William Johnson's Natchez,* two volumes (Baton Rouge, La., 1951).

28. Fields, *Slavery and Freedom on the Middle Ground,* 87. For an illuminating discussion of the difficulties facing the substantial free black population of Maryland, see 4–6. 10–14, 28–39, 68–89.

29. Among books which do emphasize the importance of changes in slavery over time are Rose, *Slavery and Freedom,* especially viii–x, 20–30; Boles, *Black Southerners;* and Berlin, *Slaves Without Masters.*

30. Oakes, *The Ruling Race,* 69–95. Even so prominent a slaveholder as James Henry Hammond was seriously tempted, on more than one occasion, by the prospect of moving from South Carolina to fresh fields in the west, perhaps in Texas. See Faust, *Hammond,* 109–14.

31. For the purposes of the present study, I have confined my discussion of the comparative history of slavery to direct comparison of Southern slavery with slavery elsewhere, and have not ventured into the broader international history of slavery, including the question of the relationship between capitalism and slavery.

32. David Brion Davis, *The Problem of Slavery in Western Culture* (Ithaca, N.Y., 1966), 229. See also Davis, *The Problem of Slavery in the Age of Revolution, 1770–1823* (Ithaca, N.Y., 1975), and *Slavery and Human Progress* (New York, 1984).

33. Orlando Patterson, *Slavery and Social Death: A Comparative Study* (Cambridge, Ma., 1982), 207.

34. Ibid., 5–14. The quotation appears on page 13.

35. Elkins, *Slavery,* third ed., 37–80, 135–7, 225–42. See also Frank Tannenbaum, *Slave and Citizen: The Negro in the Americas* (New York, 1946), and Gilberto Freyre, *The Masters and the Slaves* (New York, 1956).

36. Genovese's views, already discussed in earlier chapters, are spelt out

fully, for example, in *Roll, Jordan, Roll* and *The World the Slaveholders Made.* Carl Degler has pertinent comments on the role of the church and the law in Brazil in his *Neither Black Nor White: Slavery and Race Relations in Brazil and the United States* (New York, 1971), 26–39. For a thoughtful discussion of many of the issues raised by Elkins, see C. Vann Woodward, *American Counterpoint: Slavery and Racism in the North-South Dialogue* (Boston, 1971), chapters 2 and 3.

37. Eugene D. Genovese, "The Treatment of Slaves in Different Countries: Problems in the Application of the Comparative Method," in Laura Foner and Eugene D. Genovese, eds., *Slavery in the New World: A Reader in Comparative History* (Englewood Cliffs, N.J., 1969), 202–10, especially 203.

38. Degler, *Neither Black Nor White,* 219. See also 39–47.

39. Kolchin, "American Historians and Antebellum Southern Slavery, 1959–1984," in Cooper, Holt, and McCardell, eds., *A Master's Due,* 106.

40. Blassingame, *The Slave Community,* 49–70. Most of Genovese's writings are suffused by a powerful awareness, and a deep knowledge, of the international history of slavery. In addition to the works cited in notes 36 and 37 above, see *In Red and Black: Marxian Explorations in Southern and Afro-American History* (New York, 1971); *From Rebellion to Revolution: Afro-American Slave Revolts in the Making of the New World* (Baton Rouge, La., 1979); and, with Elizabeth Fox-Genovese, *Fruits of Merchant Capital: Slavery and Bourgeois Property in the Rise and Expansion of Capitalism* (New York, 1983).

41. Herbert S. Klein, *Slavery in the Americas: A Comparative Study of Virginia and Cuba* (Chicago, 1967).

42. Richard S. Dunn, *Sugar and Slaves: The Rise of the Planter Class in the English West Indies, 1624–1713* (Chapel Hill, N.C., 1972), 224, and, more generally, 224–62. Dunn's book is not primarily a comparative study but he does establish the contrast with the mainland colonies in both his introduction and his conclusion. See *xiii–xvi,* 335–41. In a more recent essay, he has made a detailed, and often revealing, comparison between plantations in Virginia and Jamaica. See Dunn, "A Tale of Two Plantations: Slave Life at Mesopotamia in Jamaica and Mount Airy in Virginia, 1799 to 1828," *William and Mary Quarterly,* third series, 34 (1977): 32–65.

43. Degler, *Neither Black Nor White,* especially 25–92. The quotation appears on page 89.

44. Rose, *Slavery and Freedom,* 153–5; Degler, *Neither Black Nor White,* 261–4.

45. George M. Fredrickson, *White Supremacy: A Comparative Study in American and South African History* (New York, 1981), 54–93, 136–62. The quotation appears on page 93.

46. Peter Kolchin, *Unfree Labor: American Slavery and Russian Serfdom* (Cambridge, Ma., 1987), 360.

47. See above, 78–79.

48. Kolchin, "Reevaluating the Antebellum Slave Community: A Comparative Perspective," *Journal of American History* 70 (1983): 588. Kolchin's article provides a convenient summary of many of the main themes and conclusions of *Unfree Labor.*

49. This and the preceding paragraphs are largely based on Kolchin, *Unfree Labor,* especially 17–22, 51–7, 98–102, 155–6, 184–96, 233–9, 359–75. For another comparison between Southern ·planters and a European élite, see Shearer Davis Bowman, "Antebellum Planters and Vormärz Junkers in Comparative Perspective," *American Historical Review* 85 (1980): 779–808.

7

Slavery and Southern White Society

I n the words of one prominent South Carolina planter, "Slavery informs all our modes of life, all our habits of thought, lies at the basis of our social existence, and of our political faith."[1] Millions of his Southern white contemporaries, whether or not they themselves owned large numbers of slaves, would surely have agreed, and those who viewed the South from outside would scarcely have dissented. It was after all slavery which defined the South, and which differentiated it from the rest of the United States.

There has been a tendency among some recent historians to question the extent of the differences between North and South and to draw attention to their similarities.[2] This has served as a healthy reminder of what the two sections had in common—above all perhaps their common American character. The South yielded to no other part of the country in its patriotic ardor; indeed, it can be argued that, when a feeling of Southern nationalism developed in the mid–nineteenth century, it was in fact a displaced version of Southerners' American nationalism. They felt that the Northern majority had taken over American nationality and converted it to its own ends, and that the South was the defender of the true and original American faith.[3]

It is impossible to set slavery aside from any discussion of the similarities or differences between North and South. To say that it was "only" slavery which distinguished the one region from the other is akin to saying that it is "only" religion which divides Northern Ireland from the Irish Republic. Slavery permeated almost every aspect of the

124

life of the South. Much of the recent work on the lives of the slaves themselves has focused on the two environments within which they dwelt—one controlled by the master, backed by all the weight and power of white society, and the other provided by the interior life of the slave community. Similarly, most Southern whites lived in two environments—one shaped by contact with the institution of slavery and the presence of black slaves, the other by the social, economic, and political relationships within the white community. Although the two environments were distinct, they overlapped and each entered into the other profoundly. In particular, the first often conditioned and circumscribed—and even controlled—the second.

Slavery left its mark in many places and in many different ways: on the Southern social structure, including its class divisions; in the paradoxical relationship between slavery and liberty in Southern minds; on the style and substance of Southern politics; in the compulsive need to construct elaborate theoretical defenses of the peculiar institution; and in shaping the sense of Southern identity and eventually of Southern separatism.

Conflicting images of aristocracy and democracy have often served to complicate and confuse the picture of Southern white society There has been a long-running historical debate between those who see a society dominated by slaveholding planters and those who see a more democratic society in which a large class of yeoman farmers formed the solid core. In that form, the debate has now lost much of its impetus, and certainly its terms of reference have begun to look dangerously oversimplified. A more variegated and elaborate picture of the Southern social structure has now led the way toward a more wide-ranging debate about its character and implications.[4]

As with so many other aspects of the historiography of slavery and Southern society, Eugene Genovese has played a key role in setting the terms of the modern debate—even for those who disagree with him profoundly. In his writings over many years, he has offered a more refined and subtle version of the "planter-dominance" interpretation, firmly rooted in his Marxist and Gramscian ideological soil. In his earlier work, the South was described as a precapitalist, seigneurial society, dominated by slaveholders and above all by the large planters. Such a society bred not only a paternalist relationship between masters and slaves, but a hegemonic relationship between the dominant planter class and the rest of white society. This concept of the hegemony of the planter class is central to Genovese's view of Southern society. It was not simply a matter of the economic power of the slaveholding planters, but rather of their ability to impose their values and their will on the whole society.

This renewed emphasis upon planter dominance was never likely to command universal acceptance, and over the years Genovese himself has developed an increasingly subtle and complex picture of the structure and the divisions of Southern slave society.[5] One of the most frequent criticisms of Genovese's earlier work in particular was that his class analysis tended to obscure or overshadow what most would regard as the more fundamental Southern preoccupation with race. George Fredrickson, for example, has written vividly of the emergence of the idea of what he calls a "herrenvolk democracy" among whites, based on the assumption of the racial inferiority of the blacks. Slavery regulated the relations between whites and blacks, not by promoting the establishment of a paternalist or seigneurial society but by providing the instrument of racial (or racist) control.[6]

Many critics also find Genovese guilty of blurring the distinction between the terms "planter" and "slaveholder" and thus neglecting the numerical majority of slave owners who owned only a small number of slaves. Clearly, the picture of the "ruling race" of slaveholders presented by James Oakes differs fundamentally from that painted by Genovese. Oakes emphasizes the predominance of small and medium-sized slaveholdings and the entrepreneurial and profit-hungry spirit of the slaveholding classes, as well as their social and geographical mobility. Indeed, Oakes moves rapidly to the other extreme of depicting planter paternalism as the ideology of an atypical and superannuated minority group.[7]

Questions of class and the character and extent of antebellum Southern white "democracy" have been the focus of attention for many historians during the last two decades. Forrest McDonald and Grady McWhiney have done much to restore the plain folk of the South to their proper place in the total picture, but have muddied the issue by their obsession with the Celtic origins and character of that group.[8] (Surely, the last thing Southern history needed was another set of crude racial or ethnic stereotypes!) A number of historians, including Steven Channing, William Barney, Michael P. Johnson, J. Mills Thornton, Kenneth Greenberg, Laurence Shore, and Bruce Collins, have examined divisions and pressures within Southern white society, in the context of the movement of the South toward secession in 1860–61.[9] Others, such as Steven Hahn, J. William Harris, and Randolph B. Campbell, have tackled such issues at the grass roots level in studies of particular localities.[10]

The debate ranges over many issues, and no consensus looks imminent. However, in the context of the present study, it is appropriate to concentrate on the impact of slavery—the simple fact of widespread slave ownership, the reliance on slave labor, the presence of a substantial population of black slaves—on the structure and character of Southern white society. Here at least the outlines of a realistic picture may be discerned, with the help of the findings of some of the recent work. The notions of planter dominance, or at least planter leadership, on one hand and Southern white democracy on the other may not be quite so far apart as they appear at first sight.

The first step must surely be to abandon any oversimplified model of the Southern social structure, whether it be the crude bipolar division into planters and poor whites or something just a little more sophisticated which recognizes the existence of some middle group between the two. There are various possibilities, but Randolph B. Campbell has offered a formulation which recognizes the complexities of Southern society but remains straightforward and sensible. On the basis of his study of one Texas county, he proposes a division into five classes: large planters holding twenty or more slaves, small planters with from ten to nineteen slaves, yeoman farmers (including both small slaveholders and nonslaveholders), poor whites (including tenant farmers and farm laborers), and finally nonfarmers, who would have been mainly townspeople.[11] This formulation has two particular merits. First, its middle group straddles the divide between slaveholders and nonslaveholders and thus indicates both the peculiar place of slaveholding in the whole system and the fact that it was not the only factor involved. Second, both this feature and the division into five classes, none of them rigidly fenced off from its neighbors, implies that mobility between the classes was commonly a fact and always a possibility or at least an aspiration. There was a continuum between a series of classes rather than a series of almost impassable obstacles between them.

Against this background, it may be possible to seek some accommodation between the ideas of plantation aristocracy and white democracy. First of all, one of the truly distinctive features of Southern slavery was that ownership was not concentrated in the hands of a tiny minority. Even after the relative decline in the 1850s, which caused much alarm and anxiety, a quarter of Southern white families owned slaves. In almost all the states of the Deep South, well over a third of white families owned slaves, and in Mississippi and South Carolina, almost a half owned slaves. The dramatic expansion of the South in the nineteenth century did not lead to the creation of vast estates, each with a labor force of several hundred slaves. Between 1790 and 1860, the size of the average individual slaveholding increased only from eight to ten. The social, political, and economic effects of the wide diffusion of slave ownership were profound. In the words of Otto Olsen:

> The fact is that the enslavement of black people did provide extensive economic opportunities for whites, and, viewed from its own racist context, slavery appears a good bit less oligarchical in several significant economic respects than twentieth century free labor capitalism. The ownership of slaves was spread among a remarkably broad proportion of the white population, and the extent of this white investment was central to Southern white unity before, during and after the Civil War.[12]

When the fact of widespread slaveholding is placed alongside the availability of new land and a significant degree of both social and geographical mobility,[13] some kind of pattern begins to emerge. It is possible to take the view that large-scale planters exercised great influence and power, without going so far as to depict them as a small self-perpetuating oligarchy or as a privileged caste sealed off from the rest of society. Many of the great planters were, if not self-made men, only second- or at most third-generation aristocrats. The simple fact that planter and slaveholder were not synonyms had great significance for the antebellum South. Slaveholding or the ambition to hold slaves forged a link which united a very large number of white Southerners.

Such bonds were reinforced by an intricate network of personal contacts and relationships. Genovese is prominent among many recent historians of slavery who have emphasized the role of the planter in the local community. Planters made loans to help poorer neighbors through difficult times and sometimes hired out their slaves to work for them. They also provided assistance with marketing and transportation, as well as facilities for ginning and milling.[14]

Planters and smaller farmers shared in the same annual cycle dictated by the weather and the seasons and the same pressures and crises arising from the cultivation of the same crops. Steven Hahn has pointed out that, because of the heavy dependence on slave labor, the system did not constantly array Southern whites in directly exploitative relations with each other. In this as in other ways, slavery tended to mitigate class conflict within the white community.[15]

Behind the economic relationship between the slaveholding planter and his neighbors there were any number of personal and social ties. Quite often they were ties of kinship, as the planter's neighbors might well have included various branches of his own family. Planters played a leading part in local churches, in the constant political activity which was an important part of the social life of the time, and perhaps in providing some schooling for local children. Like paternalist behavior toward slaves, such services to the local white community did not arise from disinterested benevolence. Some were simply good business, some symbolized the status and inflated the ego of the planter, and most were investments in social stability and peace and a demonstration of the essential unity of the white South in the presence of a large black slave population. In his own truculent way, James Henry Hammond took such duties seriously, though he found them irksome—not least the grand annual feast he provided for all his often coarse and unrefined neighbors. Generalizing from Hammond's example, his biographer, Drew Gilpin Faust, comments:

> Lacking less personal structures for social and economic welfare and education, the South left the relationships of plantation paternalism to fill these institutional roles. Within the microcosm of a plantation and its neighborhood originated the complex ties of interdependence that assured white solidarity in the antebellum South.[16]

Large planters and small farmers shared not only many interests but also many fears. Both often centered on the question of race. As long as the mass of yeoman farmers accepted that slavery provided not only an escalator by which they might one day rise, but also a floor beneath which they could not fall, a Southern white consensus in defense of the peculiar institution was more or less assured. Not unnaturally, slaveholders—and particularly the larger slaveholders—made it their business to propagate such beliefs by every available means. The existence of a large unfree black population in their midst gave even the humblest of white Southerners a certain status simply by dint of the fact that they were not black and not slaves.

Among the deep-rooted racial fears shared by all sections of white society, two stand out with particular clarity. The first was the constantly recurring fear of servile insurrection, which persisted in spite of the lack of any significant slave uprising in the thirty years before the Civil War. Laurence Shore has suggested that planter anxieties about slave rebellions stemmed, at least in part, from a haunting fear of divisions within white society between slaveholders and poorer whites which might prevent the white community from standing together in face of such a threat.[17] The second and even more profound fear dwelt on the consequences of the demise of slavery, if that dreaded eventuality should ever occur. Southern whites shared a nightmare vision of economic collapse, social disintegration, and race war if the regulatory mechanism of slavery should ever be removed. Steven Hahn quotes a typical warning addressed by Governor Joseph E. Brown to his north Georgia constituents: "So soon as the slaves were at liberty thousands of them would leave the cotton and rice fields . . . and make their way to the healthier climate in the mountain region [where] we should have them plundering and stealing, robbing and killing."[18]

Shared interests and shared fears intertwined with personal relationships to form what J. William Harris calls the "ligaments of community" in the white South. He cites the example of an incident in one such small community in 1851, where at a meeting local whites agreed to expel an inhabitant of Yankee origin who was accused of promulgating abolitionist sentiments. The episode, says Harris, showed the power of the planter elite, but also their sense of vulnerability:

> If slaves were contented, if nonslaveowners were united with slaveowners in their opinions about slavery, how could a Yankee mechanic possibly be a threat? The nervousness of the slaveholding elite makes apparent the ambiguity of their political position. True, slaveholders were, on the whole, *of* their communities; indeed, they were leaders of their communities. But equally true, the community was their master. They could only rule by consent; politically, they depended, simply and unequivocally, on the support of all white

men. If the mass of small farmers—their community—turned against them as *slaveholders*, slavery would be finished.[19]

Here lies a valuable clue to the relationship between the elite of slaveholding planters and the white democracy of the antebellum South. The larger slave owners were leaders in their own communities, and they or their lawyer-spokesmen occupied a disproportionately high share of elective offices and other positions of power and influence. But they did not rule with the help of massive military or police power, or by excluding the great majority from political participation, or by reliance on the trappings of traditional authority in a hierarchical society. Insofar as they ruled, they ruled by consent. The fact that such consent was generally given may owe something to a measure of deference from certain other sections of the community, but it owed much more to the common interests and common fears which have already been discussed, and to the skill with which the planter class played upon them. Perhaps the slaveholding planters of the Old South shared some of the aptitude of the English landed aristocracy in the nineteenth century for holding on to much of their influence and even their power in a changing world by applying a judicious mixture of confidence, containment, concession, and compromise—and a willingness to admit ambitious individuals and rising groups to their own charmed circle. Perhaps it is easier in the context of more traditional European societies to come to terms with the idea of a ruling class maintaining its authority by means of conciliation and consent. However, the notion of a democracy run by aristocrats is not so very far from the Jeffersonian ideal; perhaps the antebellum South was still adhering to that ideal, or something like it, while the rest of the United States was diverging from it.

The last word on this particular subject may be given to William J. Cooper:

> These landowning farmers or yeomen never wavered in their loyalty to the southern slave system. Aware and independent minded, the yeomen were not obsequious ciphers who blindly followed wherever the lordly planters led. Although wealth and prestige did give planters a powerful position in both society and politics, their ascendency remained secure only so long as the mass of southern landowners and voters supported it. Throughout the antebellum era the overwhelming majority of those landowners and voters per-

ceived a profound kinship between their interests and those of the planters. Even though some scholars argue that the slave system curbed the potential prosperity of yeomen, most yeomen did not feel restricted or inhibited. Besides they had no interest in challenging the social order guaranteed by the slave system, which provided social peace despite the presence of millions of blacks, a group the white yeomen believed absolutely inferior. An omnipotent racism convinced all whites that only bondage enabled black and white to coexist without massive social trauma.[20]

The very title of Cooper's book, *Liberty and Slavery,* may serve to introduce another, equally important, dimension of the impact of slavery on Southern white society. One of the most glaring paradoxes of the white South lay in its combination of fierce devotion to the idea of liberty, with a profound commitment to the institution of slavery. It is possible to dismiss this simply as a historical coincidence—the coexistence of two phenomena which were quite distinct but which inevitably generated a certain amount of tension. However, those historians who have probed more deeply into the relationship between liberty and slavery in the South have concluded that much more than coincidence is involved.

A good starting point is Edmund Morgan's study of colonial Virginia, *American Slavery, American Freedom.* Having analyzed the conversion of Virginia from white indentured servitude to black slavery in the late seventeenth and early eighteenth centuries, and having examined its political, social, and racial implications, Morgan concludes his study by focusing on his main theme of the relationship between slavery and freedom in Virginia. He examines the influence of the ideas of the English eighteenth-century Commonwealthmen, who saw ominous signs of tyranny and slavery in every exercise of executive power by the Crown, and who wanted the functions of government confined to the protection of liberty and property. In Morgan's view, Virginia planters were unusually receptive to such ideas in part at least because the presence on all sides of slaves who were totally subject to the will of others provided an object lesson in what it could mean to be at the mercy of a tyrant. "Virginians may have had a special appreciation of the freedom dear to republicans because they saw every day what life without it could be like."[21]

A system of racial slavery offered the further advantage that it created a measure of apparent equality among all sections of the white population. Furthermore, it took out of political society much of the labor force and most of the poor, and thus disposed of the threat of mob rule which plagued the minds of advocates of republican liberty elsewhere. Slavery enabled Virginians to declare their unbounded love of liberty without such fears and inhibitions. These two powerful lessons—that their own slaves provided a direct warning of the dangers of submission to others and that slavery provided a guarantee of their own liberty—remained firmly rooted in Virginian minds during the struggle for independence from Britain and did much to shape the distinctive character of Southern republicanism in the decades which followed. Critics have sometimes accused Morgan of implying that republican liberty in America was only made possible by racial slavery—and this would be palpably absurd, as the experience of the Northern colonies showed. Morgan is careful to say that such republican beliefs did not have to rest on slavery, but that in Virginia they did—and Virginia was uniquely influential throughout the Revolutionary era.[22]

Slavery remained a source of disquiet and embarrassment in some quarters during the Revolution and its aftermath, but despite the increase in manumissions in some parts of Virginia and Maryland, there was no fundamental challenge to the system. George Washington, Thomas Jefferson, and James Madison had little difficulty, despite their slave ownership, in maintaining their authority and their credibility as revolutionary leaders and founding fathers of a new nation conceived in liberty. The legacy of the Revolution to the South included both a more directly racial justification of slavery which defended white freedom by diminishing the humanity of the blacks, and a continuing association of the ideas of republican liberty and black slavery.[23]

Much of the Southern rhetoric before and during the Revolution took as its theme the reduction of the colonies to a condition of "abject slavery" through the repressive measures and the interference with their liberties perpetrated by the British government. Kenneth Greenberg has noted how this dread of enslavement carried over from the struggle for independence into the Southern brand of American republican ideology in the nineteenth century. The keynote of this kind of republican liberty was independence, freedom to control one's own affairs, fear of unchecked power, and avoidance of any kind of subjection to the will of others. The arguments directed against Britain in 1776 found strong echoes in much of the Southern rhetoric directed against Northern Republicans in the 1850s.

Greenberg's explanation of the relationship between liberty and slavery in the antebellum South carries strong echoes of Morgan's analysis of the colonial period:

> It is one of the most striking ironies of American history that the owners of black slaves should also have been among the most vigorous defenders of the ideal of liberty. But the connection between the institution of slavery and the love of liberty is no mere historical accident. There were good reasons why slavery and liberty should have developed in tandem. Black slavery, of course, was the essential economic underpinning for the condition of white liberty. The poorest group in American society, by its very exclusion from civil life and its relegation to a form of property, provided the economic and social base that allowed the ideal of liberty to flourish. Moreover, constant exposure to the conditions of black slaves made Southern whites peculiarly sensitive to any loss of freedom that might begin to place them in a similar condition. The heady experience of domination bred a devout commitment to freedom—at least to the freedom of masters.[24]

In his study of "plain folk and gentry" in the area around Augusta, Georgia, J. William Harris explores the connection between liberty and slavery at the grass roots level. He portrays a belief, widely shared by slave owners and non–slave owners alike, in an ideology which saw the South as a near-ideal society in which black slavery allowed liberty for whites without the danger of anarchy. This republican ideal of ordered liberty was constantly threatened by corruption, and particularly by either a concentration of national political power or excessive democracy, which would lead to anarchy and then tyranny. On one hand, slavery gave all whites a certain status and a sense of equality with each other, and removed the danger of conflict between capital and labor. On the other hand, while protecting white liberty, it also posed a potential threat to it, if divisions between slave owners and non–slave owners should ever become serious. That threat would be all the greater if some such outside force as the Northern Republicans sought to exploit it in order to sow the seeds of an antislavery party in the South.[25]

Such fears of outside interference had much to do with the relationship between slavery and the content, priorities, and style of Southern politics. In his study of the Nullification Crisis of 1832–33, William Freehling stressed that behind the immediate issue of the tariff lurked the crucial question of the defense of slavery.[26] Among recent Southern historians, no one has made a more convincing case than William J. Cooper for the central importance of slavery in Southern politics, at least from the 1820s onward. From the election of Andrew Jackson in 1828 down to the party upheaval of the mid-1850s, Southerners gave their allegiance to national political parties because they saw them primarily as instruments for the defense of Southern interests in general and slavery in particular. It was only with the breakdown of the second-party system and the emergence of the Republican party in the North that an increasing number of Southerners turned to the alternative strategy which culminated in secession.[27]

Like Morgan, Greenberg, and Harris, Cooper makes the crucial connection between slavery and that kind of liberty which gives priority to a sense of independence and freedom from outside interference. Living in close proximity to millions of black slaves made white Southerners "especially sensitive to the ultimate meaning of liberty, control of one's own affairs, one's own destiny." Cooper goes on:

> Then, in practical terms this cherished liberty depended upon the southern whites retaining unqualified domination over their peculiar institution. Their losing control of slavery would signal that an outside force directed the local affairs as well as the destiny of the white South. As a result white southerners would be shackled by someone else just as they shackled their own slaves. Free men would fall into slavery.[28]

The obsessive concern with slavery and the insistence on independence and control of one's own affairs, which Cooper describes as characteristic of the white South in general, emerge equally clearly from J. Mills Thornton's account of Alabama, *Politics and Power in a Slave Society*. Cooper and Thornton differ on a number of points, but they share similar views not only of the agenda of Southern politics but also of the style and tone of Southern political life. The style and tone, like the political agenda, was shaped largely by slavery. Cooper traces back to the colonial period a Southern political style which mixed deference and democracy. He acknowledges that by the Jacksonian era or even before, the balance had shifted decisively toward democracy, though an element of deference persisted, notably in the leadership role of the planter class. But now the planters and their lawyer henchmen had to bid for popular support in electoral contests which were often fiercely fought. There was no room for aloofness or airs of superiority; success depended on broad popular appeal and a quick response to the popular will. In Thornton's picture of Alabama politics in the Jacksonian period, the politicians saw it as their role simply to give the electorate what it wanted, while seeking to protect the interests of the state from outside attack.[29]

There is another theme stressed by Cooper, and rather less by Thornton, which is closely related to slavery and its defense. This is the concern with honor—both personal honor and the honor of the South as a whole. Cooper suggests that abolitionist attacks on slavery were seen as threats not only to Southern liberties but to Southern honor:

> In the white southern mind liberty and honor could not be pried apart. Welded together they became the tangible core of the southern psychology. A man who possessed liberty could also call himself honorable; no free man would allow his name, his reputation to be besmirched by dishonor. With honor gone, liberty became problematical. The absence of liberty and honor carried the awful connotation of degraded slave. Thus for white southerners escaping the dreaded status of slave necessitated the maintenance of their liberty and honor no matter the cost.[30]

Much the fullest and most important discussion of Southern honor is in the book of that title by Bertram Wyatt-Brown. However, for reasons which may be understandable but are surely regrettable, he chose quite specifically and deliberately to set slavery aside from his analysis of the Southern concern with honor.[31] For those who may feel that this is a case of Hamlet without the prince, it is fortunate that another recent study has taken up Cooper's point about the interrelationship of liberty and honor in the Southern mind, and the crucial connection of slavery with both. Indeed, in his *Masters and Statesmen: The Political Culture of American Slavery*, Kenneth Greenberg has made this very question one of his central themes. Insofar as republicanism and honor both laid stress on the search for personal autonomy and independence, they remained compatible. However, the idea of honor also implied the ability to command the respect and the obedience of others, and therefore the exercise of power over others. This created a tension between the concept of honor and the idea of republican liberty which, Greenberg suggests, was at the heart of a distinctive Southern political culture.

The most original and important part of Greenberg's thesis is his exploration of the relationship between the Southern vision of the ideal master, "legitimately" exercising power over slaves, and the parallel vision of the ideal statesman, "legitimately" exercising power over free people. Greenberg is at pains to say that the relationship between the two is not a simple one of cause and effect. Rather, they were interdependent and interactive. "The structure of the master-slave relationship," he finds, "seemed to echo endlessly through all areas of Southern thought and behavior." In particular, both masters and statesmen "simultaneously asserted their power and their powerlessness [and] they simultaneously asserted their independence and dependence." The master was expected to disown any lust for power propelled by greed, while at the same time demonstrating his power and superiority over his slaves in order to earn their respect and obedience. Similarly, the ideal Southern statesman should not actively have sought office and power, but at the same time he needed to assert his superiority and his authority in order to achieve honor in the eyes of white society. According to Greenberg, the constantly repeated but contradictory admonition to remain powerless and at the same time powerful "represented the embodiment in thought of a tension inherent in the master-slave relationship."

Greenberg pursues his central themes through discussions of various aspects of Southern political life and political style: the reluctance of political leaders blatantly to seek office, or to become mere mouthpieces of the popular will; their constant references to duty and to the burdens which their position thrust upon them; their propensity for grand gestures of resignation or defiance; their anti-party instincts and their particular distaste for the newer political style of manipulation, organization, and party discipline; and their liking for the idea of "virtual representation" of all the interests in a community where slavery had deadened much of the potential for internal conflict among the white electorate. Connections are also suggested between the master-statesman ideal and the practice of dueling between men of honor and independence. When he comes to examine the mounting sectional crisis of the 1850s, Greenberg sees the Southern preoccupation with both honor and republican liberty as a powerful force behind refusal to compromise and fierce resentment of interference from the "corrupt" North. The abolitionist attack on slavery as a moral evil and the Republican party campaign to keep slavery out of the territories were both regarded as insults alike to Southern honor and Southern independence.

There are aspects of Greenberg's thesis which mar a good case by overstatement, and which strain some of the attempted connections between master and statesman to the breaking point. There are times too when a chasm opens up between the ideal statesman delineated by Greenberg and the realities of Jacksonian politics in the South, as depicted, for example, by J. Mills Thornton. Greenberg relies heavily on the extreme case of South Carolina because it suits his argument so well, and like so many other historians, concentrates heavily upon the large planters to the exclusion of small and middling slaveholders. For all that, he has provided the most ingenious, stimulating, and sustained attempt to trace the configurative influence of the peculiar institution on Southern public life and political style.[32]

Greenberg also offers some intriguing observations on the motivation and presentation of the Southern proslavery argument. Like a number of other recent commentators, he treats the elaborate arguments propounded in defense of slavery as a serious contribution to the articulation of a distinctive Southern ideology.[33] This contrasts with an earlier tendency to see the proslavery argument as either a propaganda exercise or as a smoke screen to cover gnawing doubts or pangs of guilt about slavery. Charles Sellers and Kenneth Stampp are among many historians who have emphasized the importance of such feelings of guilt, and surely such feelings must indeed have existed.[34] It is, however, very difficult to prove just how widely or strongly such feelings were shared among white Southerners, and the evidence is fragmentary and elusive. Ironically, James Oakes, whose main emphasis is on the acquisitiveness and competitiveness of the slaveholding class, finds himself obliged for that very reason to rely heavily on the guilt factor to explain the inner turmoil which so many of its members felt. They found themselves trapped between their evangelical faith, which condemned materialism and proclaimed the humanity of their slaves, and their lust for material advancement, for which slave ownership was both the means and the measure. He quotes an Alabama slaveholder who confessed that "if we do commit a *sin* owning slaves, it is certainly one which is attended with great *conveniences.*"[35]

The charge that the proslavery argument was a propaganda instrument is surely true, but this does not dispose of its importance. Propaganda is not necessarily a synonym for hypocrisy or deception; the constant reiteration of certain basic themes in proslavery tracts and essays may testify to deeply held convictions as well as to a good deal of soul-searching. What is surely true is that the proslavery argument was addressed to a number of different audiences, and the main thrust of the argument was changed or modified accordingly. Defenses of slavery go a long way back in American history, but they became more elaborate and more assertive from the 1830s onward, in response to the abolitionist attack from the North. In the increasingly heated atmosphere of the antebellum decades, much of the aggressive defense of slavery as a positive good and as the true foundation of a civilized society was aimed in that direction.

The defenders of slavery came to rely on well-rehearsed responses to the two most obvious lines of attack—that slavery was incompatible with the political ideals of the American republic, which rested on the rights of the individual, and with the tenets of evangelical Christianity, which proclaimed the equality of all men in the sight of God. The response to the first of these objections drew upon the whole intricate relationship between liberty and slavery in the South, which has already been discussed. In concocting a reply to the second, Southern churchmen drew heavily upon selective biblical references, mainly from the Old Testament, to support the claim that slavery was a divinely ordained mechanism for regulating the relationship between a superior and inferior race.

Laurence Shore observes that from the 1830s onward, as the North seemed to be leaping ahead economically, the need arose for a Southern defense against the charge that slavery was the cause of the region's economic "backwardness." That defense pointed to the huge agricultural advantages the South derived from a system of racial slavery in which blacks could be used to grow crops such as cotton, sugar, and rice in climatic conditions that white men could not tolerate. Hard drudgery in such unfavorable conditions was inappropriate for white people, and in the words of *DeBow's Review,* "no white man should attempt to make a Negro of himself."[36] According to Oakes, the slaveholders themselves put their faith in slavery as part of their gospel of prosperity, and paid little heed to "the abstract ruminations of southern intellectuals."[37]

Those historians who discern significant evidence of guilt, remorse, or psychological tension within the ranks of slaveholders tend to see the proslavery argument as an exercise in boosting self-confidence or as soothing balm to assuage inner doubts. In separate but similar arguments, two recent historians have suggested that attempts at the moral justification of slavery frequently drew a distinction between the ideal and the reality and implied, if they did not explicitly express, a plea for the reform of the peculiar institution. Drew Gilpin Faust shows how the intellectual champions of slavery contrasted the way in which the community interest was fostered by the master-slave relationship with the insatiable greed which characterized Northern society. In Southern slave society, men of superior mind had to shoulder the burden of disinterested leadership and responsibility for others. If men of education and independence of mind were to exercise social control through the system of slavery, they had to take up the burden of moral stewardship over the whole community. Slaveholders must be inspired to strive toward the achievement of that ideal.[38]

According to Kenneth Greenberg, the Southern answer to the charge that the unrestrained power of master over slave was immoral and corrupting was simply to deny that the master exercised any such power. Rather, so it was claimed, there was an organic relationship between master and slave which made the two interdependent. Like Faust, Greenberg shows how the proslavery argument constantly stressed the duties and obligations of masters. The power of the master was limited by moral and legal restraints and family and community pressure—and, above all perhaps, by economic self-interest which made abuse of slaves self-defeating. Again, in much the same way as Faust, Greenberg emphasizes the Southern counterattack which compared the harmonious community shaped by slavery very favorably with the insecurity and misery which were the lot of Northern wage earners. Greenberg's interpretation of the proslavery argument chimes in neatly with his overall view of the paradox of power and powerlessness, independence and dependence, in the position of the master. It is only to be regretted that he insists on labeling this part of his thesis as "the proslavery argument as an antislavery argument;" whatever else it may have been, it was surely not that.[39]

The proslavery argument was directed at another and, in the eyes of some historians, more important target within the South itself. It was one of the main weapons in the long campaign of the slaveholding minority to maintain its authority and to convince the nonslaveholders that all white Southerners had a common interest in the preservation of the peculiar institution. Laurence Shore points out that the South had two labor systems, free and slave. It was the task of the defenders of slavery to demonstrate that free white labor could be adequately protected in a slave society—and also to ensure that the prospect of future slave ownership remained a real possibility and not an impossible dream for nonslaveholders. "All aspects of the mature proslavery argument," he writes, "involved the intellectual storm and stress of trying to make an oxymoron appear logical, of trying to justify a dual labor system's compatibility with an ethic which denied duality."

Shore quotes an article in *DeBow's Review* in 1860 which laid out the full range of the nonslaveholder's interests in slavery: the maintenance of high wages, freedom from competition with "foreign pauper labor," the protection of status based on skin color and the avoidance of "emancipation's degrading equality," the value to all Southerners of the products of slave labor, and underlying everything else, the prospect of becoming a slave owner and participating in the success of the slave economy.[40] James Oakes quotes a Richmond newspaper which, in the same year, made much the same point: "Free labor is the main support and stay of the institution [of slavery], because where the two races approximate equality in numbers, slavery is the only protection of the laboring classes against the evils of amalgamation and moral degradation."[41]

Underlying much of the discussion of the proslavery argument and its appeal to different audiences is an intellectual problem which may seem more exciting and more sharply defined in the minds of modern scholars than it did to the protagonists at the time. Was it class or race which was the foundation upon which the defense of slavery rested? Was it some patriarchal ideal which inspired the proslavery argument, or was it a system of racial control which would guarantee democracy among whites?

In conformity with his overall view of planter paternalism and the seigneurial character of Southern slave society, Genovese puts class before race, and social hierarchy before racial superiority. He draws heavily upon the work of George Fitzhugh, whose proslavery writings were devoted in large measure to a savage indictment of Northern capitalist society and the miserable existence to which it condemned its own "wage-slaves." Genovese makes no secret of his admiration for Fitzhugh's argument and his critique of Northern society and uses them to reinforce his own view of the anticapitalist, prebourgeois character of the antebellum South. Genovese is only the most conspicuous among a number of historians who have given a preeminent place to Fitzhugh among the champions of slavery—and, in view of his arresting style and the boldness of his arguments, this is hardly surprising. However, it is now widely accepted—and acknowledged by Genovese—that Fitzhugh was a special case, a man apart from the mainstream of the proslavery argument and a much less representative figure among the defenders of slavery than those included in Faust's "sacred circle"—William Gilmore Simms, James Henry Hammond, Edmund Ruffin, Nathaniel Beverley Tucker, and George Frederick Holmes. Their arguments were more philosophical, drew heavily on biblical and historical evidence, offered a measured defense of a society based on the principle of inequality, and emphasized moral stewardship as the key to the master-slave relationship.[42]

The spotlight was shifted to the racial defense of slavery by George Fredrickson in his study of *The Black Image in the White Mind.* Fredrickson suggests that, in the 1840s and 1850s, as slavery gained strength in the newer areas during its westward expansion, a new and harsher proslavery argument came to the fore, based on the scientific wisdom of the day which asserted the inherent and irredeemable inferiority of the black race. Such an overtly racial, or racist, defense of slavery paved the way, not to a highly traditional, paternalist white society, but to what Fredrickson describes as herrenvolk democracy, an egalitarian white democracy resting on the enslavement of an inferior race. Some Southerners were ready to go further and claim that "Negro slavery was not only compatible with white equality but was the very foundation of it."[43]

Logic would seem to insist that there can be no common ground between the idea of a patriarchal society based on the principle of inequality and the idea of a herrenvolk democracy based on racial differentiation. However, the distinction may have been less clear-cut—and must surely have appeared less clear-cut—at the time than it seems in retrospect. In the first place, the scientific and other "proofs" of Negro inferiority obviously have an important bearing on the proslavery argument, but the connection is not an essential or exclusive one. After all, the same scientific arguments found much favor in the North as well as the South, and buttressed Northern white racism, but they did not promote the growth of slavery there. Second, the meaning of equality requires examination in this context. It need not imply—and was highly unlikely to have meant in practice—complete social and political equality among Southern whites. In his often quoted speech on slavery as the cornerstone of the Confederacy, Alexander Stephens insists that, while subordination of the Negro was appropriate, "with us, all the white race, however high or low, rich or poor, are equal in the eyes of the law."[44] Examples abound of societies based on equality before the law which tolerate enormous social and economic, and even political, inequalities. In other words, it is possible to return to the idea of something like a democracy run by aristocrats, or more accurately, the kind of Southern white society described earlier, where the planter class wielded considerable power and influence, not as of right, but by winning and keeping broad popular support.

Fredrickson himself acknowledges that, whatever logic might dictate, there was a good deal of interweaving of, and indiscriminate resort to, both the paternalist and the racial arguments in defense of slavery. This view is more positively supported by other historians, including Drew Gilpin Faust and John McCardell. Faust thinks that the differences among those who embarked on the systematic defense of slavery were in tone and emphasis rather than substance. In McCardell's opinion, both the paternalist and the herrenvolk democratic strains were present in the writings of virtually every apologist for slavery. He does, however, suggest that there was some shift of emphasis over time toward the racist argument. Part of the explanation may be that, in earlier years, the racial basis of slavery was taken literally rather than publicly defended, and that, even later, some proslavery spokesmen hesitated to deploy it too openly. As tension between North and South grew in the 1840s and 1850s, the proslavery argument developed a sharper edge and a more aggressive tone, with an increasing emphasis on race rather than class, in order to promote the solidarity of all white Southerners, whether slaveholders or not.

Faust concludes that the proslavery argument was designed to provide the South as a whole "with a conventionalized formula of self-affirmation, to allay the anxieties of Southerners about the nature of the world in which they lived." In his study of the growth of Southern nationalism, John McCardell underlines the centrality of slavery and the proslavery argument in the increasingly sharp definition of a separate Southern identity. Slavery was "the *sine qua non* of sectional ideology," he says, but, he is careful to point out, not its only component. He quotes an article written in 1839 by the Virginian A. P. Upshur in which he describes slavery as "the great distinguishing characteristic of the Southern states, and . . . in fact, the only important institution which they can claim peculiarly as their own." For the title of his chapter on slavery and Southern nationalism, McCardell chooses the phrase "the great distinguishing characteristic," and he concludes the chapter with the claim that by 1860 slavery had become "the corner-stone of the ideology of Southern nationalism."

The defense of slavery—particularly on racial grounds—and the definition of Southern nationalism had become inextricably interwoven. In McCardell's words:

> During the 1850's a commitment to the racist defence of slavery often preceded an advocacy of Southern nationalism. Not every racist defender of slavery was a Southern nationalist; but . . . racism and Southern nationalism became jointly more fashionable. During the 1850's, more and more Southerners came to rest their advocacy of a Southern nation upon the preservation of slavery and the preservation of slavery upon the doctrine of white supremacy and enhancement at the Negro's expense.[45]

Moral condemnation from the abolitionists and political denunciations from the Republicans helped to create in Southern minds a siege mentality in which defense of their Americanism, their Southernism, and their peculiar institution all merged into one. Concern for liberty and honor, as well a pride, sensitivity to insult, and a distaste for compromise—all rooted in the traditions and values of a distinctive slave society—came together in a powerful emotional cocktail, the flavor of which is well caught by William Cooper:

> For southerners the Republican assault on their liberty was made even more unbearable because simultaneously the Republicans insulted them. . . . The Republican attacks on the South and on its major social institution made of white southerners pariahs in their own land because in the Republican lexicon black slavery and the whites involved with it violated the American creed. But southerners proudly identified themselves as Americans. They wore their American heritage as a badge of honor. . . . Knowingly and with malice aforethought Republicans besmirched the escutcheon of southern Americanism. . . . With their good name slandered southerners believed their liberty already endangered, for in the South good name and integrity of reputation were the hallmarks of free and honorable men. Facing what they could only characterize as outrageous and unprincipled assailment of their institutions, their values, their patriotism, their liberty, the collective South denounced the challenge of Republicanism. In turn southerners became even more zealous defenders of their honor and guardians of their liberty.[46]

Forced into ever greater awareness of the peculiarity of their peculiar institution, and battered by waves of criticism from outside, white Southerners had done their best to build a defensive wall around themselves during the antebellum decades. By the 1850s, if not indeed before, they had reached that dangerous mental state in which they perceived everyone as being out of step except themselves. Slavery was the fundamental cause of that state of mind, and the champions of slavery, like the prophets of Southern nationalism, saw the South as the last bastion of true values and true liberty in a world of unsettling changes and dangerous new -isms. (The closest parallel in the world of the late twentieth century must surely be found in white South Africa.) When the South finally resorted to secession and then to war, it did so in order to defend its honor and its liberties—including, preeminently if ironically, the liberty to enslave others.

146 * Slavery

NOTES

1. William Henry Trescot, quoted in Rosengarten, *Tombee*, 139.

2. See for example Edward Pessen, "How Different from Each Other Were the Antebellum North and South?" *American Historical Review* 85 (1980): 1119–49.

3. I have explored this theme somewhat further in a hitherto unpublished paper on "Southern Nationalism and American Nationalism."

4. The early champion of the yeoman-democracy thesis was Frank L. Owsley; see his *Plain Folk of the Old South* (Baton Rouge, La., 1949). Randolph B. Campbell, "Planters and Plain Folks: The Social Structure of the Antebellum South," in John B. Boles and Evelyn T. Nolen, eds., *Interpreting Southern History: Historiographical Essays in Honor of Sanford W. Higginbotham* (Baton Rouge, La., 1987), 48–77, provides an excellent review of the literature on the subject.

5. The evolution of Genovese's views may be traced through many of his writings, including *The Political Economy of Slavery; In Red and Black; The World the Slaveholders Made;* and in numerous essays.

6. George M. Fredrickson, *The Black Image in the White Mind: The Debate on Afro-American Character and Destiny, 1817–1914* (New York, 1971), 61–8, 93–6. Fredrickson attributes the term "herrenvolk democracy" to Pierre L. van den Berghe, *Race and Racism: A Comparative Perspective* (New York, 1967).

7. Oakes, *The Ruling Race,* especially chapter 2.

8. Forrest McDonald and Grady McWhiney, "The Antebellum Southern Herdsman: A Reinterpretation," *Journal of Southern History* 41 (1975): 147–66.

9. Steven A. Channing, *Crisis of Fear: Secession in South Carolina* (New York, 1970); William L. Barney, *The Road to Secession: A New Perspective on the Old South* (New York, 1972); Michael P. Johnson, *Toward a Patriarchal Republic:*

The Secession of Georgia (Baton Rouge, La., 1977); J. Mills Thornton, *Politics and Power in a Slave Society: Alabama, 1800–1860* (Baton Rouge, La., 1978); Kenneth S. Greenberg, *Masters and Statesmen: The Political Culture of American Slavery* (Baltimore, 1985); Laurence Shore, *Southern Capitalists: The Ideological Leadership of an Elite, 1832–1885* (Chapel Hill, N.C., 1986); Bruce Collins, *White Society in the Antebellum South* (London, 1985). Collins, in particular, provides a valuable synthesis of recent work, spiced by his own personal reflections.

10. Steven Hahn, *The Roots of Southern Populism: Yeoman Farmers and the Transformation of the Georgia Up-Country, 1850–1890* (New York, 1983); Harris, *Plain Folk and Gentry in a Slave Society;* Randolph B. Campbell, *A Southern Community in Crisis: Harrison County, Texas, 1850–1880* (Austin, Tx., 1983); Randolph B. Campbell and Richard G. Lowe, *Wealth and Power in Antebellum Texas* (College Station, Tx., 1977). See also some of the essays in Orville V. Burton and Robert C. McMath, eds., *Class, Conflict and Consensus: Antebellum Southern Community Studies* (Westport, Ct., 1982).

11. Randolph B. Campbell, "Planters and Plain Folks: The Social Structure of the Antebellum South," in Boles and Nolen, eds., *Interpreting Southern History,* 65. See also Campbell, *A Southern Community in Crisis.*

12. Olsen, "Historians and the Extent of Slaveownership in the Southern United States," 116.

13. See Collins, *White Society in the Antebellum South,* 83–97, for a helpful discussion of the mobility and fluidity of Southern society.

14. Ibid., 17, 37–40.

15. Steven Hahn, "The Yeomanry of the Nonplantation South: Upper Piedmont Georgia, 1850–1860" in Burton and McMath, eds., *Class, Conflict and Consensus,* 29–56.

16. Faust, *Hammond*, 131.

17. Laurence Shore, "Making Mississippi Safe for Slavery: The Insurrectionary Panic of 1835," in Burton and McMath, eds., *Class, Conflict and Consensus*, 96–127.

18. Hahn, "The Yeomanry of the Nonplantation South," 45.

19. Harris, *Plain Folk and Gentry in a Slave Society*, 94–122. The quotation appears on page 122.

20. Cooper, *Liberty and Slavery*, 248–9.

21. Morgan, *American Slavery, American Freedom*, 369–87. The quotation appears on page 376.

22. Ibid., 363–8, 380–6.

23. See above, 17–19.

24. Greenberg, *Masters and Statesmen*, 85–90. The quotation appears on page 88.

25. Harris, *Plain Folk and Gentry in a Slave Society*, 5–7, 18–19, 36–9.

26. William W. Freehling, *Prelude to Civil War: The Nullification Controversy in South Carolina, 1816–1836* (New York, 1966).

27. William J. Cooper, *The South and the Politics of Slavery, 1828–1856* (Baton Rouge, La., 1978), especially xi–xiv, 370–4. See also Cooper, *Liberty and Slavery*, 237–47, 256–8.

28. Ibid., 179–80.

29. Ibid., especially 184–7; Thornton, *Politics and Power in a Slave Society*, 160–2, 200–1. There is an interesting comparison of the views of Cooper and Thornton in Drew Gilpin Faust, "The Peculiar South Revisited," in Boles and Nolen, eds., *Interpreting Southern History*, 111–14.

30. Cooper, *Liberty and Slavery*, 180.

31. Bertram Wyatt-Brown, *Southern Honor: Ethics and Behavior in the Old South* (New York, 1982). In fairness to Professor Wyatt-Brown, it should be added that he plans to treat the relationship between slavery and honor in another book. For an interesting brief discussion of the links between slavery and honor in the Old South, see Patterson, *Slavery and Social Death*, 94–7.

32. Greenberg, *Masters and Statesmen*. The essential features of Greenberg's thesis are spelt out in the preface and in chapter 1; see, in particular, vii–viii, x–xi, 3–4, 15–16, 20–2. The basic themes are then applied to various aspects of Southern life in succeeding chapters.

33. Ibid., 85–103.

34. Charles G. Sellers, "The Travail of Slavery," in Sellers, ed., *The Southerner as American* (Chapel Hill, N.C., 1960), 40–71; Kenneth M. Stampp, "The Southern Road to Appomattox," *Cotton Memorial Papers*, No. 4 (El Paso, Tx., 1969), 3–22, reprinted in Stampp, *The Imperiled Union: Essays on the Background of the Civil War* (New York, 1980), 246–69. For a contrary view, see Bertram Wyatt-Brown, "Modernizing Southern Slavery: The Proslavery Argument Reinterpreted," in Kousser and McPherson, eds., *Region, Race and Reconstruction*, 27–49.

35. Oakes, *The Ruling Race*, 105–10, 117–22. The quotation appears on page 121.

36. Laurence Shore, *Southern Capitalists*, 40–1. See also 3–11.

37. Oakes, *The Ruling Race*, 138, and, more generally, 127–43.

38. Drew Gilpin Faust, *A Sacred Circle: The Dilemma of the Intellectual in the Old South, 1840–1860* (Baltimore, 1977), 112–26.

39. Greenberg, *Masters and Statesmen*, 92–103.

40. Shore, *Southern Capitalists*, 75–6, and, more generally, 40–78.

41. Oakes, *The Ruling Race*, 130.

42. For Genovese's extended commentary on the ideas of George Fitzhugh, see his *The World the Slaveholders Made*, 118–244. Drew Gilpin Faust offers a brief but sharp critique of Genovese (and Fitzhugh) in *A Sacred Circle*, 127–31. See also the introduction to Faust, ed., *The Ideology of Slavery: Proslavery Thought in the Antebellum South, 1830–1860* (Baton Rouge, La., 1981).

43. Fredrickson, *The Black Image in the White Mind*, 62, and, more generally, 43–70.

44. Fredrickson cites Stephens' speech in the context of his discussion of "herrenvolk democracy." Ibid., 63–4.

45. Faust, *A Sacred Circle*, 125–7, 131; John McCardell, *The Idea of a Southern Nation: Southern Nationalists and Southern Nationalism, 1830–1860* (New York, 1979), 7, 49–50, 57–8, 71–6, 85, 90, and, more generally, chapter 2, "The Great Distinguishing Characteristic."

46. Cooper, *Liberty and Slavery*, 257.

8

The Death Throes of Slavery

After a long life, slavery in the South met a sudden, violent, and unexpected death. Even the war, however, did not kill slavery with one clean blow of the executioner's axe. The South's peculiar institution came to a painful and untidy end resulting from multiple injuries inflicted by emancipation edicts, invading armies, internal deterioration, and the active pursuit of their freedom by the slaves themselves. The transitional period from slavery to freedom in the midst of a great civil war was a time of turbulence, confusion, dislocation, and distress. The process by which emancipation came to slave communities, and the immediate response of the freedmen themselves to the novel experience of liberty, can yield fresh insights into the history of slavery itself.

Without the Civil War, it is virtually inconceivable that slavery would have been terminated during the 1860s. Various historians have drawn attention to the supreme irony that it was secession and war which produced precisely the threats to liberty and slavery that the South feared most—government interference, class division, social upheaval, and ultimately the destruction of slavery itself.[1] There was little apprehension in the antebellum South, even as the sectional crisis deepened, that slavery was in imminent danger of collapse. During the secession winter of 1860–61, some Southern voices were raised in warnings against the risks being taken with the future of slavery, but they went largely unheeded.

However, there had been a good deal of anxiety in the 1850s about some of the internal stresses and strains of Southern slave society and the disturbing possibility of their exploitation by outsiders. The diminishing proportion of white families who held slaves and the widening gap between the wealth of slaveholders and nonslaveholders have been discussed in Chapter 4.[2] If the road to slave ownership became severely constricted or even closed, then Southern white society faced the prospect of serious class conflict. Such fears were aggravated by the Free Soil policy of the Republican party, which would deny slavery any possibility of further territorial expansion. The belief that slavery must expand or die had many disciples in the South, and in particular, ambitious young men still saw westward migration as the best hope for their future. In the background, with John Brown's raid on Harper's Ferry in 1859 in the forefront of Southern minds, lurked the chronic fear of servile insurrection.

The unifying theme of all these fears and concerns lay in their potential for creating the kind of disunity among Southern whites which Northern Republicans might turn to their own advantage. Might the Republicans be able to persuade frustrated and disappointed nonslaveholders in the South to make common cause with their Northern counterparts under the banner of free white labor? Was the relative decline of slavery in the border states and the upper South another warning of the power of free white labor and a dangerous portent of the steady erosion of the peculiar institution? Would all groups in Southern white society stand shoulder to shoulder in face of any threat of slave rebellion?[3]

In the one and a half years between John Brown's raid on Harper's Ferry and the outbreak of the Civil War, the South was swept by rumors of slave plots, slave violence, and slave arson. This near-hysteria was accompanied by a crackdown on slaves and free blacks, backed by new laws and imposed by state and local authorities, as well as by a resurgence of vigilante activity. In some states, including South Carolina and Georgia, there were moves toward the enslavement of all free blacks. Anxiety and panic over slave unrest and the passions aroused by the movement toward secession fueled each other.[4] When the Southern states seceded and then went to war, they carried behind the mask of aggressive self-confidence a troublesome burden of internal turmoil and insecurity over their peculiar institution.

In his study of slavery in wartime Georgia, Clarence Mohr describes a state of affairs common to most of the Confederate states: "Plantation society can be seen in retrospect as a vessel for the containment of powerful warring impulses, contradictory forces which were augmented and magnified under the pressures of a war environment."[5] What Mohr and others have made abundantly clear is that, under the strain of four years of military conflict and domestic upheaval, Southern slavery underwent disruption and erosion and even started to crumble into disintegration, before the emancipation imposed by invading Northern armies took full effect.

In one form or another, the feverish activity and constant mobility of a society at war steadily undermined the stability and order on which slavery rested. In those areas threatened by federal troops, masters often moved their slave property to "safer" areas in the interior. This loosened the supports upon which the system relied and the discipline which regulated slave life. Masters could not always find land in new areas on which their "refugee" slaves could be put to their accustomed agricultural work and were forced to hire them out to other forms of employment in the towns or in industry. These wartime upheavals pushed slaveholders into choices between their immediate economic self-interest and their image of themselves as paternalists—and it was the latter which usually suffered. If a master could not transfer all his slaves to safer locations, he was inclined to give the highest priority to his most skilled or valued workers. He often felt obliged to separate husbands from wives or parents from children; the old and infirm, and sometimes the women and children, were simply abandoned. For their part, slaves gained fresh insight into the vulnerability and insecurity of their owners and the limitations of the owners' power.

The influx of slaves into the towns and cities intensified all the old white anxieties about the incompatibility of slavery with the urban environment. Overcrowding and housing shortages weakened social and racial barriers and aggravated problems of law and order. Despite objections from the white community, more slaves in the towns were able to hire themselves out and to live virtually independent lives. The employment of more slaves in industry reinforced the same trend toward looser discipline and declining stability. Slaves were extensively used in the munitions industry, mining, ironworks, textile mills, and food processing, and particularly in such areas as transportation, railroad construction and repair, and hospital work, where large numbers of unskilled workers were needed. Resort to financial incentives became widespread, and a kind of implicit bargaining often dictated terms and conditions of labor. In a number of places there was friction between free and slave workers.

Nothing was more indicative of the destabilizing effects of war upon a slave society than the drafting or impressment of slaves to work on the building of fortifications or in other forms of military labor. Hard physical labor, often in wretched conditions dangerously close to the front line, encouraged some slaves to make a dash for freedom. Many of those who did return to their owners after their spell of such labor were in poor health and an unsettled frame of mind. In the earlier part of the war, the use of slaves as military laborers and auxiliaries was arranged by contracts between owners and the state or Confederate authorities. However, as the pressures of war mounted, the authorities resorted to forced impressment of slaves for such purposes. Implementation of the policy produced the worst of both worlds. It was not pursued rigorously enough to cope with severe labor shortages, but it was widespread enough to outrage many slaveholders.

Indeed, the irony of the situation was surely lost neither on slaves nor their owners. Slaves were required to play an essential part in a war effort aimed to secure the indefinite continuation of their enslavement—and yet their mobilization for this purpose eroded the very foundations of that system of bondage. Slaveholders had supported secession and the fight for independence largely because of their resentment at federal government interference, actual or threatened, with their peculiar institution. Now the Confederate government was interfering with their slave property in ways which Washington had never contemplated. The impressment of slaves under the orders of the local military authorities was a profound shock to slaveholders, and a deep humiliation, not only in their own eyes but in the eyes of their slaves, too. It was another assault on the psychological underpinnings of slave society. There is something both ironic and particularly revealing about the story of the planter whose five sons had been taken into the army but whose support for the Confederate cause wavered only when the government impressed his slaves.[6]

For all the transient slave population on the move within the South, and for all the urban and industrial slaves and the military laborers, it was still true that, in large areas of the Confederacy and for much of the war, the bulk of the slave population remained down on the farm or the plantation. But even here the war exerted a far-reaching, if less dramatic, influence. The depletion of the white male population as more and more men left to join the army raised problems both in the supervision of the labor force and the maintenance of order through slave patrols. A substantial and visible white presence had always been one of the mainstays of an orderly slave society. Discipline on the plantations and farms was inevitably relaxed, and slaves generally worked less hard than before. White women were often left in somewhat precarious control at precisely the time when slaves saw the opportunity to assert themselves and when some of the old assumptions about white authority faced serious challenge. Rumors of slave plots and insurrections were commonplace. J. William Harris describes one such conspiracy in Hancock County, Georgia, in October 1863. Linton Stephens wrote to his brother, the vice president of the Confederacy, expressing his anxiety about such a plot at a time when the countryside was stripped of white men:

> Our negro population are going to give us great trouble. They are becoming extensively corrupted. The necessary pains to keep them on our side and in order have been unwisely and sadly neglected . . . I believe that the institution of slavery is already so undermined and demoralized as never to be of much use to us, even if we had peace and independence today. The institution has received a terrible shock which is tending to its disintegration and ruin.[7]

The authors of two excellent state studies—Clarence Mohr on Georgia and C. Peter Ripley on Louisiana—are in broad agreement in their analysis of the crumbling of slavery under the stresses and strains of war. In his discussion of refugee slaves, as elsewhere, Mohr suggests that the basic norms and rhythms of an established rural society were disrupted and the assumption that "Southern whites were in control of society as actual or potential wielders of ultimate power—that they were in the most basic sense 'masters' " was irretrievably undermined. Ripley observes that "the sustaining qualities of isolation, dull routine, and monotonous plantation labours were threatened by moving about, changing jobs, and communication with other slaves"—and the various mechanisms of paternalism and slave control were seriously impaired.[8]

The Confederacy wrestled for four years with the insoluble problems of conducting a struggle to preserve its basic institutions by means which themselves threatened the viability of those very institutions. The final irony came with the proposal to employ slaves as soldiers in that struggle. In 1861 any such idea would have been laughed out of court, but during the last eighteen months of the war it was widely discussed within the army and in political circles. In 1865, Robert E. Lee himself gave his support to the proposal, and the Richmond Congress finally enacted the measure; but the war came to an end before it could have any significant effect. Sheer necessity inspired the invention of various justifications of the enlistment of slaves to fight for Confederate freedom, but the irony and the inconsistency were by no means lost on all Southerners. Howell Cobb favored the use of slaves in every aspect of the war effort except military service; he would even have preferred to have "purchased" British and French aid by abolishing slavery rather than resort to the arming of blacks: "The day you make soldiers of them is the beginning of the end of the revolution."[9]

The history of slavery within the Confederacy exposed many of its inner tensions and contradictions and questioned many of its basic and long-standing assumptions. Equally revealing is the experience of those parts of the South which came under Union control during the first two or three years of the war, and which either contained substantial slave populations or became magnets for slaves making their own bid for freedom. From early 1862, there were three main testing grounds of the de facto freedom of the slaves: the sea islands and the coastal areas of the Carolinas and Georgia, the delta area of Louisiana, and large parts of western and central Tennessee. As it happened, the first two did contain large slave populations, many of them concentrated on unusually large plantations.[10] After the success of the Vicksburg campaign in the summer of 1863, further areas of large slaveholding in the lower Mississippi Valley came under permanent Union control. During the last twenty months of the war, as Northern armies penetrated further and further into the heartland of the Confederacy, many thousands more slaves made the transition from slavery to freedom. Meanwhile, the decline and eventual abandonment of slavery in the border states—Maryland, Kentucky, Missouri—unfolded in a separate chapter of the story of emancipation. Barbara Jeanne Fields has graphically described the collapse of slavery in Maryland during the war years.[11]

In the context of the present study, it is not necessary to examine the evolution of Union policy on slavery. Abraham Lincoln's Emancipation Proclamation and the various pieces of congressional legislation were of crucial importance as declarations of intent and as a framework for action. However, for each slave community and slave family liberation came about as a result of the movement of the armies and against the background of an often highly unstable local situation. Emancipation was a piecemeal process taking place over months or even years—not a single glorious day of jubilee. It was in the nature of the Emancipation Proclamation that this should be the case, for Lincoln declared free only those slaves who were at the time still under Confederate control. Their actual freedom depended on the progress and the eventual outcome of the war.

The federal authorities lacked the administrative machinery, the political will, and the positive conception of the role of government which would have been required to manage an orderly transition from slavery to freedom, backed by welfare programs to assist the adjustment of the freed slaves to their new status.[12] For many slaves, their baptism into freedom took place amid all the suffering, misery, dislocation, and confusion which have commonly been the fate of the refugees, the homeless, and the other defenseless victims of warfare throughout history. The joy of liberation was often swiftly followed by fear, insecurity, and disillusion. In most areas, the approach of the Union army produced a feeling of restless excitement; some slaves took off to claim their freedom without delay, while the majority stayed where they were. First contact with Yankee liberators produced a rapidly changing kaleidoscope of emotions: relief at the discovery that they were just ordinary men and women rather than the monsters depicted in the slaveholders' propaganda; eagerness to help the freedom-bearing army on its way; the euphoria of the first taste of freedom mixed with bewilderment about what would happen next; a welter of confused and contradictory feelings toward former masters and their families, who had hitherto defined so much of the world of the slaves; and a growing disenchantment as the ex-slaves encountered the racial prejudice, or simply the ignorance and indifference of their liberators.[13]

It did not take long to discover that freedom did not by itself fill stomachs or provide shelter. Many freed slaves gave immediate expression to their newfound freedom simply by wandering away from the plantation which had restricted their horizons for so long. Many more found themselves herded into contraband camps, often in overcrowded and unhealthy conditions; some did not live to enjoy their liberty for very long. The invading Northern forces were in many instances overwhelmed by the problem of coping with thousands of ex-slaves and, sadly but inevitably, often saw them as an impediment to the pursuit of their military objectives. When it came to impressing supplies, or to looting, pilfering, and vandalism, the behavior of Yankee soldiers was no worse, and probably rather better, than the normal standard of conquering armies; but they frequently showed little discrimination between their black and white victims.

When it came to the question of enabling or requiring freed slaves to support themselves, three main options, none of them overwhelmingly attractive, were placed before them. All three shared an increasing element of compulsion which blurred more than a little the distinction between erstwhile bondage and newly acquired freedom. Under the first option, large numbers of freed slaves were put back to work on the land they had recently tilled as slaves, now under the control either of their old masters or of new masters to whom plantations were leased. In Louisiana, slaves were put to work under contracts which severely restricted their freedom. As Ripley describes the operation of this system, "increasingly, Federal regulations governing the labor force resembled a throwback to the slave codes and a preview of the black codes."[14] Elsewhere in the Mississippi Valley, ex-slaves working on the plantations were often brutally treated and were lucky if they received even a part of the pitifully low wages to which they were entitled. Fundamentally, the policies of the federal authorities, military and civilian, were directed toward military objectives, cotton speculation, the imposition of some kind of order, and the prevention of an influx of freed blacks into the Northern states, rather than toward the promotion of the economic independence of the former slaves.[15]

The second form of employment for freed slaves was as military laborers, employed by the Union army as many thousands had been by their Confederate opponents, in the construction of fortifications or in a variety of auxiliary roles. The work was often arduous and sometimes dangerous, and many military laborers were ill-fed and badly treated. As many as two hundred thousand ex-slaves may have served the Union armies for shorter or longer periods in this way. A substantial number did so, not by choice but through coercion, as the military resorted to impressment of labor to meet its urgent needs. C. Peter Ripley's description of military labor in Louisiana could no doubt be replicated elsewhere:

> But for the absence of corporal punishment, military treatment of contraband laborers was not unlike slavery. Although blacks were not bought and sold, they were impressed, moved about, and assigned jobs indiscriminately.[16]

In addition to military labor or wage labor on the plantations, there was a third possibility for adult male slaves. This was recruitment into the Union army, which offered the freedman the opportunity of active participation in the fight for freedom and the clearest affirmation possible of his own new status. Much Northern opinion, including that of Lincoln himself, came around only slowly and warily to what was one of the most revolutionary steps of the whole war. The argument in favor of recruiting black troops was clinched largely by the recognition that they would leave less work to be done, and less blood to be spilled, by white soldiers. Over 180,000 black soldiers served in the Union army, where they experienced discrimination and prejudice in many forms. A very large proportion were former slaves, and their contribution to the war effort was militarily and morally important. It was, however, disfigured by the fact that some of them were forced, even at gunpoint, to enlist in the army, and were dragged away from their families very shortly after their own "liberation."[17]

Enough has been said to indicate that the wartime experience of emancipation induced trauma at least as often as euphoria. However, for all its shocks and disappointments, the Civil War surely added up to "a revolution of profound dimensions," as Willie Lee Rose describes it. "Surely," she continues, "the difference between slavery and freedom is about the greatest difference in status we can imagine, no matter how kindly a view some historians might want to take of slavery, no matter how limited and curtailed freedom may have turned out to be."[18] She has also suggested how much there may be yet to learn about many aspects of the history of slavery and the life of the slave community from an examination of the immediate consequences of, and responses to, emancipation.[19] The revolutionary upheaval of the war years may be employed as a probe with which to examine some of the inner workings of the peculiar institution.

The very diversity of the slave response to the prospect and the fact of liberation offered abundant evidence of the variety of the slave experience and the slave personality. The thousands of slaves who abandoned their familiar surroundings and made their way through the Union lines to claim their freedom took many risks and displayed great courage in their leap into the unknown. Similarly, if less spectacularly, the resilience and resourcefulness displayed by many more slaves as the prospect of emancipation came near surely undermines the credibility of the Sambo stereotype—except perhaps as a piece of playacting by the slaves. Leon Litwack has painted a remarkably intricate and complex picture of slave behavior in the immediate aftermath of slavery. Rejecting simple classifications of slaves as docile or militant, Uncle Toms or Nat Turners, Litwack argues that individual slaves experienced many different emotions and expressed (or concealed) them in many different ways:

> If the vast majority of slaves refrained from aggressive acts and remained on the plantations, most of them were neither "rebellious" nor "faithful" in the fullest sense of those terms, but rather ambivalent and observant, some of them frankly opportunistic, many of them anxious to preserve their anonymity, biding their time, searching for opportunities to break the dependency that bound them to their white families.[20]

The habits of deception and dissembling, and the basic survival instinct, learned over generations of bondage, were put to good use as the war swirled around the slaves' home area. Many among those slaves who stayed switched overnight from apparent submission and loyalty to their owners to help and cooperation cheerfully offered to the Yankee soldiers. Slaves were active participants in their emancipation and its aftermath and not just passive objects of government policy or military authority.

Eyewitnesses at the time and later historians have commented on the low incidence of violence by slaves against their former owners. There was no blood-soaked retribution for age-old wrongs, although there were isolated instances where personal vengeance was exacted. Litwack cites the example of the seizure by a detachment of black troops of a slaveholder who had a few days earlier whipped some of his female slaves. The wretched man was tied to a tree and himself whipped, first by a soldier who had once been his slave and then by the women who had suffered at his hands. In many areas the presence of black soldiers excited particular fears among the white community.

Generally, the freed slaves were satisfied with the destruction or appropriation of their former masters' property, rather than attacks upon him or his family. Reports of plunder, looting, and arson were common, and understandably enough, slaves usually showed little compunction about engaging in such activities. Having been treated as property themselves for so long, former slaves regarded it as no more than rough justice that they should now take possession of some of their owners' other possessions.[21] Willie Lee Rose has suggested that, before the moment of liberation came, slaves resisted their owners during the war by an escalation of their traditional methods—malingering, petty theft, sabotage, and flight—with only occasional thought of violent rebellion. When freedom came, they adapted themselves to the new situation and acted in the same moderate vein, without resort to mass violence.[22]

Although the behavior of ex-slaves in the aftermath of emancipation sheds much light on various aspects of the master-slave relationship, the evidence does not point to any single overriding conclusion. In some cases the restraint the freed slaves displayed may well have indicated the strength or even the warmth of the personal relationship between owner and owned. On the other hand, many slaveholders were shocked, disgusted, or simply bemused by what they regarded as the disloyalty or ingratitude of their former slaves. One owner lamented that "in truth the Negroes did not care as much about us as we did for them," and another complained that "they didn't even ask my advice about going away." (Neither betrayed any consciousness of the irony of such remarks.) Sometimes it was the most trusted and favored slaves who took the lead in assisting the Yankee soldiers or in seizing the master's property. At times, long-standing personal ties or a reputation for benevolence as an owner seemed to count for little or nothing. A harshly treated slave might have regarded a more kindly owner as the height of his or her aspirations; a well-treated slave would have yearned for freedom. One master deplored the defection of a female slave who had shared his bed until his marriage.[23]

Shock and bewilderment made owners unsure what to expect. As Litwack says, "when property suddenly assumed a personality, nothing seemed certain any longer."[24] Slaveholders had long convinced or deluded themselves with a romanticized view of the master-slave relationship and were now totally dismayed at the discovery of what so many slaves really felt about that relationship. Some owners rapidly switched to complaints about "uppity" ex-slaves who no longer knew their place. Others soon dropped the habits, or the pretenses, of the old paternalism and abandoned any responsibility for aged or sick former slaves, or set about exploiting the new relationship by offering only pitifully low wages to their former slaves.

Explanations of the bitterness, resentment, and confusion in the minds of former slaveholders are not too difficult to find. Their whole world was collapsing around them. Their plight as they watched the disintegration of their cherished peculiar institution has been perceptively described in James Roark's *Masters without Slaves*. In one of her essays, Willie Lee Rose has written that for the slaveholder "nothing less than his own significance in the only world he knew was at stake." The planter experiencing the collapse of slavery was, she says, like "a man undergoing severe trauma. Not only were his finances in chaos. So was his superego." Seeking to explain but not to excuse the behavior and the mistakes the planters made at this critical time, she writes that they displayed "the psychological defensiveness of a displaced elite whose world-view was shaken not only by their conquerors but also by their erstwhile slaves."[25]

At the moment of its demise, slavery revealed more still about the nature and complexity of the master-slave relationship. Many masters came to see the war and the impending collapse of slavery as a judgment of God, not necessarily on the wickedness of slavery *per se* but rather on evil features of the system which the South had tolerated for too long, such as excessively brutal punishments or the breakup of slave families. During the war years, the movement for the humanitarian reform of slavery attracted new followers. More generally, the harshness of slavery was moderated as, in Mohr's words, "whites concealed their loss of mastery beneath a cloak of greater permissiveness."[26]

Leon Litwack has written a full and often moving account of the reactions of slaves to the experience of emancipation. His massive book defies summarization because its main message is to convey something of the remarkable variety and diversity of the freed slaves' feelings and actions. One passage may serve to illustrate this basic theme:

The war revealed, often in ways that defied description, the sheer complexity of the master-slave relationship, and the conflicts, contradictions and ambivalence that relationship generated in each individual. The slave's emotions and behavior invariably rested on a precarious balance between the habit of obedience and the intense desire for freedom. The same humble, self-effacing slave who touched his hat to his "white folks" was capable of touching off the fire that gutted his master's house. The loyal body servant who risked his life to carry his wounded master to safety remounted his master's horse and fled to the Yankees.

Litwack goes on to describe the slave nurse protecting the white children whom she had suckled as babies, and yet showing no disapproval at the threat of the Yankee soldiers to burn her master's house. It ought to be burned, she said, because "there has been so much devilment there."[27] If there was one lesson taught by emancipation, it was surely that the slaveholders knew less about the lives of their slaves, and understood less of their thoughts and feelings, than they had fondly imagined.

The ending of slavery also sheds a good deal of retrospective light on the life of the slave community. In his study of the slave family, Herbert Gutman relied heavily on evidence drawn from the period of adjustment from slavery to freedom. Some slaves traveled considerable distances and expended much time and effort in the search for partners from whom they had been separated by sale or some other cause. Even more striking is the large number of slaves who sought some form of legal registration, and religious blessing, on "marriages" which had survived, often for many years, under slavery but without any formal legal or divine sanction. Gutman also emphasized the concern of slave parents to protect their children during the period of uncertainty and instability which often accompanied liberation, and the persistence of the wider kinship networks which were an important feature of slave society.

In many ways the family was sorely tested during the war years. The movement of some slaves to "safe" areas often disrupted families, and the general increase in the mobility of the slave population led to other separations. The impressment of adult male slaves by both armies for use as military auxiliaries and laborers was a particularly unwelcome interference with family life, and the recruitment or conscription of freedmen into the Union army had a similar effect. However, the opportunity to fight for the freedom of one's family was one of the more persuasive arguments used to persuade ex-slaves to enlist in the army.

The social upheaval and insecurity generated by the war made the family all the more important as a bulwark of the slave (or the ex-slave) community. Herbert Gutman underlines the importance of the family in the adaptation of slaves to changing circumstances over many generations, and that role was never more necessary than during the Civil War and the transition from slavery to freedom.[28] C. Peter Ripley makes much the same point in his study of Louisiana:

> From slavery to freedom the black family, more than any other facet of the Louisiana experiment, exemplifies a sense of black community, a sense that black Americans brought with them out of bondage, a feeling of what their lives should be about.

He adds that, at the same time, wartime disruptions and many of the policies pursued by both Confederate and Union authorities constantly threatened the integrity and security of the slave or ex-slave family. "In matters of the family," he writes, "blacks had an immediate and real awareness of their best interests; but those interests were frequently frustrated by both blues and grays."[29]

Religion was another of the pillars of the slave community which became more important than ever amid all the dangers of war and the uncertainties which followed liberation. Black churches provided some of the organization, and black preachers much of the leadership, which saw the freed slaves through the troubled years following emancipation. With its deliberate double meaning, both earthly and supernatural, deliverance had long been one of the dominant themes of slave religion, as Genovese has shown,[30] and their faith helped to keep alive the slaves' longing for freedom, and their perception of what it would mean, through generations of bondage.

Any discussion of the moment of emancipation and what it may reveal about the character and impact of slavery itself must come finally to the question of the perception of freedom in the minds of the freed slave themselves. Some of their immediate responses, such as the inclination simply to move around and break away from the physical confinement of servitude, are very illuminating. So too is the determination to hold on to the family, and to consolidate its position, as a source of stability and reassurance in a rapidly changing world. The appetite for education and the effort which went into securing it is a particularly suggestive example of the former slaves' understanding of the opportunities and the challenges of freedom. The yearning for land as the only secure basis for economic freedom also suggests lessons drawn from the slaves' own experience and from their observation of the whites' world.[31]

Attitudes to work, once the compulsions of slavery had been removed, are somewhat harder to analyze. Former slaveholders desperately needed to believe that blacks were inherently idle and could only be made to work by the constant supervision and tight discipline of slavery—and they were determined to show that their prophecies on this subject had been fulfilled.[32] It was the search for confirmation of their long-held views which probably inspired stories of ex-slaves who believed that they would become wealthy simply by not working, because from their observation of white society, the richest men were the great planters who engaged in no physical labor at all.

In fact, the ex-slaves generally took a much more practical and realistic view of the necessity for labor and of the process of adjustment to a free labor system—although they were scarcely helped by the ill-managed and exploitative schemes of contract labor into which they were often pressed after emancipation. Longer-term developments during and after Reconstruction are beyond the scope of this study, but it is worth noting one or two aspects of the adjustment from slave to free labor. If mothers gave up work in the fields to care for their children, if slaves used their newly won freedom to opt for rather less work and rather more leisure, and if they showed a preference for self-sufficiency and subsistence farming rather than production for a distant market—even though after emancipation, as Roger L. Ransom and Richard Sutch have shown, blacks received a somewhat larger share of the income generated by Southern agriculture—some questions may arise not only about the economics of slavery but other aspects of the legacy slavery left behind.[33] Such reactions to emancipation cast a fresh light upon assertions about the rate of expropriation, the extent to which slaves absorbed a belief in the Protestant work ethic, and the "negative non-pecuniary income" of the slaves.

Mobility, education, land, and work were all involved in the perception and meaning in the minds of the former slaves. In the words of Clarence Mohr:

> What the ex-slaves sought was a kind of limited self-determination or autonomy that would preclude any whites from controlling their lives or exploiting their labor. Such aspirations were a natural outgrowth of antebellum servitude, but they ran counter to the dominant force shaping Southern life in the wake of emancipation.[34]

The confusion and chaos of war meant that, even in areas under Union control, many slaves felt insecure in their newfound freedom. For those in other areas, freedom only came when the war ended. Litwack makes the point that it was only the final Confederate surrender which convinced many Southern blacks of the reality of freedom.[35] That realization was to be followed all too quickly by disillusionment as freedom was diminished or undermined in practice. Slavery has cast a long shadow over the whole of subsequent American history, but for present purposes the story must conclude in 1865.

It is truly extraordinary that the idea of freedom persisted in the minds of the slaves so vigorously through two centuries until the destruction through war of a system of slavery which had lost the power and the will, if it ever possessed them, to liquidate itself. Beginning in the colonial era as the available answer to a labor problem, slavery had become by the nineteenth century the foundation of a way of life, an economic and social system, and a pattern of human relationships which were truly distinctive, if not indeed unique. Any study of slavery must surely begin and end with a reminder of its fundamental injustice and inhumanity, its brutality and barbarity. However, as its modern historians have demonstrated, it must also be regarded as a remarkable chapter in the history of human resistance to adversity, and of human resilience, adaptability, and endurance under pressure.

The achievement of the slaves was to have survived their long ordeal, to have defied their enslavers by creating a community life and a culture of their own, and to have cherished a clear vision of freedom until the day of liberation and beyond. The achievement of the historians of slavery during the last generation has been greatly to deepen and enrich—if scarcely to simplify—our understanding of the system, the society which rested upon it, and the lives of those who were its victims. It has been one of the greatest historical endeavors of modern times, and it still continues.

NOTES

1. For one recent example see Harris, *Plain Folk and Gentry in a Slave Society,*190–1.

2. See above, 60–61.

3. For a spirited account of the mounting anxieties of slaveholders on the eve of secession and Civil War, see Oakes, *The Ruling Race,* 227–42.

4. Channing, *Crisis of Fear,* provides a vivid account of this process in South Carolina. (Cf. chapter 5, note 18.) For Georgia, there is an equally good account in Clarence L. Mohr, *On the Threshold of Freedom: Masters and Slaves in Civil War Georgia* (Athens, Ga., 1986), 3–50.

5. Mohr, *On the Threshold of Freedom,* xv. The discussion in the following paragraphs of slavery within the Confederacy relies heavily on Mohr's excellent study of Georgia. See also James H. Brewer, *The Confederate Negro: Virginia's Craftsmen and Military Laborers, 1861–1865* (Durham, N.C., 1969). There is still a great deal of useful information to be found in the much older study by Bell I. Wiley, *Southern Negroes, 1861–1865* (New Haven, 1938).

6. Frank L. Owsley, *State Rights in the Confederacy* (Chicago, 1925), 264–5.

7. Harris, *Plain Folk and Gentry in a Slave Society,* 167–70. The Linton Stephens quotation appears on page 167.

8. Mohr, *On the Threshold of Freedom,* 118; C. Peter Ripley, *Slaves and Freedmen in Civil War Louisiana* (Baton Rouge, La., 1976), 13.

9. Robert F. Durden, *The Gray and the Black: The Confederate Debate on Emancipation* (Baton Rouge, La., 1972), 184.

10. There is a classic study of the situation in the South Carolina sea islands by Willie Lee Rose, *Rehearsal for Reconstruction: The Port Royal Experiment* (Indianapolis, 1964); Louisiana is well covered in Ripley, *Slaves and Freedmen.*

11. Fields, *Slavery and Freedom on the Middle Ground,* 90–130.

12. On the policy of the federal government and its implementation, see LaWanda Cox, *Lincoln and Black Freedom: A Study in Presidential Leadership* (Columbia, S.C., 1981), and Louis S. Gerteis, *From Contraband to Freedman: Federal Policy Toward Southern Blacks, 1861–1865* (Westport, Ct., 1973).

13. The description of first responses to liberation in this and following paragraphs relies heavily on Leon F. Litwack, *Been in the Storm So Long: The Aftermath of Slavery* (New York, 1979). Litwack provided a briefer statement of some of the main themes of his major study in his "Free at Last," in Tamara K. Hareven, ed., *Anonymous Americans: Explorations in Nineteenth-Century Social History* (Englewood Cliffs, N.J., 1971), 131–71.

14. Ripley, *Slaves and Freedmen,* 58, and, more generally, 37–9, 43–68.

15. Gerteis, *From Contraband to Freedman;* Lawrence N. Powell, *New Masters: Northern Planters During the Civil War and Reconstruction* (New Haven, 1980).

16. Ripley, *Slaves and Freedmen,* 42.

17. Litwack, *Been in the Storm So Long,* 64–103. The standard work on black soldiers in the Union army is Dudley T. Cornish, *The Sable Arm: Negro Troops in the Union Army, 1861–1865* (New York, 1966).

18. Rose, *Slavery and Freedom,* 94.

19. Ibid., 110–111. There is no more sensitive or perceptive brief account of the immediate impact of emancipation upon slaves and their owners than in two of the essays in *Slavery and Freedom:* "Masters without Slaves," 73–89, and "Blacks without Masters: Protagonists and Issue," 90–111. Eugene Genovese and Herbert Gutman are two other major historians of slavery who have made very effective use of evidence drawn from the time of emancipation.

20. Litwack, *Been in the Storm So Long,* 162.

21. Ibid., 18–20, 65, 140–4.

22. Rose, *Slavery and Freedom,* 94.

23. Ibid., 85, 86. See also Litwack, *Been in the Storm So Long*, 151–9.

24. Litwack, "Free at Last," 144.

25. James L. Roark, *Masters without Slaves: Southern Planters in the Civil War and Reconstruction* (New York, 1977), especially chapters 2 and 3; Rose, *Slavery and Freedom*, 76, 89.

26. Mohr, *On the Threshold of Freedom*, 236. See 235–71 for a full discussion of the movement for slavery "reform" during the Civil War.

27. Litwack, *Been in the Storm So Long*, 162–3.

28. Gutman, *The Black Family*, 9–24, 34–5, 139–43, 204–7, 402–25.

29. Ripley, *Slaves and Freedmen*, 158–9, and, more generally, 146–59.

30. Genovese, *Roll, Jordan, Roll*, 248–55, 272–84.

31. Discussion of these topics is scattered through the pages of Litwack, *Been in the Storm So Long*, and various studies of particular localities, including Rose, *Rehearsal for Reconstruction*, on the South Carolina sea islands, and Ripley, *Slaves and Freedmen*, on Louisiana.

32. This point is effectively made in Dan T. Carter, *When the War Was Over: The Failure of Self-Reconstruction in the South, 1865–1867* (Baton Rouge, La., 1985), 149–50, 159, 164, 177–9, 182–3, 205–7, 226–7.

33. Roger L. Ransom and Richard Sutch, *One Kind of Freedom: The Economic Consequences of Emancipation* (Cambridge, 1977), 1–39, 203–36.

34. Mohr, *On the Threshold of Freedom*, 96.

35. Litwack, *Been in the Storm So Long*, 167–87.

Bibliographic Essay

As the subject matter of the book itself is the recent historiography of slavery in the Old South, the main purpose of this bibliography is to draw together and, where necessary, to supplement information and evaluation scattered through the various chapters and their notes. This short essay does not set out to provide a comprehensive bibliography of slavery; like the book itself, the bibliography concentrates on the more important book length studies and refers to articles only where they are absolutely essential, and where the topic or the views of a particular historian would not otherwise be adequately covered. For studies of some of the more specialized topics, the reader will be referred to the relevant note or notes in a specific chapter.

It is not easy to digest the full implications of the expansion and transformation of the study of slavery which has taken place during the last generation. Until at least the second World War, the conventional wisdom on the subject derived above all from the work of Ulrich B. Phillips and his followers. It was essentially a view of slavery from above, focusing on the place of slavery in the Southern economy and in Southern white society, which was based on exclusively white sources, particularly plantation records, and which accepted the racial assumptions of the prevailing Southern white culture. It is true that this view was already under challenge in the inter-war period. The new impetus owed much to a small but growing band of black historians, inspired by a remarkable pioneer, Carter G. Woodson, and sustained by the Association for the Study of Negro Life and History and the *Journal of Negro History,* and led into the next generation by a figure of towering authority in John Hope

Franklin. The political and intellectual climate of the New Deal years, and then the second World War, provided further encouragement. An early essay by the young Richard Hofstadter, "U. B. Phillips and the Plantation Legend," *Journal of Negro History* 29 (1944), mounted a direct attack on the hitherto prevailing point of view. The overturning of the Phillips interpretation was completed by Kenneth Stampp's *The Peculiar Institution,* published in 1956.

New approaches were also encouraged by contributions from other disciplines, mainly in the social and behavioral sciences—economic history, sociology, social psychology, and anthropology—which offered novel techniques and a different methodological framework.

The revolution in our thinking about and understanding of Southern slavery since the 1950s has stemmed from many sources, including changing intellectual currents, the influential work of major scholars, the exploration of new sources (including slave sources), and the continuing application of new techniques and multidisciplinary approaches. It has probably owed even more to the changing political, social, and racial environment of modern America. The civil rights movement, black power, black nationalism, the spread of black studies courses, the general rise in black consciousness, and the continuing concern with racial injustice in contemporary American society, have all exercised a powerful influence. A high proportion of the modern historians of slavery are men and women of a liberal or radical persuasion; explicitly or implicitly, virtually all of them adopt attitudes toward race which have advanced beyond all recognition compared with the prevailing assumptions of fifty or sixty years ago.

In short, there has been a historiographical revolution of dramatic proportions. The main focus of the present study has been on the interpretations and arguments articulated in the rich and diverse modern literature on Southern slavery, rather than on the personal and ideological backgrounds of individual scholars. For a fascinating discussion of these matters, based partly on interviews with some 175 historians, see August Meier and Elliott Rudwick, *Black History and the Historical Profession, 1915–1980* (Urbana, Ill., 1986), especially chapter 4. Meier and Rudwick assess the relative influence upon the reinterpretation of the history of slavery of intellectual interchange between scholars and the influence of leading historians on one hand, and, on the other, the changing social, political, and intellectual climate in which historians have lived and worked. They come down firmly on the side of the latter as the predominant influence. Their revealing account provides a valuable context for the present study.

1. Bibliographical Aids and Guides

For works published before the 1970s, expert guidance may be found in James M. McPherson et al., *Blacks in America: Bibliographical Essays* (Garden City, N.Y., 1971). Full and up-to-date listings of books and articles on slavery may be found in the voluminous notes in John B. Boles and Evelyn T. Nolen, eds., *Interpreting Southern History: Historiographical Essays in Honor of Sanford W. Higginbotham* (Baton Rouge, La., 1987). See in particular the text and the notes in Charles B. Dew, "The Slavery Experience," also Randolph B. Campbell, "Planters and Plain Folks: The Social Structure of the Antebellum South," and Drew Gilpin Faust, "The Peculiar South Revisited: White Society, Culture and Politics in the Antebellum Period, 1800–1860." The excellent index in *Interpreting Southern History* enables the reader to track down particular items and the work of individual historians.

There is an extensive bibliography in Allen Weinstein, Frank O. Gatell, and Lewis Sarasohn, eds., *American Negro Slavery: A Modern Reader,* third ed. (New York, 1978). John Boles, *Black Southerners: 1619–1869* (Lexington, Ky., 1983), has a valuable bibliography essay. Peter Kolchin, "American Historians and Antebellum Southern Slavery, 1959–1984," in William J. Cooper, Michael F. Holt, and John McCardell, eds., *A Master's Due: Essays in Honor of David Herbert Donald* (Baton Rouge, La., 1985), 87–111, is a perceptive review, which is not unwilling to challenge some of the assumptions of the new orthodoxy, especially the "community and culture" emphasis of much recent work.

2. General Works

The first major scholarly history of Southern slavery was Ulrich B. Phillips, *American Negro Slavery: A Survey of the Supply, Employment and Control of Negro Labor as Determined by the Plantation Regime* (New York, 1918; paperback reprint, Baton Rouge, La., 1966). See also Phillips's *Life and Labor in the Old South* (Boston, 1929; reprint, 1963). The characteristics of Phillips's work—a sympathetic view of

Southern white society, belief in white supremacy as the central theme of Southern history, and extensive research in plantation records—are mirrored in a number of the older state histories of slavery, among the best of which are Charles S. Sydnor, *Slavery in Mississippi* (New York, 1933), and James B. Sellers, *Slavery in Alabama* (Tuscaloosa, Ala., 1950).

The next major landmark was Kenneth M. Stampp, *The Peculiar Institution: Slavery in the Ante-Bellum South* (New York, 1956), which was so methodical in its rebuttal of Phillips that it sometimes verged on becoming the captive of the earlier work. Labelled on first publication as a "neo-abolitionist" interpretation of slavery, *The Peculiar Institution* may now strike the reader as a moderate, even cautious, assessment. In some respects, it may even seem a little dated; more accurately, one might say that its message has been rapidly absorbed into the mainstream of slavery historiography. After more than three decades, it remains one of the basic texts for the student of the subject.

The intensity and diversity of slavery studies during the last thirty years have greatly magnified the difficulties of achieving an overall synthesis—still more of arriving at a new consensus. However, if one historian has a claim to be regarded as the dominant, if seldom uncontroversial, influence during the last twenty years at least, it is surely Eugene Genovese. His magnum opus, Roll, Jordan, Roll: The World the Slaves Made (New York, 1974), paints the most evocative and many-sided picture of slave life which has yet appeared. Despite its considerable bulk, it remains, among all the major works on the subject, the most popular with students, whether or not they sympathize with the author's ideological standpoint. It also continues to yield many insights to those who think that they know the subject quite well. Genovese's other, briefer and often more polemical writings include *The Political Economy of Slavery: Studies in the Economy and Society of the Slave South* (New York, 1967); *The World the Slaveholders Made: Two Essays in Interpretation* (New York, 1969); *In Red and Black: Marxian Explorations in Southern and Afro-American History* (New York, 1968); and, with Elizabeth Fox-Genovese, *Fruits of Merchant Capital: Slavery and Bourgeois Property in the Rise and Expansion of Capitalism* (New York, 1983). For an interesting discussion of Genovese's earlier work, see Richard H. King, "Marxism and the Slave South," *American Quarterly* 29 (1977), 117–31.

The work of other leading modern historians of slavery, including John Blassingame, Stanley Elkins, Robert Fogel and Stanley Engerman, Herbert Gutman, Lawrence Levine, and Willie Lee Rose, is referred to below, in the appropriate sections of this essay. The one outstandingly successful recent attempt at synthesis is John B. Boles, *Black Southerners,* which compresses many of the findings of recent studies into a volume of modest proportions and still finds room to express a distinctive and challenging point of view on some questions. Its approach is not, however, overtly historiographical in the manner of the present volume.

A number of general surveys place slavery in the context of the broader sweep of black history in America. In the latest edition of John Hope Franklin's distinguished text, he has acquired a coauthor: John Hope Franklin and Alfred A. Moss, *From Slavery to Freedom: A History of Negro Americans,* sixth ed. (New York, 1988). A shorter survey, with a somewhat different emphasis indicated by its title, is August Meier and Elliott Rudwick, *From Plantation to Ghetto,* revised ed. (New York, 1970). Vincent Harding *There Is a River* (New York, 1981) is a work of prophecy as much as history, and is suffused by a kind of messianic nationalism.

3. Essays, Readings, Anthologies

Some of the leading historians of slavery have demonstrated that they are superb exponents of the essay form—for example, Eugene Genovese whose work is discussed in section 2, above. Willie Lee Rose, *Slavery and Freedom,* edited by William H. Freehling (New York, 1982), is a collection of essays which contains more wisdom and insight than many volumes several times its length. The collected essays of two distinguished elder statesmen of the American historical profession include important discussions of various aspects of slavery: C. Vann Woodward, *American Counterpoint: Slavery and Racism in the North-South Dialogue* (Boston, 1971), and Kenneth M. Stampp, *The Imperiled Union: Essays on the Background of the Civil War* (New York, 1980).

Perspectives and Irony in American Slavery, Harry P. Owens, ed. (Jackson, Miss., 1976), is a collection of outstanding essays by leading historians. The 1960s and '70s saw the publication of a number of useful collections of essays or readings. Weinstein, Gatell, and

Sarasohn, *American Negro Slavery: A Modern Reader* has already been mentioned in section 1, above. See also Nathan I. Huggins, Martin Kilson, and Daniel M. Fox, eds., *Key Issues in the Afro-American Experience,* two volumes (New York, 1971), and August Meier and Elliott Rudwick, eds., *The Making of Black America: Essays in Negro Life and History,* two volumes (New York, 1969).

4. Slavery in the Colonial and Revolutionary Periods

There is no single authoritative history of slavery in the seventeenth and eighteenth centuries. The earlier chapters of Boles's *Black Southerners* provides an admirable brief account. On Virginia, the most important, if controversial, modern study is Edmund S. Morgan, *American Slavery, American Freedom: The Ordeal of Colonial Virginia* (New York, 1975), but see also Gerald W. Mullin, *Flight and Rebellion: Slave Resistance in Eighteenth-Century Virginia* (New York, 1972), which is revealing on many aspects of slave life, and Thad W. Tate, *The Negro in Eighteenth-Century Williamsburg* (Charlottesville, Va., 1966). Various articles taking diverse points of view on the early evolution of slavery in Virginia are conveniently listed in Boles, *Black Southerners,* 218–9.

On the early development of slavery in South Carolina, see the massively impressive study by Peter H. Wood, *Black Majority: Negroes in Colonial South Carolina from 1670 through the Stono Rebellion* (New York, 1974). See also Daniel C. Littlefield, *Rice and Slaves: Ethnicity and the Slave Trade in Colonial South Carolina* (Baton Rouge, La., 1981). For Georgia, see the valuable study by Betty Wood, *Slavery in Colonial Georgia, 1730–1775* (Athens, Ga., 1984). The varying patterns of development of colonial slavery are put into clear perspective in Ira Berlin, "Time, Space and the Evolution of Afro-American Society on British Mainland North America," *American Historical Review* 85 (1980): 44–78.

For the period of the American Revolution, much useful information may still be found in Benjamin Quarles, *The Negro in the American Revolution* (Chapel Hill, N.C., 1961). An outstanding collection of essays, examining many aspects of slavery from the mid-eighteenth century to the early nineteenth century, can be found in Ira Berlin and Ronald Hoffman, eds., *Slavery and Freedom in the Age of the American Revolution* (Charlottesville, Va., 1983). See also Ira

Berlin, "The Revolution in Black Life," in Alfred H. Young, ed., *The American Revolution: Explorations in the History of American Radicalism* (DeKalb, Ill., 1976). The tangled and often paradoxical relationship between slavery and the winning of American independence is explored with considerable discrimination by Duncan J. MacLeod, *Slavery, Race and the American Revolution* (Cambridge, 1974), and in considerable detail by Donald L. Robinson, *Slavery in the Structure of American Politics, 1765–1820* (New York, 1971). See also Robert McColley, *Slavery and Jeffersonian Virginia*, second ed. (Urbana, Ill., 1973). A seminal article on the legacy of the Revolution and the subsequent transformation of slavery is William H. Freehling, "The Founding Fathers and Slavery," *American Historical Review* 77 (1972): 81–93.

5. The Economics of Slavery

The historiography of the economics of slavery inevitably divides into the periods before and after *Time on the Cross*. Discussion of such questions as the efficiency of slave labor, the profitability of slavery, and the relative priorities of profit and paternalism have taken new directions and acquired a new impetus since the publication of that highly controversial work in 1974 and the massive critical response which it provoked.

Despite the prime importance of slavery as a labor system, some of the recent studies of slave life say curiously little about the actual work of the slaves. If one returns to earlier accounts, Phillips still offers much useful information, and, in *The Peculiar Institution*, Kenneth Stampp devotes a long and highly informative second chapter to the subject. There is a wealth of both information and comment on the subject in Genovese, *Roll, Jordan, Roll*.

Similarly, the works of Phillips, Stampp, and Genovese, cited above, all contain much important material and set out contrasting positions on profitability and other controversial topics. In contrast to Stampp's conclusion that the use of slave labor could be, and often was, profitable, Genovese's writings, from *The Political Economy of Slavery* onward, have explored in depth the economic implications of slaveholder paternalism and expressed serious doubts about the performance of the Southern slave economy. Harold D. Woodman, "The Profitability of Slavery: A Historical Perennial," *Journal of*

Southern History 29 (1963), 303–25, established sensible criteria for assessment of this thorny question. Important pioneering work in the application of statistical methods to the study of Southern slavery appeared in Alfred H. Conrad and John R. Meyer, "The Economics of Slavery in the Ante Bellum South," *Journal of Political Economy* 66 (1958), 95–130, and in their *The Economics of Slavery and Other Studies in Econometric History* (Chicago, 1964).

Academic argument exploded into popular sensation when the case for the efficiency and profitability of slavery was pressed further than ever before in Robert W. Fogel and Stanley L. Engerman's two-volume work, *Time on the Cross:* volume I, *The Economics of American Negro Slavery;* volume II, *Evidence and Methods* (Boston, 1974). The authors hoped to make their book a demonstration model of the new techniques of "cliometrics," but the ensuing controversy in fact exposed their fallibility. Because of their apparent exactitude, statistics can exercise a kind of tyranny over the unsuspecting, but the figures which are presented are often not exact at all. They are the end product of calculations based on information which is inevitably patchy and inadequate and carried on through a process of weighting one factor against another, which may not be much above the level of a hunch. The extent to which a small initial error can in consequence be magnified many times over in the final outcome perhaps deserves to be measured by a "geometric index of historical fallibility."

Some of the most telling blows against *Time on the Cross* were dealt by other quantitative historians. A particularly formidable critical barrage was delivered by the contributors to Paul A. David et al., *Reckoning with Slavery: A Critical Study in the Quantitative History of American Negro Slavery* (New York, 1976). See also Herbert G. Gutman, *Slavery and the Numbers Game: A Critique of* Time on the Cross (Urbana. Ill., 1975), and Thomas L. Haskell, "The True and Tragical History of *Time on the Cross,*" *New York Review of Books,* 2 Oct. 1975, 33–39. A less well-known but particularly thorough and penetrating critique may be found in Donald J. Ratcliffe, "The *Das Kapital* of American Negro Slavery? *Time on the Cross* after Two Years," *Durham University Journal* 69 (1976), 103–30. A major new study of slavery by Professor Fogel is eagerly awaited, and it is to be hoped that it may set the seal on the evolution of a more harmonious relationship between quantitative methods and the sources and techniques of more conventional historical research.

The most important study of the economics of slavery since *Time on the Cross* has been Gavin Wright, *The Political Economy of the Cotton South: Households, Markets and Wealth in the Nineteenth Century* (New York, 1978). Even if parts of the book are impenetrable to all but the most experienced and expert trackers through the cliometrical jungle, the basic arguments are clear and generally convincing, particularly in their interweaving of economic and noneconomic factors. On the other hand, the case for the slaveholder as capitalist is pressed rather too hard in James B. Oakes, *The Ruling Race: A History of American Slaveholders* (New York, 1982). See also the important essay by Otto H. Olsen, "Historians and the Extent of Slaveownership in the Southern United States," *Civil War History* 18 (1972), 101–16.

For references to works on the management of slave labor, see chapter 3, note 10, and for studies of the internal slave trade, see chapter 4, notes 30, 32, and 33.

6. The Life of the Slaves: Personality, Community, Culture

The delineation of a slave's eye view of slavery and concern with the slave community and slave culture have been dominant features of the historiography of slavery during the last two or three decades. If the vigorous reaction to Stanley Elkins was one of the inspirations of this development, it also owed much to the political and racial preoccupations of the time and to the fresh attention paid to source material emanating from slaves and ex-slaves themselves.

Once again, it should not be thought that earlier historians had entirely neglected such topics, and Kenneth Stampp's *The Peculiar Institution* has important things to say on many aspects of slave life, though almost entirely on the basis of evidence from white sources. He remains stubbornly skeptical about the value of the slave sources, although it has been pointed out that conventional white sources, such as plantation records, individual diaries and memoirs, and travellers' accounts, need to be scrutinized just as carefully, to test their reliability, authenticity, and typicality.

In the mere sixty pages of part III of Stanley Elkins, *Slavery: A Problem in American Institutional and Intellectual Life*, third ed. (Chicago, 1976), a whole new chapter in the study of the slave personality and slave life was opened. The third edition includes two fascinating chapters in which Elkins reflects on the development of the debate over slavery in the period since his book first appeared. There is a good selection of the views of Elkins's critics in Ann J. Lane, ed., *The Debate over Slavery: Stanley Elkins and His Critics* (Urbana, Ill., 1971), which also includes Elkins's essay on "Slavery and Ideology," reprinted in the third edition of *Slavery*. See also the two important essays by Kenneth Stampp and Eugene Genovese cited in chapter 5, note 19. There is a thoughtful reassessment of the whole question of the slave personality, stressing the diversity of reactions to servitude, in Bertram Wyatt-Brown, "The Mask of Obedience: Male Slave Psychology in the Old South," *American Historical Review* 93 (1988), 1228–52.

The urge to rebut Elkins and the exploration of slave sources were among the factors which, during the 1970s, encouraged the publication of a number of fresh studies of slave life. John W. Blassingame, *The Slave Community: Plantation Life in the Antebellum South* (New York, 1972; revised and enlarged ed., 1979) originally set out, almost too deliberately, to refute Elkins, but the fuller and rounder picture presented in the revised edition elevates it to the front rank of books on the subject. Like Elkins, Blassingame has earned the sometimes painful accolade of a book devoted to the views of his critics: Al-Tony Gilmore, ed., *Revisiting Blassingame's The Slave Community: The Scholars Respond* (Westport, Ct., 1978). See also Blassingame's stimulating essay on "Status and Social Structure in the Slave Community: Evidence from New Sources," in Owens, ed., *Perspectives and Irony in American Slavery*.

One of Blassingame's critics had already offered his own very different interpretation in George P. Rawick, *From Sundown to Sunup: The Making of the Black Community* (Westport, Ct., 1972), which takes an uncompromising black nationalist view and which serves somewhat uneasily as the introduction to a massive collection of source material, *The American Slave: A Composite Autobiography,* edited by Rawick, forty-one volumes (Westport, Ct., 1972–9). Access to this material has been immensely facilitated since the publication of Donald M. Jacobs, ed., *Index to "The American Slave"* (Westport, Ct., 1981).

Much the fullest and richest picture of slave life by any of the modern historians is of course to be found in Genovese, *Roll, Jordan, Roll.* Other useful studies are Leslie H. Owens, *This Species of*

Property: Slave Life and Culture in the Old South (New York, 1976); Paul D. Escott, *Slavery Remembered: A Record of Twentieth Century Slave Narratives* (Chapel Hill, N.C., 1979); and Thomas L. Webber, *Deep Like the Rivers: Education in the Slave Quarter Community, 1831–1865* (New York, 1978), which is broader in coverage than its title indicates, but narrow in its focus as a result of its virtual exclusion of white influences. Deborah Gray White, *Ar'n't I a Woman? Female Slaves in the Plantation South* (New York, 1985) is a brief pioneering study of an important subject which needs much fuller investigation.

Most of the studies referred to above provide information on the physical conditions of slave life and the health of the slaves. Owens, *This Species of Property* is particularly helpful—and so too is Boles, *Black Southerners*. For the contrasting views expressed in *Time on the Cross* and *Reckoning with Slavery*, see the references in chapter 5, note 3. On health and medical treatment (or mistreatment), see Todd L. Savitt, *Medicine and Slavery: The Diseases and Health Care of Blacks in Antebellum Virginia* (Urbana, Ill., 1978), and Kenneth F. Kiple and Virginia H. King, *Another Dimension to the Black Diaspora: Diet, Disease and Racism* (Cambridge, 1981).

In *Roll, Jordan, Roll,* Genovese evaluates with subtlety and insight the nature, variety, and limitations of slave resistance. In *From Rebellion to Revolution: Afro-American Slave Revolts in the Making of the New World* (Baton Rouge, La., 1979), he sets the problem in a broad comparative context, but ties his interpretation of it to a much more rigid ideological framework. Blassingame and Owens both have useful brief discussions of resistance, and there are important essays in Lane, ed., *The Debate over Slavery*. The fullest account of slave rebellion is in Herbert Aptheker, *American Negro Slave Revolts* (New York, 1943), but its value is greatly diminished by excessive zeal to demonstrate the strength of a tradition of servile rebellion.

The treatment of slave religion in Genovese, *Roll, Jordan, Roll,* is of fundamental importance, and Albert J. Raboteau, *Slave Religion: The "Invisible Institution" in the Antebellum South* (New York, 1978), provides additional information. See also Mechal Sobel, *Trabelin' On: The Slave Journey to an Afro-Baptist Faith* (Westport, Ct., 1979). In his *Black Southerners,* Boles questions the emphasis on the "underground" religion of the slave community and examines the interaction of white and black religion in the Old South. There is a new collection of essays, edited by Boles, *Masters and Slaves in the House of the Lord: Race and Religion in the American South, 1740–1870* (Lexington, Ky., 1988). See also Kenneth K. Bailey, "Protestantism and Afro-Americans in the Old South: Another Look," *Journal of Southern History* 41 (1975), 451–72.

Herbert G. Gutman, *The Black Family in Slavery and Freedom, 1750–1925* (New York, 1976), has placed the family squarely in the center of slave life and used it as a tool to open up other aspects of slave culture. In a massive, difficult but ultimately rewarding book, Gutman may have been inclined to assert more than his evidence always demonstrated. The debate which his book aroused has led to a proliferation of articles on the slave family, but, as yet, no new book-length study.

One of the most exciting and illuminating discussions of slave culture is to be found in the earlier chapters of Lawrence W. Levine, *Black Culture and Black Consciousness: Afro-American Folk Thought from Slavery to Freedom* (New York, 1977), which makes ingenious and effective use of slave songs, spirituals, and folk tales. See also Levine's essay "Slave Songs and Slave Consciousness," in Tamara K. Hareven, ed., *Anonymous Americans: Explorations in Nineteenth-Century Social History* (Englewood Cliffs, N.J., 1971); and Dena J. Epstein, *Sinful Tunes and Spirituals: Black Folk Music to the Civil War* (Urbana, Ill., 1977). Sterling Stuckey also makes extensive use of evidence from folklore in his *Slave Culture: Nationalist Theory and the Foundations of Black America* (New York, 1987) which, for all its wealth of ideas and fascinating detail, succeeds better as a deeply felt and powerful plea for a cause than as a straightforward historical investigation. In contrast, a recent study of eighteenth-century slavery emphasizes the interpenetration of black and white culture: see Mechal Sobel, *The World They Made Together: Black and White Values in Eighteenth-Century Virginia* (Princeton, N.J., 1987). Surely, the debate over the sources and character of slave culture must eventually recognize that the people whose culture is under investigation were, at one and the same time, African, American, Southern, and unfree. Whatever were the distinctive elements of that remarkable culture may have come from any one of those sources—or, more likely, from some combination of all of them, formed in a shared historical experience.

7. Local Studies

One of the pleasing developments of recent years has been the appearance of local studies of high quality which throw fresh light on the operation of the slave system, the life of the slave community, and the problems and tensions of a slave society. Four outstanding, but very disparate, examples may be given pride of place; they are respectively a study of a slave community on a group of neighbouring plantations; a biography of a prominent South Carolina planter; an examination of white and black society in one quite small area; and a study of the unusual history of slavery in a border state.

The first is Charles Joyner, *Down by the Riverside: A South Carolina Slave Community* (Urbana, Ill., 1984), which blends history, social anthropology, and folklore to paint a remarkable picture of slave life on the great rice plantations along the Waccamaw River. The second is Drew Gilpin Faust, *James Henry Hammond and the Old South: A Design for Mastery* (Baton Rouge, La., 1982), which devotes two superb chapters to Hammond as planter and slaveholder. The third is J. William Harris, *Plain Folk and Gentry in a Slave Society: White Liberty and Black Slavery in Augusta's Hinterlands* (Middletown, Ct., 1985), which probes deeply into the relationship between slavery and liberty, and much else besides, at the grass-roots level. The fourth is Barbara Jeanne Fields, *Slavery and Freedom on the Middle Ground: Maryland During the Nineteenth Century* (New Haven, 1985), which demonstrates how much may be revealed about slavery by an intelligent study of one of its exceptional situations. Books such as these may give the 1980s a reputation in the historiography of slavery fit to compare with that earned by the large-scale, synoptic works of the previous decade.

Other local studies include: Orville V. Burton, *In My Father's House Are Many Mansions: Family and Community in Edgefield, South Carolina* (Chapel Hill, N.C., 1985); Theodore Rosengarten, *Tombee: Portrait of a Cotton Planter* (New York, 1986); John S. Otto, *Cannon's Point Plantation, 1794–1860: Living Conditions and Status Patterns in the Old South* (Orlando, Fla., 1984); James M. Clifton, ed., *Life and Labor on Argyle Island: Letters and Documents of a Savannah River Rice Plantation, 1833–1867* (Savannah, Ga., 1978); Julia Floyd Smith, *Slavery and Rice Culture in Low Country Georgia, 1750–1860* (Knoxville, Tenn., 1985); and Randolph B. Campbell, *A Southern Community* in Crisis: Harrison County, Texas, 1850–1880 (Austin, 1983). The great majority of these studies deal with the Atlantic seaboard and South Carolina in particular. It would be immensely helpful if there were similar local studies of communities in, for example, Alabama and Mississippi.

Elinor Miller and Eugene D. Genovese, eds., Plantation, Town and Country: Essays on the Local History of American Slave Society (Urbana, Ill., 1974), is a useful collection of older local studies. A more recent compilation, Orville V. Burton and Robert C. McMath, eds., Class, Conflict and Consensus: Antebellum Southern Community Studies (Westport, Ct., 1982), has essays by Steven Hahn, Laurence Shore, and others on various aspects of slavery.

8. Variations and Exceptions

The deviations from the prevailing pattern of agricultural slavery have been unusually well covered in recent historical writing. However, there has been no overview of the whole picture of urban and industrial slavery, the practice of slave hire, and the varied experience of the free blacks. There are questions to be asked and answered about the cumulative effects and significance of these various exceptions to the Southern rule.

On urban slavery, Richard C. Wade, Slavery in the Cities: The South, 1820–1860 (New York, 1964), has stood up well to the counterarguments of more recent historians, including Claudia D. Goldin, Urban Slavery in the American South, 1820–1860: A Quantitative History (Chicago, 1976). The situation varied considerably from one city to another; see for example David R. Goldfield, Urban Growth in the Age of Sectionalism: 1847–1861 (Baton Rouge, La., 1977), and John W. Blassingame, Black New Orleans, 1860–1880 (Chicago, 1973).

There are a number of excellent studies of industrial slavery. See in particular: Robert S. Starobin, Industrial Slavery in the Old South (New York, 1970); Ronald L. Lewis, Coal, Iron and Slaves: Industrial Slavery in Maryland and Virginia, 1715–1865 (Westport, Ct., 1979); and Fred Bateman and Thomas Weiss, A Deplorable Scarcity: The Failure of Industrialization in the Slave Economy (Chapel Hill, N.C., 1981). Genovese, The Political Economy of Slavery, has a stimulating discussion of the subject in part III. Another major historian of industrial slavery, Charles B. Dew, has written a number of important articles, including "Disciplining Slave Ironworkers in the Ante-Bellum South: Coercion, Conciliation and Accommodation," *American Historical Review* 79 (1974), 393–418; "David Ross and the Oxford Iron Works: A Study of Industrial Slavery in the Early Nineteenth Century South," *William and Mary Quarterly*, third series, 31 (1974), 189–224; and "Sam Williams, Forgeman: The Life of an Industrial Slave in the Old South," in J. Morgan Kousser and James M. McPherson, eds., *Race, Region and Reconstruction: Essays in Honor of C. Vann Woodward* (New York, 1982). See also relevant sections of Dew's *Ironmaker to the Confederacy: Joseph R. Anderson and the Tredegar Iron Works* (New Haven, 1966).

The free blacks of the South have also received extensive and outstanding coverage in recent years. Ira Berlin, *Slaves without Masters: The Free Negro in the Antebellum South* (New York, 1974), is a superb general study which establishes a clear contrast between the upper and lower South. Michael P. Johnson and James L. Roark, *Black Masters: A Free Family of Color in the Old South* (New York, 1984), is a fascinating study of an exceptional case; see also the companion volume of letters: Johnson and Roark, eds., *No Chariot Let Down: Charleston's Free People of Color on the Eve of the Civil War* (Chapel Hill, N.C., 1984). Edwin A. Davis and William R. Hogan, *The Barber of Natchez* (Baton Rouge, La., 1954), chronicles the life of another truly exceptional case, William Johnson. Other studies include: Marina Wikramanayake, *A World in Shadow: The Free Black in Antebellum South Carolina* (Columbia, S.C., 1973); Leonard P. Curry, *The Free Black in Urban America, 1800–1850: The Shadow of the Dream* (Chicago, 1981); and Suzanne Lebsock, *The Free Women of Petersburg: Status and Culture in a Southern Town, 1784–1860* (New York, 1984), which deals with both black and white women. Fields, *Slavery and Freedom on the Middle Ground,* provides fascinating insights into the situation in Maryland, where the slave and free black populations were almost equal in 1860.

9. Comparisons

There is a rich literature comparing or contrasting Southern slavery with slavery in other societies. Elkins, *Slavery,* emphasized the contrast between slavery in North and South America. Genovese has written very widely on the comparative history of slavery, and his work on Southern slave society always shows an awareness of the international context. See in particular his *The World the Slaveholders Made; In Red and Black; From Rebellion to Revolution;* and, with Elizabeth Fox-Genovese, *Fruits of Merchant Capital.* The major works of David Brion Davis are listed in chapter 6, note 32. By far the most wide-ranging of modern comparative studies is Orlando Patterson, *Slavery and Social Death: A Comparative Study* (Cambridge, Ma., 1982), but inevitably the Old South does not figure very prominently on such a broad canvas. C. Duncan Rice, *The Rise and Fall of Black Slavery* (New York, 1975), is a readable general survey.

There are a number of useful collections of writings on the comparative history of slavery, including Laura Foner and Eugene D. Genovese, eds., *Slavery in the New World: A Reader in Comparative History* (Englewood Cliffs, N.J., 1969); Stanley L. Engerman and Eugene D. Genovese, eds., *Race and Slavery in the Western Hemisphere: Quantitative Studies* (Princeton, N.J., 1975); and Robin W. Winks, ed., *Slavery, a Comparative Perspective: Readings on Slavery from Ancient Times to the Present* (New York, 1972).

Important comparisons with Caribbean slavery may be found in Herbert S. Klein, *Slavery in the Americas: A Comparative Study of Virginia and Cuba* (Chicago, 1967), and Richard S. Dunn, *Sugar and Slaves: The Rise of the Planter Class in the English West Indies, 1624–1713* (Chapel Hill, N.C., 1972). See in particular Dunn's fascinating article, "A Tale of Two Plantations: Slave Life at Mesopotamia in Jamaica and Mount Airy in Virginia, 1799 to 1828," *William and Mary Quarterly,* third series, 34 (1977), 32–65. For a sustained and wideranging comparison with the largest South American slave society, see Carl N. Degler, *Neither Black Nor White: Slavery and Race Relations in Brazil and the United States* (New York, 1971). A different point of view is presented in Stuart B. Schwartz, "Patterns of Slaveholding in the Americas," *American Historical Review* 87 (1982), 55–86.

Although other parts of the Americas have provided the obvious basis for most comparisons with Southern slavery, horizons have been greatly extended by recent studies focusing on other societies. George M. Fredrickson, *White Supremacy: A Comparative Study in American and South African History* (New York, 1981), sheds a revealing light on two slave systems which were essentially racial. On the other hand, the most elaborate and sustained—and also the most remarkable—comparative study of recent years involves a society where the race factor was not present: Peter Kolchin, *Unfree Labor: American Slavery and Russian Serfdom* (Cambridge, Ma., 1987). This is undoubtedly one of the major works on slavery to appear during the 1980s. Some of its main themes were set out in earlier articles by Kolchin, especially in "Reevaluating the Antebellum Slave Community: A Comparative Perspective," *Journal of American History* 70 (1983), 579–601. Another intriguing American-European comparison may be found in Shearer Davis Bowman, "Antebellum Planters and Vormärz Junkers in Comparative Perspective," *American Historical Review* 85 (1980), 779–808.

10. Slavery and Race

Many works cited in earlier sections devote considerable attention to the interconnections of slavery and race in Southern society. In addition there are a number of studies which take this as one of their central themes. Winthrop D. Jordan, *White over Black: American Attitudes Toward the Negro, 1550–1812* (Chapel Hill, N.C., 1968), is a superb study covering the earlier period. An abridged version was published under the title of *The White Man's Burden* (New York, 1974). For the nineteenth century, the most important study is George M. Fredrickson, *The Black Image in the White Mind: The Debate on Afro-American Character and Destiny, 1817–1914* (New York, 1971). See also the thoughtful and thought-provoking essays in C. Vann Woodward, *American Counterpoint: Slavery and Racism in the North-South Dialogue* (Boston, 1971). Ronald T. Takaki, *Iron Cages: Race and Culture in Nineteenth-Century America* (New York, 1979), is somewhat idiosyncratic, but stimulating. James M. McPherson, "Slavery and Race," *Perspectives in American History* 3 (1969), 460–73, is a thoughtful review essay, emphasizing the racial dimension of Southern slavery.

Joel Williamson, *New People: Miscegenation and Mulattoes in the United States* (New York, 1980), deals with one important aspect of relations between the races. See also the early pages of his *The Crucible of Race: Black-White Relations in the American South since Emancipation* (New York, 1984).

11. Slavery and Southern White Society

Once again, the writings of Eugene Genovese are central to the modern debate on this particular topic. See chapter 7, note 5. For a listing of a number of other relevant studies of the antebellum South, see chapter 7, notes 8 through 10, and for an excellent discussion, with extensive references to other works, see Randolph B. Campbell, "Planters and Plain Folks: The Social Structure of the Antebellum South," in Boles and Bolen, eds., *Interpreting Southern History*.

Bruce Collins, *White Society in the Antebellum South* (London, 1985), compresses the fruits of a hugely impressive range of reading into a brief discussion, but possibly strains a little too hard in pursuit of a consensus view of Southern white society. James B. Oakes, *The Ruling Race: A History of American Slaveholders* (New York, 1982), paints a somewhat overdrawn picture of a highly fluid and mobile society in which small and middling slaveholders played a much more important part than great planters. However, he does offer a valuable corrective to some earlier interpretations. Otto H. Olsen, "Historians and the Extent of Slaveownership in the Southern United States," cited in section 5 above, is of basic importance.

On the relationship between slavery and Southern white ideas about liberty, Morgan, *American Slavery, American Freedom,* is essential reading for the colonial period. William J. Cooper, *Liberty and Slavery: Southern Politics to 1860* (New York, 1983), is a judicious study which links politics to broader social and racial concerns. Kenneth S. Greenberg, *Masters and Statesmen: The Political Culture of American Slavery* (Baltimore, 1985), offers an original and challenging interpretation which is generally persuasive despite its occasional overenthusiasm. It also depends excessively on the example of South Carolina, which was an exception to (or a gross exaggeration of) almost every Southern rule. John McCardell, *The Idea of a Southern Nation: Southern Nationalists and Southern Nationalism, 1830–1860* (New York, 1979), includes a penetrating discussion of the relationship between slavery and the Southern identity.

The impulses behind the proslavery argument and the various audiences to which it was addressed have been the subject of extensive historical debate. A useful anthology of proslavery writings, with an excellent introduction is Drew Gilpin Faust, ed., *The Ideology of Slavery: Proslavery Thought in the Antebellum South, 1830–1860*

(Baton Rouge, La., 1981). See also Faust, *A Sacred Circle: The Dilemma of the Intellectual in the Old South, 1840–1860* (Baltimore, 1977), especially chapter 6. Genovese has always taken the proslavery argument very seriously; see for example *The World the Slaveholders Made*. There are interesting observations on various elements in the proslavery argument in Laurence Shore, *Southern Capitalists: The Ideological Leadership of an Elite, 1832–1885* (Chapel Hill, N.C., 1986). Two illuminating recent essays are: Bertram Wyatt-Brown, "Modernizing Southern Slavery: The Proslavery Argument Reinterpreted," in Kousser and McPherson, eds., *Region, Race and Reconstruction*, 27–49, and Peter Kolchin, "In Defense of Servitude: American Proslavery and Russian Proserfdom Arguments, 1760–1860," *American Historical Review* 85 (1980), 809–27.

12. The End of Slavery

The varied and far-reaching effects of the Civil War upon slavery within the Confederacy are thoroughly examined in Clarence L. Mohr, *On the Threshold of Freedom: Masters and Slaves in Civil War Georgia* (Athens, Ga., 1986), and also James H. Brewer, *The Confederate Negro: Virginia's Craftsmen and Military Laborers, 1861–1865* (Durham, N.C., 1969). The controversy over recruitment of African-Americans into the Confederate army is covered in Robert F. Durden, *The Gray and the Black: The Confederate Debate on Emancipation* (Baton Rouge, La., 1972).

Among local studies of areas of the South which came under Union control, Willie Lee Rose, *Rehearsal for Reconstruction: The Port Royal Experiment* (Indianapolis, 1964), is a marvellously evocative and perceptive account; C. Peter Ripley, *Slaves and Freedmen in Civil War Louisiana* (Baton Rouge, La., 1976), is a lucid brief study; Fields, *Slavery and Freedom on the Middle Ground,* is very illuminating about the situation in Maryland; and Victor B. Howard, *Black Liberation in Kentucky: Emancipation and Freedom in Kentucky, 1862–1884* (Lexington, Ky., 1983), deals with another border slave state.

The African-American experience, in all its variety, during the transition from slavery to freedom is examined with sensitivity as well as massive thoroughness in Leon F. Litwack, *Been in the Storm So Long: The Aftermath of Slavery* (New York, 1979). See also Litwack's essay "Free at Last," in Tamara K. Hareven, ed., *Anonymous Americans:*

Explorations in Nineteenth-Century Social History (Englewood Cliffs, N.J., 1971), 131–171. There is still useful material in a much older study, Bell I. Wiley, *Southern Negroes, 1861–1865* (New Haven, 1938). Important studies of the impact of federal policy in the South during and after the war include Louis S. Gerteis, *From Contraband to Freedman: Federal Policy Toward Southern Blacks, 1861–1865* (Westport, Ct., 1973); James L. Roark, *Masters without Slaves: Southern Planters in the Civil War and Reconstruction* (New York, 1977); and Lawrence N. Powell, *New Masters: Northern Planters During the Civil War and Reconstruction* (New York, 1980).

Dudley T. Cornish, *The Sable Arm: Negro Troops in the Union Army, 1861–1865,* is an informative account. James M. McPherson, ed., *The Negro's Civil War: How American Negroes Felt and Acted During the War for the Union* (New York, 1965), is a well-chosen selection of source material.

A number of books focusing mainly on the Reconstruction period take as their starting point the wartime experience of emancipation. See for example Joel Williamson, *After Slavery: The Negro in South Carolina During Reconstruction, 1861–1877* (Chapel Hill, N.C., 1965), and Peter Kolchin, *First Freedom: The Response of Alabama's Blacks to Emancipation and Reconstruction* (Westport, Ct., 1972). Roger L. Ransom and Richard Sutch, *One Kind of Freedom: The Economic Consequences of Emancipation* (Cambridge, 1977), is of particular value.

Important general works which draw lessons about the character of Southern slavery from the period of the war and emancipation include: Genovese, *Roll, Jordan, Roll;* Gutman, *The Black Family in Slavery and Freedom;* and Rose, *Slavery and Freedom,* especially chapters 5 and 6.

13. Conclusion

Intellectual indigestion is possible after even the most nutritious and skillfully prepared historiographical feast. The best antidote to a surfeit of historiographical controversy is a return to the primary sources. There is no better introduction than Willie Lee Rose, ed., *Documentary History of Slavery in North America* (New York, 1976). Another well-edited selection is Michael Mullin, ed., *American Negro Slavery: A Documentary History* (Columbia, S.C., 1976). John W.

Blassingame, ed., *Slave Testimony: Two Centuries of Letters, Speeches, Interviews and Autobiographies* (Baton Rouge, La., 1977), is a massive, varied, and fascinating collection. For those who wish to immerse themselves in larger collections of source material, there are the forty-one volumes of Rawick, ed., *The American Slave: A Composite Autobiography* (see section 6, above). Two of the best-known sources presenting white views of slavery and Southern society are: C. Vann Woodward, ed., *Mary Chesnut's Civil War* (New York, 1981), and Robert M. Myers, ed., *The Children of Pride: A True Story of Georgia and the Civil War* (New Haven, 1972).

For all the prodigious output of new work on slavery in the last two or three decades, coverage of the subject is still uneven. Lively controversy encourages concentration on whatever may be the dominant or fashionable issues of the moment, while other potentially important topics are neglected. It may be appropriate to conclude this survey of the recent historiography of slavery by suggesting some of the gaps which remain to be filled and some of the areas where more investigation is needed. The list which follows is by no means exhaustive.

In terms of geographical spread, there is need for local studies of communities or areas in Mississippi, Alabama, Louisiana, and the Southwest generally, in order to redress the balance after all the recent work on localities in the Atlantic seaboard states, and in particular in South Carolina. As far as coverage of various periods is concerned, the recent attention to the seventeenth and eighteenth centuries is welcome, but there is surely a case for more work on the period from, say, 1790 to 1830, when the prospects, economic function, and geographical spread of slavery underwent a transformation.

As far as slave life is concerned, it is noteworthy that many recent studies pay scant attention to the actual labor of the slaves, which, in the eyes of their owners at least, was their main *raison d'etre*. Within the life of the slave community, there is surely room by this time for another overview of the slave family, which would absorb the results of the detailed studies carried out since Herbert Gutman's book was published. There may be scope for further study of the character, including the day-to-day reality, of the master-slave relationship. The internal slave trade may also be ripe for further investigation and for a fresh attempt at synthesis—and the subject of slave-hiring is crying out for a book-length study. Finally, there is the long-standing and inevitable concern about the overemphasis on the larger slaveholders and the great plantations; unless the inadequacy of the sources rules it out, there must surely be a major concentration of effort on the small and middling slaveowners. At present, we know more about the great planters and the slaves themselves than about the substantial and important groups in between—the smaller slaveowners and the non-slaveholding white majority.

Index

Printed in the United States
56690LVS00002B/22-24

9 780064 301824